THE
EVERYTHING®
HEALTH GUIDE TO
SCHIZOPHRENIA

Dear Reader,

A diagnosis of schizophrenia for someone you care about will change your life forever. As a caregiver, you first may need to overcome feelings of despair. You face a difficult path that will undoubtedly involve setbacks as well as progress. Prepare for both.

You will learn that although schizophrenia is a serious condition, it is not necessarily a hopeless one.

Learning about the nature of this disease is a good place to start. Accept the challenge and arm yourself with as much knowledge as you can. Get to know the mental health care system well enough to make it work for you. Take advantage of everything it has to offer: the educational programs, the medications, the many varieties of therapy, and the assistance that is available for you and the one you care for.

No one is to blame for a mental disorder. Medical research has provided overwhelming evidence that schizophrenia and related mental disorders have a biological basis, just as heart and liver disease do.

With effort, you will be in a position to help not only yourself and your loved one but others you will meet in the years to come. With good treatment, adequate resources and information, and their own bravery and determination, most people with schizophrenia can live independent or semi-independent lives. With understanding and support, you can help them reach that goal.

Dean A. Haycock, PhD

THE

EVERYTHING

Series

These handy, accessible books give you all you need to tackle a difficult project, gain a new hobby, or even brush up on something you learned back in school but have since forgotten. You can choose to read from cover to cover or just pick out information from our four useful boxes.

 Alerts: Urgent warnings

 Essentials: Quick handy tips

 Facts: Important snippets of information

 Questions: Answers to common questions

When you're done reading, you can finally say you know **EVERYTHING**®!

PUBLISHER Karen Cooper

DIRECTOR OF ACQUISITIONS AND INNOVATION Paula Munier

MANAGING EDITOR, EVERYTHING SERIES Lisa Laing

COPY CHIEF Casey Ebert

ACQUISITIONS EDITOR Katrina Schroeder

DEVELOPMENT EDITOR Elizabeth Kassab

EDITORIAL ASSISTANT Hillary Thompson

Visit the entire Everything® series at *www.everything.com*

THE
EVERYTHING®

HEALTH GUIDE TO
SCHIZOPHRENIA

The latest information on treatment,
medication, and coping strategies

Dean A. Haycock, PhD

with Technical Review by Elias K. Shaya, MD

Avon, Massachusetts

11-4-10

An Everything® Series Book.
Everything® and everything.com® are registered trademarks of F+W Media, Inc.

Published by Adams Media, a division of F+W Media, Inc.
57 Littlefield Street, Avon, MA 02322 U.S.A.
www.adamsmedia.com

ISBN 10: 1-60550-036-4
ISBN 13: 978-1-60550-036-2

Printed in the United States of America.

J I H G F E D C B A

Library of Congress Cataloging-in-Publication Data
is available from the publisher.

This publication is designed to provide accurate and authoritative information with regard to the subject matter covered. It is sold with the understanding that the publisher is not engaged in rendering legal, accounting, or other professional advice. If legal advice or other expert assistance is required, the services of a competent professional person should be sought.

—From a *Declaration of Principles* jointly adopted by a Committee of the American Bar Association and a Committee of Publishers and Associations

Many of the designations used by manufacturers and sellers to distinguish their products are claimed as trademarks. Where those designations appear in this book and Adams Media was aware of a trademark claim, the designations have been printed with initial capital letters.

The Everything® Health Guide to Schizophrenia is intended as a reference volume only, not as a medical manual. In light of the complex, individual, and specific nature of health problems, this book is not intended to replace professional medical advice. The ideas, procedures, and suggestions in this book are intended to supplement, not replace, the advice of a trained medical professional. Consult your physician before adopting the suggestions in this book, as well as about any condition that may require diagnosis or medical attention. The author and publisher disclaim any liability arising directly or indirectly from the use of this book.

This book is available at quantity discounts for bulk purchases.
For information, please call 1-800-289-0963.

Contents

Does Mental Illness Really Exist?

Most scientists ignore people who claim mental disorders are not diseases or do not even exist. But the stakes are high. Some people in need of treatment may not get it if they adopt these questionable views. Understanding the views of people who do not believe that mental illness is a serious medical condition is the first step in fighting their misperceptions.

An Understandable Reaction to Stress

Thomas Szasz discounts the suggestion that schizophrenia and other mental disorders recognized by the American Psychiatric Association are true diseases. He introduced this idea in his first book, published in 1961, called *The Myth of Mental Illness*.

Szasz claims that society creates stresses that cause some people to react negatively. However, according to Szasz, these negative reactions are not mental illness and there is nothing amiss with the people who experience them. They merely have trouble coping with problems other people handle routinely, if not always comfortably. He faults society and the medical establishment for labeling and treating people who have problems living in the modern world as being mentally ill.

 Fact

Szasz suggested that the troubling behavior of some individuals upsets other people. Mainstream society therefore invented the concept of mental illness to explain their behavior and offer a rationale for "controlling" them.

Mainstream psychiatrists and many others, including people who care for patients, see treatment, not "control," as the reason for diagnosing mental illness. It is true that many patients claim there is nothing wrong with them. These claims often change after successful treatment. And many people who once suffered terribly from schizophrenia and other mental disorders have testified in interviews and in memoirs about the seriousness of the illnesses that once incapacitated them.

Scientology

The Church of Scientology claims that in 1969, Szasz joined forces with it to create the anti-psychiatry organization called the Citizens Commission on Human Rights (CCHR). There are reports that Szasz has disavowed a link with the Scientology group, although his name was still listed on the website when this book went to press.

The misinformation that this and other anti-psychiatry groups propagate can easily be dismissed by people who are familiar with the field. The problem is that many consumers of mental health care are upset by their illness and therefore vulnerable to misinformation. Unproven assertions could potentially have serious negative consequences for people who are dealing with paranoia and other delusions.

Do Drugs Do More Harm than Good?

In some cases, modern medicines may do more harm than good. But years of experience have proven that the majority of people with schizophrenia do better by taking antipsychotic medications than they do by not taking them. There are exceptions, and good psychiatrists should always look for ways to avoid medicating anyone who does not need it.

 Fact

It is undeniable that antipsychotic drugs have been misused in poorly run institutions by overwhelmed or incompetent mental health care providers. In such instances, excess doses of drugs like Thorazine and Haldol have been used to "manage" uncontrollable patients by making them semiconscious. Such abuses are not acceptable and are not the norm today.

Table 12-1: Misconceptions about Antipsychotic Medications

Myth	Fact
They are addictive.	They are not habit-forming.
They make users "high."	They do not produce euphoria.
They control peoples' minds.	At the right doses, they do not act as "chemical straitjackets."
They are "knock out" drugs.	Some can have sedating effects, but their value is in diminishing psychotic symptoms.
They take away free will.	They help patients overcome debilitating symptoms so they can deal with problems rationally.

Sources: the New York State Office of Mental Health and the National Institute of Mental Health

Thousands upon thousands of examples and case records attest to the ability of antipsychotic drugs to give patients a chance at living without the worst symptoms of schizophrenia.

Do Pharmaceutical Companies Control Modern Psychiatry?

It is no secret that individual pharmaceutical companies try to influence psychiatry by getting psychiatrists to prescribe the medications they manufacture and provide. This is how the companies make money. They do the same thing in all fields of medicine, from general practice to cardiology.

A good psychiatrist will not prescribe an inappropriate medication in response to pressure by a drug company. A problem arises when doctors take money from pharmaceutical companies as consulting fees or other payments for services rendered and do not disclose that fact to their colleagues, the public, or their patients. Everyone has the right to know if a potential conflict of interest exists. Fortunately, such unethical doctors are in the minority.

Other Possible Conflicts of Interest

Many mental health advocacy groups have accepted funding from pharmaceutical companies. Many of these groups do an outstanding job educating the public and promoting the cause of better mental health care. There is, however, an appearance of a conflict of interest when an advocacy group accepts money from a company that would profit financially from a recommendation.

In an ideal world, communities or the federal government would assure the health care treatment of its citizens, and conflict of interest would not be a problem. But in the real world, organizations compromise in order to survive financially. People worry that groups and individuals who accept money may be more inclined, even if in a subtle way, to favor that company's products when making recommendations or writing prescriptions. They worry about what an organization may not say in deference to a sponsor. Because it is difficult to know if an organization has self-edited itself, the appearance of a conflict of interest can be troubling for some watchdogs.

In the summer of 2008, even the American Psychiatric Association attracted criticism because it accepted money from pharmaceutical companies.

Influencing Doctors' Choices

In 2007, the *New York Times* found evidence that payments from pharmaceutical companies can influence the drugs doctors prescribe. Reporters analyzed prescription data and payments from drug companies to psychiatrists in Minnesota. They found that psychiatrists who received $5,000 or more from the manufacturers of atypical antipsychotic medications issued, on average, three times the number of prescriptions for this class of drugs for use in children than did psychiatrists who received less than $5,000 from the companies.

However, it also reasonable to consider the possibility that the drug companies observed their data first and identified those doctors who seem to prescribe their drugs more than others. The companies may then have picked those doctors to be on their speakers' bureau or their advisory boards because they had more experience with the company's drugs. If so, the fact that the doctors are paid

Dedication

For Florence Moratelli and Marie Culver

Acknowledgments

Marie E. Culver, MA, encouraged and supported me during this project and others. She read the manuscript with great care and cleared it of many flaws. Charles Ouimet, PhD, was always available to offer advice and encouragement. My friend Ismail Shalaby, MD, PhD, introduced me to Elias Shaya, MD, the technical reviewer for this book. Steve Stock shared helpful impressions and insights. Several people living with schizophrenia helped me better understand the challenges and victories they experience.

Many organizations, including the National Alliance on Mental Illness, National Alliance for Research on Schizophrenia and Depression, and others devoted to the improving the lives of people with schizophrenia and other severe mental illnesses served as inspirations for this book, as did the experts and advocates who have devoted their professional lives to helping people with schizophrenia and other brain diseases.

Introduction

Mental illness, neuropsychologist R. Walter Heinrichs concluded, "is among us and diminishes to the extent that we care for those who endure it."

Unfortunately, far too many people have to endure one of the most serious mental illnesses: schizophrenia. The National Institute of Mental Health estimates that today in the United States 2.2 million individuals suffer from this brain disease. Other estimates place the figure above 3 million.

It appears in approximately one of every 100 people in the world today. The disease takes a shocking emotional and financial toll on those affected by it. The image of the homeless, untreated person with schizophrenia is too often accurate, but it does not reflect the full impact of this disease. While some individuals with psychiatric illnesses are homeless and have no caregivers, many live independently and have committed caregivers and adequate support. Because the disease tends to strike in late adolescence or early adulthood, millions of patients have friends and family members—parents, grandparents, or siblings—who support them. A diagnosis of schizophrenia presents unwanted and unexpected challenges for everyone who cares for a friend or relative living with the disease.

Because schizophrenia strikes just as people are planning and training for careers, it takes an additional toll on individuals and society.

Lack of work experience compounds their problems as they struggle to recover the basic social skills necessary to live a satisfying life.

In the United States, the disease removes an estimated $32.5 billion from the economy each year. While the total financial cost has been estimated in excess of $100 billion, the cost in terms of human suffering for patients and family is incalculable. Without adequate care, lives are disrupted, careers are cut short, and people are lost to each other.

To the uninformed, schizophrenia brings to mind a raving, dangerous lunatic or someone with a split personality. In reality, some people with the disease experience few psychotic episodes and are lucid and rational for much of their lives. Between 20 percent and 35 percent recover—some completely. While this can be a devastating disease for some, it is effectively treatable for most. There are many success stories.

Yet by some estimates, the severe symptoms and the persistent nature of the disorder mean that up to 80 percent of people with schizophrenia may experience varying levels of disability, possibly for their entire lives. Sadly, the percentage of patients with schizophrenia who commit suicide is 10 percent or higher.

You, as a caregiver, may have to assume responsibilities you never imagined or wanted as you help your loved one get treatment and learn skills that will help her regain control of her life. With your help, and with effort by the patient, the illness may be brought under control.

The purpose of this book is to help you educate yourself to find, get, and give the best possible care. For most patients, a combination of counseling or therapy, a social support network, and the short- or long-term use of antipsychotic medications offers the best option for lessening the impact of this most serious of psychiatric disorders. Arm yourself with knowledge so you can begin to counter the effects of this disease. With it, you may be able to reduce the frequency of hospitalizations and possibly eliminate them. You can gain a measure of control by advocating for better treatment, social services, and more money for research.

If one observation, suggestion, opinion, or reference in this book helps you move toward achieving any of those goals, it will have been worth the effort of writing it.

CHAPTER 1

Schizophrenia Basics

SCHIZOPHRENIA IS A severe, often chronic brain disease that can make a person unable to function at work or school, maintain interpersonal relationships, and even take adequate care of her personal needs. This major change is the result of a disruption in basic brain function, which leads to loss of touch with reality. It includes psychotic symptoms such as hallucinations, delusions, disorganized speech, and bizarre, disorganized behavior. The brain dysfunction may also lead to impaired thinking, blunted emotions, and loss of motivation, interest, or pleasure. Together, these effects of the disease make successful social interactions difficult or impossible.

A Brief Overview of Schizophrenia

Normally, social behaviors and the brain functions that control them are taken for granted because they are automated, like our heartbeat. People do not usually have to make an effort to make these behaviors and functions happen. Schizophrenia, unfortunately, disrupts this automation; considerable effort and treatment become necessary to control, restore, or maintain normal social behavior and thought processes. Fortunately, effective treatments are available, and researchers continue to search for better ones.

In most cases, treatment consists of antipsychotic medication and various forms of therapy. Schizophrenia is a disease that, although it is not curable, can be effectively controlled in many cases.

 Question

What one symptom do all people with schizophrenia share?
No one symptom characterizes the disease. Hallucinations and delusions are some of the more common symptoms associated with schizophrenia. These and other psychotic symptoms may also be seen with psychiatric conditions other than schizophrenia.

No one knows exactly what causes schizophrenia, but approximately one out of every 100 people on the planet will suffer from the disease. Schizophrenia strikes regardless of geographic location, culture, religion, race, or ethnicity. Approximately 3 percent of all people will experience psychotic symptoms—not necessarily schizophrenia—at some point in their lives. Eight out of ten of these episodes will occur between the ages of sixteen and thirty. Thus, there is great concern about correctly diagnosing someone's symptoms as schizophrenia.

DSM-IV: The "Bible" of Psychiatric Diseases

Physicians and other clinical providers, as well as researchers in the field of psychiatry, use the same book to decide what to call various mental illnesses and how to diagnose them. This is the *Diagnostic and Statistical Manual of Mental Disorders*, fourth edition (*DSM-IV*). The *DSM-IV* was created based on consensus by approximately 1,000 experts in the field and is updated periodically. The fourth edition, revised in 2000, provides detailed information about hundreds of different mental disorders in its 943 pages.

This book provides a common language and a common guide for the great variety of people involved in treating psychiatric illnesses.

These include psychiatrists, other physicians, nurses, psychologists, social workers, counselors, and occupational and rehabilitation therapists. The *DSM-IV* is used in clinical settings such as hospitals and offices, as well as in research facilities. It is also used for administrative purposes by insurance companies and government agencies.

Features of the Disease

One of the most dramatic symptoms of schizophrenia described in *DSM-IV* is the presence of psychosis, a disturbing mental state in which a person may be fully alert but his contact with reality is lost or very seriously distorted. Common examples are hallucinations (such as hearing voices), delusions (such as feeling that one is being controlled and/or threatened by outside forces), and disorganized thinking or incoherent speech (such as belief in very strange ideas; irrational thoughts). Psychiatrists refer to these as positive symptoms.

The disease is also characterized by negative symptoms, which at first examination may seem less dramatic than positive psychotic symptoms. Negative symptoms include apathy and lack of speech, motivation, and emotional display. Unfortunately, they can be just as debilitating as positive symptoms over the course of a patient's lifetime. Intellectual abilities also can be affected, making it difficult for someone with schizophrenia to concentrate, remember, and learn new tasks. In young people, this typically results in a drop in grades and poor academic performance.

Symptoms of Schizophrenia

- Delusion
- Hallucinations
- Disorganized thinking
- Disorganized speech
- Social withdrawal
- Lack of emotional expression
- Apathy, lack of motivation

Adapted from the *DSM-IV.*

Targeting Adolescents and Young Adults

Roughly half of the people who develop schizophrenia first show symptoms before age twenty. However, the disease can appear as early as the mid- to late teens and as late as the mid-thirties. Most cases develop between ages fifteen and twenty-five.

Varied Outcomes

The disease manifests itself differently in different people for reasons that are not yet understood. Some patients experience episodes of worsening symptoms that last days or weeks, but in between these serious episodes they experience minimal symptoms or no symptoms. Others may have symptoms that are milder but more chronic. Usually, medications can readily control symptoms in these people. There will be times, however, when patients' symptoms may suddenly get worse and their treatment needs to become more intense.

Essential

After a diagnosis of schizophrenia, some people experience only one or a few episodes of worsening symptoms. Others have repeated episodes but live productive, independent lives between these troubling events. Other patients face a greater challenge. These patients may require lifelong support and assistance in order to improve the quality of their lives.

Some people recover relatively quickly. Some may respond to treatment and resume normal lives. For many, however, schizophrenia is a chronic condition whose symptoms may range widely in severity. Nevertheless, symptoms are almost always improved by treatment.

Negative symptoms tend to linger longer than psychotic symptoms. One reason the disease is so challenging is the lack of a single symptom common to all of its subtypes.

A Person, not a Disease

Many mental health care providers and advocates refer to people who have been diagnosed with schizophrenia as "consumers of mental health care" or just "consumers." At least one study indicates that this is preferred by patients and their relatives. Others discussing the topic avoid using "consumers" because it can be confused with other types of consumers, such as shoppers. Some people use a version of the phrase "people with (or diagnosed with) schizophrenia." All of these are used in this book.

 Fact

The word "schizophrenia," while outdated in its meaning compared to today's understanding of the disease, it is still used. In 1911, a Swiss psychiatrist named Eugen Bleuler created the word from the two Greek words—schizein, which means "splitting," and phren, which means "the mind." The literal translation is "split mind." Early descriptions of the disease referred to the splitting of the mind from reality.

Most experts and patients agree that it is best to avoid equating a person with the disease that affects him. Avoid calling someone with schizophrenia a "schizophrenic." It is like calling someone being treated for breast cancer a "cancer" or a "tumor." It dehumanizes people by equating them with the disease they are fighting. It also stereotypes them. In a society that still places a stigma on mental illness, stereotyping someone in this way makes her struggle to regain health and independence even more difficult than it already is.

Schizophrenia's Effect on Relationships

The symptoms of schizophrenia do not just separate people with the disease from others; they construct giant barriers between them. Overcoming these barriers is often one of the biggest challenges for consumers of mental health care.

Shock

The first months or years of dealing with the disease can be the most challenging. First, you find that you are facing a serious disorder with which you have no experience. You need time to learn about the nature of the disease, its treatments, and the strengths and weaknesses of the mental health care system. In addition, you must handle the psychological stresses caused by the appearance of the disease and its implications.

Second, it often takes time to settle on effective therapies. Antipsychotic medications may need to be tried and their doses adjusted. Side effects, if they appear, need to be treated. And it may take time to find a psychiatrist and other mental health care workers you feel comfortable working with.

Until fairly recently, a diagnosis of schizophrenia promised a good chance of serious mental impairment for life. Fortunately, that has changed. Most people who are diagnosed with schizophrenia today respond well to treatment and are able to function nearly as well as they did before the disease began to wreak havoc on their lives.

Serious Internal Distractions

Hallucinations, delusions, and bizarre behavior turn people inward. It is impossible to focus on routine tasks and social interactions when you are dealing with voices that comment on your every action, or when you are living with the knowledge that special messages just for you are being broadcast on the news or hidden in street signs.

Many people know little about mental illness. What they do know is often colored by inaccurate depictions they have seen in films or read about in the media. The average person does not make an effort to establish or even maintain a casual or intimate relationship with someone struggling with severe mental illness. Consequently, people struggling with psychosis often lose established relationships, and more than half never marry.

Lost Social Skills

Most people learn how to socialize in adolescence and early adulthood. This is just when schizophrenia is most likely to appear. As a result, some social skills are never learned and others are lost.

Old friends fall away. Finding new, good friends takes a lot of work, and it is made more difficult by lingering symptoms. The result may be a loss of interest in previously enjoyable activities and a lack of initiative. It may become difficult to concentrate and plan, to understand and adapt.

This makes meeting people, getting to know them, and participating in the give-and-take of social interaction very difficult. Until they learn about the nature of schizophrenia, even family members can become alienated from someone dealing with the disorder. Schizophrenia changes people, but there is hope. With symptom control, therapy, and practice, patients can regain many of these skills.

A Brief History of Schizophrenia

No one knows how long schizophrenia has been around. It is possible to find descriptions of mental illness in tablets, carvings, and other writings from the ancient world, but these brief observations never describe enough symptoms and features of schizophrenia to definitively establish its existence thousands of years ago.

From Prehistory to the Eighteenth Century

Records from the ancient world are sketchy. It has been suggested that the mentally ill may not always have been considered ill. In some cultures they may have been seen as people in close touch with higher, mystical forces.

In the absence of convincing early written descriptions of the disease, many researchers are ready to concede that the disease may have been around in the late Middle Ages. But even these claims are disputed. While clear cases of some forms of mental illness are described in the sixteenth century—in Shakespeare's plays, for example—what looks like schizophrenia to one modern psychiatrist looks like another, similar illness to another. Torrey believes, the first unmistakable descriptions of schizophrenia appeared only in the early nineteenth century when Englishman John Haslam and Frenchman Philippe Pinel described people with schizophrenia-like symptoms.

The Nineteenth Century to the Early Twentieth Century

In the second half of the nineteenth century, schizophrenia began to accumulate the labels that are familiar to psychiatrists today. A French psychiatrist born in Austria, Benedict-Augustin Morel, observed the "early deterioration of the mind" in a patient and used the phrase *démence précoce* (early or premature dementia) to describe what he observed. He used the word "dementia" to describe a chronic, progressive deterioration of intellectual ability. Morel believed that heredity, drug use, and previous medical history all played a part in the development of the condition he described.

Paranoid psychosis was described in 1868. Three years later, disorganized schizophrenia, then called hebephrenia, was characterized. Three years after that, catatonic schizophrenia entered the medical literature. For the next two decades, these illnesses were considered separate mental disorders.

 Fact

In 1834, Russian author Nikolai Gogol provided one of the most complete early descriptions of schizophrenia in his short story "Diary of a Madman." Gogol's Axenty Ivanovich Poprishchin experiences auditory hallucinations (dogs talk to each other) and delusions (he believes he is the king of Spain).

In 1896, a forty-year-old German psychiatrist named Emil Kraepelin proposed that paranoid psychosis, hebephrenia, and catatonia
were forms of the same disease. He translated Morel's French phrase
démence précoce into Latin, *dementia praecox*, which he considered
an incurable disease caused by organic changes in the brain.
In 1883, Kraepelin had written the *Psychiatric Compendium*, a
textbook that associated mental dysfunction with physical causes.
He was the first to bring together a useful system for describing and
classifying mental disorders and abnormal behavior. Kraepelin's
influence can still be seen today in classification systems used
throughout the world. His influence is apparent in the two best-
known diagnostic manuals of mental disorders, the American Psychiatric Association's *Diagnostic and Statistical Manual of Mental
Disorders* and the World Health Association's *International Statistical
Classification of Diseases and Related Health Problems*.

The next big steps in shaping our present view of the illness
were taken by the Swiss psychiatrist Eugen Bleuler in the twentieth
century. He introduced the word "schizophrenia" in 1911 to replace
Kraepelin's phrase *dementia praecox*.

One of the reasons Bleuler introduced a new word to describe
the disease was his observation that *dementia praecox* did not always
result in full premature dementia or chronic, progressive mental
deterioration. The disease was not a one-way path downward for
everyone, even in the era before effective antipsychotic medications,
cognitive rehabilitation, and psychosocial therapies were developed.
Some patients, Bleuler observed, recovered or stopped deteriorating
on their own.

Bleuler described aspects of disorganized thinking characteristic of schizophrenia. He chose the name "schizophrenia" to reflect a
key feature of disease's effect on a person's thought processes rather
than on the assumed outcome of the illness. It seemed to Bleuler that
the disease caused a "splitting of the mind" from reality. This allusion
to a "split" may have contributed to the widely held misconception
that schizophrenia is a "split personality." In fact, Bleuler intended
the notion of split to apply to a separation between brain functions

such as thought and feelings, or to a separation between the ability to tell the real from the unreal.

Bleuler's choice of the word "schizophrenia" as a label reflects his efforts to understand the abnormal thinking processes characteristic of this mental illness. Bleuler noted the symptoms of thought disorder in the loose associations and illogical thinking that modern psychiatrists recognize in people with schizophrenia.

Interestingly, Bleuler believed schizophrenia consisted of more than one disease, a notion that went against the generally accepted view of his time. Today, more medical researchers think this idea is a possibility than did Bleuler's contemporaries.

Bleuler disagreed with his colleagues about another aspect of schizophrenia. Most of his contemporaries, like many medical researchers today, thought the causes of schizophrenia could be traced to specific areas of brain damage. Bleuler, a follower of Sigmund Freud, didn't think so; he said it could be the result of psychological problems.

Today, medical imaging and neuroanatomical studies have provided evidence that tilts the argument toward brain damage as being a significant factor in the development of the disease. There are no strong research findings that support the view that schizophrenia is the product of purely psychological problems, although these are generally recognized as potentially significant factors.

Early Treatments and Explanations

Doctors could do nothing to treat schizophrenia in the nineteenth and early twentieth century, although they did try to come up with some effective procedures.

Insulin Coma Therapy

Polish psychiatrist and neurophysiologist Manfred Joshua Sakel developed insulin-shock or insulin-coma therapy for schizophrenia in the 1930s. After accidentally inducing an insulin coma in a drug addict undergoing withdrawal, Sakel noted that his patient's mental state improved. Too much insulin drastically lowers the amount of sugar in the blood, which the brain and body use for energy. Deprived of its energy source, the brain begins to shut down, passing through states of mental confusion, listlessness, seizures, coma, and, unless blood sugar is provided, death.

Sakel began to induce convulsions and coma in people with schizophrenia by injecting them with insulin. For a little while it seemed to work and many clinicians followed his lead. Sakel reported improvement in symptoms in nearly nine out of ten patients. Doctors eventually found that the procedure didn't have much effect over the long term. The technique was abandoned when powerful tranquilizing drugs became available.

Lobotomy

Another approach to treating schizophrenia and other mental disorders was popularized and over-promoted in the 1940s and early 1950s by the American neurologist Walter Freeman. Looking for a way to help mentally ill patients who had no hope of recovery, the ambitious Freeman adapted a psychosurgical procedure pioneered in Europe by two Portuguese physicians, Antônio Egas Moniz and Almeida Lima. This radical procedure involved cutting the nerve connections between the area of the brain above the eyes, known as the prefrontal cortex, and the rest of the brain.

Freeman developed a surgical variation called transorbital lobotomy that simplified the procedure. Using an ice pick-like instrument, he pierced the thin bone behind the eye socket and then inserted the instrument into the brain and moved it back and forth to sever the connections. The procedure was over in minutes. With Freeman's enthusiastic promotion, it became a medical fad, widely performed before any well-planned scientific studies were conducted to establish its effectiveness or determine its long-term effects. It could pacify some psychotic patients and even help a few. Unfortunately, many undergoing the procedure were irreversibly harmed by it. They were left passive, apathetic, emotionally stunted, and unable to concentrate.

The lobotomists confused the passivity they produced with relief of symptoms of mental illness. Unfortunately, it took years for it to become clear that rather than targeting and alleviating specific symptoms of mental diseases, the procedure amounted to little more than the production of brain damage that quieted patients and suppressed cognitive function.

 Question

How long were frontal lobotomies performed?
Lobotomy, or prefrontal leukotomy, was introduced in 1935. More than 18,000 lobotomies were performed in the United States between 1939 and 1951 before doctors realized it did more harm than good. Nevertheless, Moniz won the 1949 Nobel Prize in Physiology or Medicine for pioneering the procedure.

Poor Parenting

In the 1950s, mainstream psychologists and psychiatrists promoted one influential "cause" of schizophrenia: a poor upbringing blamed on the parents, particularly a cold, distant mother.

The American psychiatrist Seymour Kety, by contrast, promoted the idea that schizophrenia was a brain disease, not the result of bad parenting. His research helped promote understanding of the contribution of genetic factors in predisposing some people to the illness. He also laid the groundwork in the 1940s and 1950s for imaging the living brain using positron emission tomography (PET scanning) with his research on measuring blood flow to specific parts of the brain. PET scanning has since provided important insights into the differences in brain function in schizophrenia and in health.

Drug Therapy and Deinstitutionalization

In the United States in 1955, state mental institutions held approximately 560,000 patients. By the start of the twenty-first century, that number had dropped by nearly 90 percent.

The introduction of antipsychotic and other mental health medications accounts for a significant portion of the decline. Other reasons for the decline in long-term hospitalizations are public policies concerning deinstitutionalization and improvement in understanding and care.

 Question

Who first saw the potential benefit of an antipsychotic drug? The drug that began the modern revolution in psychopharmacology—the use of drugs to improve mental health—was first used to relieve anxiety and prolong sleep in patients undergoing surgery and anesthesia. Chlorpromazine (Thorazine) was so effective in turning anxious patients into "disinterested" patients that French surgeon Henri Laborit advocated its use in psychiatry. The first tests took place in 1951.

A big move away from institutionalizing patients followed passage of the Community Mental Health Act in 1963. Some civil libertarians and other activists fought for the release of patients from hospitals because they claimed patients' rights were being violated by involuntary admission. Some politicians wanted to save government money that was used to maintain large hospitals.

Whatever the intentions or rationale, the results were mixed. Some patients benefited if they responded to antipsychotic drugs and could find a support network on the outside. Others dropped out of the health care system entirely. They were left to live on the streets because community mental health care programs hadn't been developed to provide needed services.

What Schizophrenia Is Not

Schizophrenia is not well understood. In fact, it might be one of the most misunderstood mental disorders in the DSM-IV.

It might be a syndrome or a collection of different but related diseases that have been grouped together, like cancer. It's also possible that the different subtypes might be variations of one underlying brain abnormality. The disease's secrets are slowly being revealed, but schizophrenia is still surrounded by stigma and misunderstanding.

Schizophrenia is not

- Anyone's fault
- Contagious
- Untreatable
- Caused by bad parenting or bad upbringing
- Caused by childhood trauma
- Caused by poverty
- Caused by laziness or personal weakness
- Caused by drug abuse
- The same as having a split personality

Sources: the British Columbia Mental Health and Addiction Services and the National Alliance for Research on Schizophrenia and Depression.

The Split Personality Myth

Perhaps the most common misconception about schizophrenia concerns the nature of the disease itself. Polls conducted in 2005 and 2008 suggest that between 40 percent and 64 percent of the general population believe having schizophrenia is the same as having a split personality. Split personality is an inaccurate term for what psychiatrists used to call multiple personality disorder but now call dissociative identity disorder, and it is a type of mental disorder entirely different from schizophrenia.

Dissociative personality disorder was made famous by the book and film versions of *The Three Faces of Eve* and *Sybil*, accounts of women who had experienced terrible abuse as children and developed multiple, distinct personalities as a result. These personalities coexist in one person and manifest themselves at different times. This is in no way similar to the psychotic episodes people with schizophrenia endure. The "split" in schizophrenia is a gap between reality and what a patient's hallucinations and delusions lead him to believe.

The Bad Drug Experience Myth

Some illegal drugs—for example, stimulants such as cocaine and amphetamine and hallucinogens such as LSD and psilocybin—may produce symptoms in some otherwise healthy users that are similar to those seen in schizophrenia. The drug effects are usually short-lived and most often disappear after a matter of hours or days. These experiences do not produce or result in schizophrenia. It is true, however, that people with schizophrenia are particularly sensitive to the effects of many illegal and some legal drugs, which can seriously compromise their physical and mental health and interfere with successful therapy.

CHAPTER 2

What Causes Schizophrenia?

NO ONE KNOWS what causes schizophrenia. Recent studies involving brain anatomy and brain development will be combined with knowledge about the effects of antipsychotic drugs to someday provide a more complete answer than we can offer today. What we now know, however, provides intriguing clues about possible causes of mental disorders. Far less information is available about possible environmental, sociocultural, or psychological influences on the development of schizophrenia. It is now assumed that biological factors in combination with stresses and outside events contribute to the onset and development of the disease.

The Role of Genetics

There are undeniably strong links between the genes a person is born with and her risk of developing schizophrenia, yet the connection is not absolute. If one of your relatives has schizophrenia, it does not mean you will have schizophrenia. It only means that you may have a slightly greater chance than the average person of developing the disease. This depends on how closely you are related to the person with schizophrenia.

The genetic link becomes most striking when twin siblings or both parents have the disease. Two parents with schizophrenia give their children as much as a 46 percent chance of developing the same disorder. A person whose identical twin has schizophrenia has a 50 percent chance of receiving the same diagnosis. These family members have the most genes in common. It is clear that the closer the genetic link, the greater the risk of developing this disorder.

Adoption Studies

Another very strong indication that genetics play a big role in developing schizophrenia comes from studies of adopted infants. Because adopted children are not raised with their biological relatives, key elements of environmental influence are removed from consideration when investigating biological factors that influence the development of the disease.

Comparisons of the incidence of schizophrenia in a child's biological and adoptive families show a strong genetic link. In other words, if an adopted child develops schizophrenia, the biological relatives—who did not raise the child—are more likely to have been diagnosed with schizophrenia or a schizophrenia-like illness than is the child's adoptive family. This indicates that there is something in a patient's genetic makeup that predisposes him to schizophrenia. Researchers at the National Institute of Mental Health estimate that "at least 60 percent of the factors that give rise to schizophrenia may be related to a genetic susceptibility."

No One "Schizophrenia Gene"

Scientists have identified potential genetic defects on a dozen or so chromosomes that might play a role in increasing someone's chances of developing schizophrenia.

It has been difficult to identify specific genes linked to schizophrenia because the disorder is very complicated and has a wide range of symptoms and potential environmental influences. If specific genes closely associated with the disease were known, it might be possible to develop a genetic test. Individual genes may work in concert to increase a person's susceptibility to the disease rather than condemn them to developing it.

Table 2-1: Genetic Risk of Developing Schizophrenia

Your Relationship to the Person with Schizophrenia	Your Risk
None	0.6–1%
First cousin, uncle, or aunt	2%
Nephew or niece	4%
Grandchild	4–5%
Half sibling	6%
Parent	6–8%
Full sibling	6–9%
Child with one ill parent	13%
Fraternal twin	17%
Child with two ill parents	39–46%
Identical twin	48–50%

Sources: Adapted from Comer, *Fundamentals of Abnormal Psychology* and the National Alliance for Research on Schizophrenia and Depression.

Teams of scientists from the International Schizophrenia Consortium and a company called deCODE Genetics in Reykjavik, Iceland, have managed to identify specific variations in the genes of less than 1 percent of patients with schizophrenia compared to the genes of people who are not affected by the disorder. It's important to note that these variations involving missing sections of DNA are rare even in schizophrenia patients. The effect of the deletion, however, is not subtle: it may increase the risk of getting the disease by up to fifteen times the normal risk.

These findings indicate that people with schizophrenia and similar psychotic disorders tend to have one missing section of DNA on chromosome 1 and two missing sections on chromosome 15. Both groups also confirmed a previously identified missing section on chromosome 22.

Scientists working at Cardiff University in the United Kingdom identified three places on patients' DNA molecules that appear to increase the risk for developing schizophrenia. One of these sites is near—and may involve—a gene that controls the activity of other genes. Interestingly, if people with schizophrenia and people with bipolar disorder are both included in the analysis, the link between this genetic site and the risk of mental illness gets stronger. This suggests that different mental disorders may have common genetic risk factors.

More Than Genes

All of these findings provide striking evidence that inheritance plays a role in influencing who gets schizophrenia and who does not. Yet not everyone who has a relative who is affected by the disease goes on to develop it. Looking at the same research findings from an optimistic perspective highlights the fact that even when both parents are affected, a child has better than a 50 percent chance of *not* developing the disorder. Strikingly, the same is true for a person who inherits the exact same genes as someone with schizophrenia—an identical twin. Again, there is a 50/50 chance that one twin will not develop the disease despite the fact that both were born with identical sets of genes.

A Look at the Brain

On the cellular level, the human brain impresses even most neurobiologists as a nearly inconceivably complex structure. Many key questions about its function remain unanswered and are likely to remain so for a long time. Neuroscientists, however, are making impressive progress in uncovering more and more details about the brain's structure and function every year. The payoff of this research has been incremental progress in uncovering clues to what causes schizophrenia.

Like all organs in the body, each of the parts of the brain is composed of cells. In the brain, the two main types of cells are neurons and glial cells. Neurons make up the brain's gray matter. People equate gray matter with intelligence, but the cells that make up gray matter also are responsible for all kinds functions of the brain. They regulate thinking, moving, and even involuntary actions such as breathing. The other type of brain cells, glial cells, are very active supporters of neurons. Among their many jobs is to act as insulation for nerve fibers that carry electrical and chemical messages between neurons.

The Brain from the Outside

The following description provides a quick tour of brain structure by pointing out major anatomical landmarks. Remember that in a structure as complex as the human brain, many structures have multiple roles in processing information and performing intellectual tasks. The structures of the brain interact with each other through nerve fibers, creating a network like an enormously complex electrical circuit. The left side and right side of the brain also have different specialized functions. An abnormality on one side can cause different problems than does an abnormality on the other. The description in this section includes major features that have been implicated in some of the proposed causes of schizophrenia.

The most obvious structure you see when you look at the brain is the cerebral cortex. *Cortex* is the Latin word for "bark," as in the bark of a tree. The wrinkly cerebral cortex, between 3/32- and 3/16-inch thick, is wrapped around deeper and evolutionarily older brain structures.

The cerebral cortex is itself subdivided into four parts—the frontal cortex, the parietal cortex, the temporal cortex, and the occipital cortex. The frontal cortex is the outermost part of the frontal lobe. The frontal lobe is located above the eyes and immediately behind the forehead. It helps people see the consequences of their actions and to plan ahead. In most people the left side of the frontal lobe helps us form words, while the right side allows us to use gestures and intonations to reflect emotional expression. The frontal lobe works with other structures in the brain to motivate us and spark initiative, among other important intellectual tasks.

Two strips of brain tissue separate the frontal lobe from the parietal lobe. The first one is a strip of motor cortex, which controls voluntary movement. Next to it is a strip of sensory cortex, which recognizes and processes feelings of touch. The parietal lobe, located about three-quarters of the way toward the back of the brain, processes aspects of language, touch, and spatial orientation.

 Fact

Researchers have discovered a link between reduced cortical thickness and the development of schizophrenia. This is apparently connected to cognitive problems that are related to schizophrenia, including attention deficits and impaired memory.

The temporal lobes lie under the skull opposite the temples and ears. They play an important role in memory, speech, and emotions. Parts of the temporal lobes are reported to be smaller in some patients with schizophrenia.

The occipital lobes at the very back of the brain process visual information. Tucked underneath the occipital lobe is the cerebellum, a structure that assists in controlling movements and carrying out tasks that depend on precise timing, as well as language and other intellectual functions.

The Brain from the Inside

Deeper layers below the cortex are descriptively called subcortical structures. These include the basal ganglia, which, among other functions, help regulate movement. The loss of certain neurons in part of the basal ganglia is the cause of Parkinson's disease. Another subcortical structure, the pons, has bundles of nerves that connect the cerebral cortex to the cerebellum and spinal cord. It plays a key role in arousal and in maintaining automatic nerve functions such as breathing and heartbeat. Each of the subcortical structures is made up of several smaller structures or groups of nerve cells that are essential for various functions involving emotions, emotional expression, language, intellect, motivation, and other aspects of behavior.

The limbic system is a part of the brain that is made of both cortical and subcortical structures. It is believed to be the site of abnormalities in several psychiatric disorders, including schizophrenia. Included in the limbic system are structures such as the hippocampus, amygdale, mammillary bodies, and thalamus, all of which are involved in functions like memory, motivation, emotional regulation, aggression, sexuality, and cognitive tasks.

Altered Brain Structure in Schizophrenia

Many scientists have reported research findings that suggest schizophrenia is related to changes in the structure of the brain. This insight follows the development of advanced neuroimaging technologies that allow neuroscientists to study pictures of living, functioning brains without compromising the health of research volunteers or patients.

Visible Differences

Fluid-filled spaces called cerebral ventricles in the center of the brain are a normal feature of everyone's central nervous system. These chambers, filled with cerebrospinal fluid, appear to be enlarged in some people affected by schizophrenia.

Having larger spaces in the center of the brain implies less area is available for the brain's other structures. Indeed, there are reports that associate smaller brain mass with schizophrenia.

Because these studies are time-consuming and expensive, research reports must frequently concentrate on changes in one brain region at a time. It is important to remember, however, that the brain is an intricately interconnected structure in which different regions are linked by extensive nerve cell projections. It is therefore unlikely that there is one place in the brain that is responsible for schizophrenia.

Rather, it is likely that flaws in brain structure and chemistry make functioning in several parts of the brain defective. Chemical messenger systems such as dopamine, serotonin, glutamate, and perhaps others may be impaired in the many different brain regions such as the limbic structures (involved closely with emotions), basal ganglia, prefrontal cortex, temporal lobes, and even the cerebellum, a part of the brain neuroscientists once believed did nothing more than control fine muscle movements. Its involvement might explain changes in coordination, reflexes, body postures, and other functions detected in some people with schizophrenia.

 Fact

The frontal lobe is reported to be smaller in some patients with schizophrenia. This part of the brain plays a unique and important role in determining personality, social interactions, and planning for the future. Smaller temporal lobes have also been observed in some people diagnosed with schizophrenia.

Other studies indicate that there is a lower level of activity in certain parts of the brain in some patients with schizophrenia. Compared to those of people who don't have schizophrenia, these brain regions receive less blood flow when the brain is thinking, feeling, reasoning, and telling the body what to do.

The differences in structure found in the brains of people with schizophrenia are not necessarily very big differences. In fact, some are very subtle, and similar variations can be seen in the brains of some people who are unaffected by mental illness.

Microscopic Differences

Structural abnormalities detected on the microscopic level are also very subtle. Some of these differences involve small changes in numbers of neurons and the way they are positioned in certain regions of the brain.

Pierce J. Howard, PhD, explains in his book *The Owner's Manual for the Brain* how this may happen. Some scientists suggest that in schizophrenia something goes wrong with the natural process that normally does away with unneeded connections between nerve cells—synapses—in young people. This "synaptic pruning" phase begins before puberty and extends to around the age of twenty-five. Unused, unneeded synapses shrivel and disappear, while synapses that get a lot of use become stronger. It is estimated that around 15 percent of an adolescent's cerebral gray matter is pruned in the healthy brain.

In a brain affected by schizophrenia, however, as many as 25 percent of the synapses may be eliminated. Microscopic examination of brains affected by schizophrenia reveal further anomalies, such as out-of-place neurons in the cerebral cortex and in the hippocampus, which deals with memory formation and learning.

Even though brain imaging and other studies have demonstrated several differences between brains of patients with schizophrenia and those unaffected by the disease, none of these differences are big enough or consistent enough to be used to diagnose the condition. The diagnosis of schizophrenia continues to be made by clinical interviews and examinations. Research studies continue to provide clues and improve our understanding of the brain malfunctions associated with this disease.

Due to structural and chemical flaws, communication pathways between many parts of the brain are compromised in schizophrenia. Thus, neurotransmitter systems such as dopamine, serotonin, norepinephrine, glutamate, and perhaps others appear to be impaired. Such chemical malfunctions could affect the brain regions critical in schizophrenia. One scenario suggests that brain abnormalities seen in schizophrenia—if they contribute to disease symptoms—may be the result of problems that begin before birth, while the brain of a genetically susceptible individual is developing. These developmental problems may be the result of—or may combine with—input or damage caused by something present or absent in the environment, such as a virus or some missing essential nutrients.

Wiring Problems?

Neuroscientists at the Harvard Brain Tissue Resource Center may have found an anatomical basis for several symptoms of schizophrenia, including the unusually intense perception of sights and sounds experienced by some people with the disease. Tissue from the brains of individuals with schizophrenia had more excitatory neurons compared to tissue from the brains of people who did not have the disease. Perhaps too many excitatory neurons contribute to excess stimulation and hallucinations in schizophrenia.

Another potential contributing factor in schizophrenia described by J. Pierce Howard, PhD, in *The Owner's Manual for the Brain* is the increase in the establishment of neuronal pathways that occurs during the adolescent years. While the number of brain synapses or points of contacts between neurons is pruned at this stage of life, the "wiring" or communication pathways between neurons is strengthened. The nerve fibers that convey these connections, called axons, are insulated by non-neuronal brain cells called glial cells. Glial cells wrap around axons, insulate them, and allow electrical signals to travel faster.

 Question

Are the brains of people with schizophrenia wired differently from those of other people?
During the late teen years and early twenties, the brain experiences a burst of nerve cell insulation, a process called myelination. Some scientists speculate that the sudden, improved connections resulting from this new myelination might help explain the onset of the disease. The connections may cause malfunction in a brain already weakened by genetic susceptibility and environmental factors.

Perhaps a brain in the process of developing schizophrenia could not handle the power of the new brain wiring. This might explain some early warning signs of the disease, such as heightened senses. This can result in an unusual—and not necessarily unpleasant—feeling of amazement and wonder associated with familiar objects and sights. Later, this pleasant aspect of heightened sensations can be replaced by hallucinations and delusions.

Normal Chemical Signals

Many of the parts of the brain are big enough to see with the naked eye, but the individual sites in the brain that are affected by psychoactive drugs can't be seen without the aid of powerful microscopes.

These are the key points of contact between two neurons, a tiny gap called the synaptic cleft. An electrical impulse in one brain cell, the presynaptic neuron, causes the release of a chemical messenger, a neurotransmitter, into this space. The neurotransmitter released by the first neuron drifts across the gap and makes contact with a second, target brain cell, which is called the postsynaptic neuron.

Into the Gap

Once across the gap, the neurotransmitter contacts a specific receptor molecule that sticks out from the surface of the postsynaptic neuron. The interaction between the neurotransmitter and its receptor starts a sequence of biochemical changes in the neuron on the receiving end. This contributes to its becoming more or less electrically excitable.

 Question

What are neurotransmitters?
Messages between brain cells are carried by electrical and chemical signals. The chemicals that carry signals between brain cells are called neurotransmitters. They are released by one neuron and travel a short distance to make contact with a second neuron. Most psychiatrists and neuroscientists are convinced that a neurotransmitter called dopamine plays an important role in causing some serious symptoms of schizophrenia.

If the sum total of the thousands of neuronal messages that come into a postsynaptic neuron tells it to fire, then the postsynaptic cell initiates its own electrical signal and becomes the presynaptic cell with respect to the next neuron down the line.

This process is conducted continuously, even while you sleep, on an unimaginably vast scale involving billions of brain cells. In ways we don't understand, it helps the brain produce consciousness, dreams, thoughts, feelings, and emotions. When the mechanism malfunctions, the result can be hallucinations, paranoia, depression, and other symptoms of mental illness.

Altered Brain Chemistry in Schizophrenia

Every drug now available to treat psychotic symptoms targets a sub-type of dopamine neurotransmitter receptor called the D2 receptor. The correlation between a drug's interactions with D2 receptors and its ability to ease psychotic symptoms at low doses is greatest for the older antipsychotic medications. Newer drugs probably owe many of their good and bad effects to their tendency to bind more strongly to serotonin and other types of receptors instead of the D2 receptor.

Symptoms and Receptors

Schizophrenia symptoms fall into two main classes, positive and negative. Some research suggests that positive symptoms might be traced to changes predominantly centered in one part of the brain and negative symptoms to another part.

Some clinical observations support this scheme: antipsychotic drugs that predominantly block a subset of dopamine receptors in the basal ganglia are better at controlling positive symptoms. Medications that seem to be better at controlling negative symptoms block different chemical messengers in the brain and may exert their anti-schizophrenia effects in the prefrontal cortex.

The Role of Environment

Genes alone cannot account entirely for schizophrenia. It is likely that a combination of factors interacting with an inherited predisposition to the disease will someday explain who becomes ill and who remains healthy. Factors in the environment that produce physiological and/or psychological stress may cause one person to develop the disease while sparing another. Perhaps other genes help some people resist environmental factors that would push another person toward mental illness. At this time, we just don't know.

Question

If genes contribute to schizophrenia, how can one identical twin have it and not the other?
Genes produce all the proteins that determine how the body works. Identical twins are born with the same genes, but after that, things change. Exposure to stress, for example, can influence how the activity of genes is regulated. In other words, personal experience can change how genes work.

It has been suggested that a long list of stress-inducing factors in the environment promote schizophrenia in susceptible individuals. These range from exposure to environmental toxins to viral infections.

Some Proposed Schizophrenia Triggers
- Nutrition
- Viruses and parasites
- Maternal stress
- Maternal viral infection during pregnancy
- Advanced parental age
- Development problems before birth
- Complications during birth
- Environmental toxins

Adapted from Ronald J. Comer's *Fundamentals of Abnormal Psychology.*

A parasite called *Toxoplasma gondii* is suspected of playing a role in at least some cases of schizophrenia. It is a common organism; more than 60 million people in the United States have the parasite in their bodies. Most of them are not affected by this microscopic organism because their immune systems suppress it. Still, the U.S. Centers for Disease Control and Prevention believes it is among the top three causes of death from food-borne illness. The protozoa can be found in undercooked meat and cat feces.

T. gondii infection in humans can produce psychotic symptoms. Haloperidol, an antipsychotic drug, targets the protozoan. This leads some researchers to suspect that the parasite might be one of the reasons these drugs relieve some of the symptoms of schizophrenia. A couple of scientific reports conclude that among the risks in the environment for schizophrenia is exposure to cats during childhood.

Nearly a dozen studies have found significantly elevated levels of antibodies to *T. gondii* in people with schizophrenia. More research is needed, but it seems plausible that exposure to this parasite might contribute to the development of schizophrenia in some susceptible individuals.

Viruses

There is no evidence for a specific "schizophrenia virus" in the environment. There is a fair amount of evidence, however, that a virus or viruses can contribute to development of the disease. Viruses could work in combination with genes that increase susceptibility to the disease. Or they might interact with other environmental factors that promote its development. Multiple studies indicate that pregnant women who get influenza during the first half of their pregnancy give birth to children who are more likely to develop schizophrenia than children whose mothers did not suffer from the flu.

Stress

A woman exposed to a significant amount of stress during the first six months of her pregnancy has an increased risk of giving birth to a child who will develop schizophrenia later in life. This phenomenon was demonstrated in children born to Dutch women who lived through the invasion of their country by the German army in World War II.

What Might Cause Schizophrenia?

Schizophrenia is a complex disorder, perhaps a complex of disorders. Sometimes people who separate and categorize concepts miss the fact that these possibilities are not necessarily mutually exclusive. No one explanation of the biological cause of the disease necessarily must invalidate other explanations.

A Chemical Hypothesis

One of the oldest biochemical explanations of what causes schizophrenia is based on our understanding of how antipsychotic medications work. In short, it says there is something wrong somewhere along the chemical messenger pathway. Somehow, neurons located in key parts of the brain receive abnormal signals or do not effectively process chemical signals from other neurons. This breakdown or miscommunication somehow results in the myriad symptoms seen in schizophrenia. In theory, straightening out these signaling systems should correct the problem. Currently available medications can do this to some extent, but only partially and imperfectly. Perhaps we haven't developed drugs that target the chemical abnormality effectively enough, or perhaps there is more to the underlying problem in schizophrenia than described by this scheme.

A Genetic Hypothesis

This explanation emphasizes the inheritance of genes that increase a person's susceptibility to developing some form of schizophrenia. This hypothesis has been strengthened in recent years with the identification of genes that are suspected of playing a role in the disease. Perhaps the drugs now used to treat schizophrenia target some of the proteins made by these very genes. If we could pin down exactly which genes are associated with schizophrenia, it might someday be possible to design drugs that target them specifically.

A Brain Connection Hypothesis

This explanation suggests that schizophrenia results from faulty wiring or connections between crucial areas of the brain. Such improper wiring probably occurs early in life, making schizophrenia a neurodevelopmental disorder.

Multiple events could account for changes in brain connections. This hypothesis fits easily into a combined hypothesis that might explain the biological basis of the disease: A genetic predisposition makes some people sensitive to factors such as prenatal or childhood infections, nutritional deficiencies, or exposure to toxins and/or psychological stresses. These factors affect brain development, leading to faulty connections and structural and chemical abnormalities.

The drugs now available may be capable of acting on only one or a few of the resulting functional abnormalities. Furthermore, the medications may do so imperfectly.

Other Explanations

In the past, some psychologists have suggested that many of the problems experienced by people with schizophrenia can be traced to their reactions to stress, social pressures, family dynamics, labeling, or upbringing. Data supporting these views is very limited compared to data supporting biological theories. It is likely that psychological factors—reactions to stress, for example—are a factor in the development and expression of the disorder's symptoms. Explanations that rely purely on psychological or sociocultural factors that fail to consider known biological factors, however, remain unconvincing to most scientists and others who are familiar with the disease.

CHAPTER 3

What Type of Schizophrenia Are You Dealing With?

SCHIZOPHRENIA IS NOT a simple disease. Most psychiatrists recognize five or so general subtypes of the disorder. A subtype diagnosis is assigned based on a patient's most recent clinical evaluation. In other words, the symptoms a patient displays when he sees a psychiatrist determine the diagnosis. A key factor in assigning a subtype diagnosis is the nature of the most prominent symptoms. These can change over time. Furthermore, a patient may have features of more than one subtype, and the most severe symptoms of psychosis sometimes fade with age.

Diagnosing Schizophrenia

For a psychiatrist to make a diagnosis of schizophrenia, the patient must have experienced specific symptoms over a defined period of time. An accurate diagnosis also requires the elimination of other medical conditions that could produce similar symptoms. Therefore, the patient should have a complete physical examination, including blood and urine analyses for the presence of commonly abused drugs.

A good psychiatrist will interview the patient and her family, examine the medical records, and consider the patient's history to determine if schizophrenia is the right diagnosis. According to the most recent edition of the *Diagnostic and Statistical Manual of Mental Disorders*, a diagnosis of schizophrenia can be made only if a person meets the following criteria:

- At least two of the following five symptoms are evident for thirty days (or less if effectively treated): hallucinations, delusions, negative symptoms, disorganized behavior, or disorganized speech.
- Some signs and symptoms of the illness have been present for a minimum of six months.
- There must be no indication of bipolar disorder, that is, symptoms of mania alternating with depression.
- There must be no other identifiable medical or neurological cause of the symptoms.
- The symptoms are not caused by use of illegal drugs, alcohol, or medications.

Instead of a minimum of six months' duration of symptoms, the World Health Organization requires only one month's duration to make the diagnosis of schizophrenia.

Alert

An accurate diagnosis of schizophrenia must be made by a qualified psychiatrist. There are many psychiatric and medical conditions that can be easily confused with schizophrenia but have very different causes and outcomes. You, as a relative, acquaintance, or friend cannot make a diagnosis, but you can help your loved one find an effective diagnosis and good medical care.

Paranoid Schizophrenia

People with a paranoid type of schizophrenia hear voices and have delusions of persecution. The voices are usually related to delusions that others are plotting against them or people close to them. Paranoid schizophrenia is often the least difficult form of the disease to treat. It is also easier to predict how well a patient will fare with this form of schizophrenia compared to other subtypes. Symptoms tend to appear later than in other forms; the age at diagnosis tends toward the mid-thirties instead of early adulthood.

People with pure paranoid schizophrenia have no negative symptoms, can speak coherently with no sign of disorganized speech, and demonstrate no catatonic behavior, that is, immobility or repetitive movements.

A successful interview will reveal a delusion of persecution. Except for their delusions and the voices they hear, people suffering from paranoid schizophrenia can be difficult to distinguish from anyone else. They can maintain a pleasant appearance and take care of themselves. This often allows them to hold on to their jobs and function in society much more successfully than do people suffering from other forms of the disease. It also raises the question of whether paranoid schizophrenia is a distinct disease.

A Patient with Paranoid Schizophrenia

- Meets general criteria for schizophrenia
- Hears voices frequently (auditory delusions) or is convinced she is being persecuted or plotted against
- Demonstrates no disorganized speech or behavior
- Shows no sign of inappropriate or unexpressive emotional response (flat affect)
- Shows no sign of catatonia (bizarre behavior, odd postures, excited or excessively subdued behavior)

Adapted from the *DSM-IV*.

Disorganized Schizophrenia

This category includes the most psychotic and difficult to treat patients. Once called hebephrenia, disorganized schizophrenia typically appears at a younger age than the paranoid form of the disease. An untreated person with this subtype generally has poor hygiene and an unkempt appearance, which makes him seem clearly disturbed. Deterioration can be steady and quick without treatment.

A Patient with Disorganized Schizophrenia
- Meets the general criteria for schizophrenia
- Has disorganized speech
- Demonstrates disorganized behavior
- Shows inappropriate or little emotion
- Shows no signs of catatonic behavior

Adapted from the *DSM-IV.*

A person with disorganized schizophrenia may intersperse speech with laughter or silliness. The humor is called inappropriate by psychiatrists because it has no connection to the topic of conversation, if conversation is even possible. The speech itself will be disorganized. Behavioral disorganization will be so severe that bathing, grooming, and nutritional intake suffer.

If hallucinations and/or delusions are present, they are not as organized, elaborate, and consistent as they are in other forms of the disease, such as paranoid schizophrenia. In keeping with the disorganized nature of this subtype, psychotic symptoms, when present, are disconnected and patchy.

Catatonic Schizophrenia

The symptom that sets catatonia apart from other forms of schizophrenia is the presence of odd physical movements or postures. Some people affected by this subtype of the disease become immobile. Patients with such psychomotor disturbances were seen much more often in the first half of the twentieth century than they are today. This is probably due to earlier and more effective treatment with antipsychotic medication.

Patients displaying the hyperactivity sometimes seen in this subtype of schizophrenia move incessantly in a way that appears to be unconnected to any outside influence. This is called agitated or hyperactive catatonia. Others have a "waxy flexibility." In these cases, while it is possible to physically adjust the posture and limb positions of a patient, the limbs move with wax-like resistance. The patient maintains that posture for prolonged periods of time no

matter how uncomfortable it may be. Another symptom sometimes seen in this relatively rare variety of mental illness is a state
psychiatrists call "extreme negativism." The person resists all outside attempts to adjust her rigid stance. These patients also do not
respond to instructions to change their posture. Patients with catatonic schizophrenia meet the general criteria for schizophrenia and
have at least two of the following symptoms.

Symptoms in a Patient with Catatonic Schizophrenia
- Lack of voluntary movement, which allows the patient to be
  placed in odd physical positions (waxy flexibility)
- Trance-like state
- Excess mobility or hyperactivity that appears to have no pur-
  pose and does not respond to outside influences
- Lack of response or resistance to commands, instructions,
  and physical adjustments of posture
- Complete lack of speech with no response to attempts to
  communicate
- Assumption of odd physical postures, pointless repetitive
  movements, or exaggerated facial expressions (grimacing)
- Apparently pointless copying and repetition of another per-
  son's words or movements

Adapted from the *DSM-IV.*

Voluntary movements may also appear; a person will adopt
inappropriate or odd postures. The patient's face may be contorted
by obviously exaggerated grimaces.

Other symptoms involve mimicry. The person copies what
someone else says or does and repeats the words or actions incessantly. If the patient parrots a word, she is said to show echolalia. If
she repeatedly imitates someone's physical movement, she is said to
have echopraxia.

Undifferentiated and Residual Schizophrenia

Both of these subtypes of the disorder are used to describe the disease in patients whose symptoms do not match the criteria outlined in previous sections. In a sense, they are classifications used to make sure everyone with schizophrenia is given a diagnosis that conveys as much information about the nature and history of his condition as possible. As with other subtypes, these diagnoses can change as symptoms change.

Undifferentiated

If a patient's symptoms cannot be placed convincingly into any of the other categories—paranoid, disorganized, or catatonic—a diagnosis of undifferentiated schizophrenia is made. The patient may not have symptoms of paranoia, disorganization, or catatonia, but he will, over the course of a month, have two or more of the following: delusions, hallucinations, disorganized speech or behavior, or negative symptoms.

Residual

This is a category that describes people whose symptoms have improved enough so they cannot be classified as paranoid, disorganized, catatonic, or undifferentiated. They still have enough remnants of the disorder, however, to register with mental health professionals as not fully recovered. Negative symptoms, for example, such as social withdrawal, reduced or limited emotional range, lack of ambition for large and small projects, and reluctance to speak may be present. Alternatively, a patient with residual schizophrenia may have "watered down" versions of psychotic symptoms: odd ideas or occasional, fleeting hallucinations. These symptoms differ from those seen in other types of schizophrenia because they are not as severe, incapacitating, organized, or persistent.

It is also possible that this subtype represents "a transition between a full-blown episode and complete remission," according to the American Psychiatric Society's *DSM-IV*.

Symptoms in a Patient with Residual Schizophrenia
- Has been diagnosed with another subtype of schizophrenia in the past
- Shows no signs of hallucinations, delusions, disorganized speech, or grossly disorganized or catatonic behavior
- Has negative symptoms
- Has two or more very low-key versions of classic positive schizophrenia symptoms such as odd beliefs, strange perceptual experiences, or peculiar behavior

Adapted from the *DSM-IV*.

Type I and Type II

Some systems for classifying different types of schizophrenia are not recognized by the American Psychiatric Association (APA) and so do not appear in the Diagnostic and Statistical Manual. One that you may come across is the Type I and Type II classification.

This system for describing subtypes of schizophrenia can be found in some psychology textbooks, research papers, or certain websites. It may be used because some people are dissatisfied with the usefulness of the *DSM-IV* classifications, which critics claim do not provide adequate indication of a patient's chances of recovery or the course her disease is likely to take. The *DSM-IV* classifications, some people say, are more descriptive than clinically useful. The APA's system also largely ignores overlap of symptoms in some people. The Type I/Type II classification approach emphasizes the relative predominance of positive and negative symptoms in a particular patient.

Type I Schizophrenia

Patients with lots of hallucinations, delusions, and/or disorganized or bizarre behavior—that is, positive symptoms—are included in the Type I category. People in this subset often functioned fairly well before becoming ill. They tend to develop schizophrenia later than Type II patients and generally experience a faster onset of disease.

Disease symptoms tend to wax and wane for patients with Type I disease; troubling episodes are interspersed with remissions. Patients function normally in society during remissions. They have a better chance of recovery even though they are more likely to be diagnosed with one of the classical subtypes of schizophrenia: paranoid, undifferentiated, catatonic, disorganized, or residual. Their cognitive or intellectual abilities are more likely to be only minimally impaired compared to people with Type II schizophrenia.

The biological basis of Type I schizophrenia is assumed to involve significant biochemical abnormalities as well as less detectable— perhaps more subtle or even minimal—structural brain abnormalities. The underlying biochemical flaw may be related to too much dopamine activity in a network of sites in the brain called the limbic system, which is closely associated with emotion. Proponents of this classification system say this is consistent with the greater effectiveness of typical or older antipsychotic medication in Type I patients.

Type II Schizophrenia

Patients with Type II disease show more negative symptoms than do Type I patients. Their faces are unexpressive. They lack initiative and motivation, don't pay attention, are withdrawn, can't find pleasure in life, and don't talk much. When they do speak, it is in a monotone. Rather than being diagnosed with paranoid, disorganized, undifferentiated, catatonic, or residual schizophrenia, they are more likely to meet criteria for a type of schizophrenia dominated by negative symptoms.

 Fact

Type II patients are more likely to be men than women and are more likely to have had problems functioning in school, at work, and in their social life before being diagnosed with schizophrenia. They also tend to develop the illness at an earlier age.

Type II patients generally experience a steadily worsening condition, which eventually causes undeniable impairment and dysfunction so severe it couldn't be explained as eccentricity or disinterest in social interactions. It is harder for people with Type II schizophrenia to regain the level of functioning they had before the illness was diagnosed. Disease symptoms tend to be chronic; they don't come and go as they do with Type I.

The biological basis of Type II schizophrenia has been hypothesized to involve too little dopamine activity in the frontal cortex, a part of the brain that plays an important role in intellectual functioning. This would be consistent with observations that cognitive problems are significantly worse in Type II schizophrenia than in Type I. As a consequence, social functioning in all areas of life is likely to suffer.

Other factors that might someday be included in alternative descriptions of schizophrenia subtypes include the likely course of the illness and the likelihood of schizophrenia being present alongside other psychotic and personality disorders. These factors are not well understood and therefore not well described in current descriptions of the disease.

CHAPTER 4

Related Psychotic Disorders

OTHER DISORDERS CAN easily be mistaken for schizophrenia if a patient's symptoms are not examined closely. It is not clear how these other psychotic disorders are related to schizophrenia. They do have features in common, but they also show significant differences. It might be useful to think of schizophrenia as a spectrum of diseases that blend into each other. The spectrum might include the subtypes of schizophrenia, delusional disorders, schizoaffective disorders, and other diseases that show a close association with schizophrenia through common traits and inheritance patterns.

Brief Psychotic Disorder

Brief psychotic disorder appears suddenly and goes away quickly. At least one psychotic symptom—hallucination, delusion, disorganized speech or behavior, or catatonic behavior—appears and disappears within a period of one to thirty days.

The symptoms are not lasting; patients recover and go back to the same level of functioning they had before the symptoms appeared. General medical conditions that could account for the symptoms, such as a drug reaction or a blow to the head, must be eliminated before this diagnosis is made.

Brief psychotic disorder is not often seen by doctors in developed countries, including the United States. Because it can appear and disappear in a matter of days, it is possible some cases are never seen in a medical setting. Like schizophrenia, it can strike adolescents and young adults, but the average age is somewhere around thirty years.

The Stress Factor

Sometimes, brief psychotic disorder follows major stress in someone's life. The horror of combat or a crime or accident could be enough to evoke such a response from some people. For others, the loss of a loved one could precipitate the short-lived symptoms. More than one severely troubling event could also add up to major stress.

For a psychiatrist to diagnose brief psychotic disorder with marked stressors, the precipitating stressful event must be so bad that it would produce significant stress in anyone. In these cases, the disorder might be thought of as a reactive psychosis that doesn't last very long. If there is no record or indication of stressful events preceding the symptoms, the diagnosis is made "without marked stressors," according to the *DSM-IV*. If the disorder appears in a woman a month or less after she has given birth, a diagnosis of brief psychotic disorder with postpartum onset is made.

Short but Troubling

Although the symptoms can be over in a few days, the experience of this disorder is usually overwhelming. The patient is terribly confused and emotionally upset by what is happening to her. The trauma is so severe it is often necessary to closely watch the patient so she doesn't harm herself. The suicide rate among this group is high, particularly among the young.

Shared Psychotic Disorder

Also known as folie à deux, shared psychotic disorder is relatively rare. It affects an otherwise healthy person who shares delusions with a close relative or friend. The dominant partner in a close relationship between a pair of relatives or domestic partners often suffers from schizophrenia or a similar disease. Over time, the less dominant partner begins to believe some or all aspects of the delusions afflicting the more dominant person.

A Close Relationship

The pair has often lived together for a long time with little or no social contact with others. Not many people seek treatment for their shared delusions, but when the primary partner is treated, the shared psychosis often fades away.

Sartre's Folie à Deux

French novelist and philosopher Jean Paul Sartre provides an account of a case of incipient folie à deux in "The Room". In the story, Eve's husband, Pierre, suffers from a mental illness. It becomes apparent as the story progresses that Eve is getting very close to accepting Pierre's psychotic experiences as real.

Schizophreniform Disorder

Schizophreniform disorder is just like schizophrenia except the symptoms have been present for more than one month but less than six. There is also no requirement for impaired functioning at work or in everyday life, although most people with the disorder have problems in these areas. If the symptoms were to last longer than six months, a diagnosis of schizophreniform disorder would be changed to schizophrenia.

Clues to Recovery

Medical researchers have noted that the absence or presence of certain traits can provide a good indication of the outcome of this disorder. If a person with schizophreniform disorder has two or more of the following traits or specifiers, the patient has a good chance of a smoother recovery:

- Prominent psychotic symptoms appear less than a month after the first observable changes in behavior or ability to function.
- The patient is confused or baffled as the psychosis reaches its highest level.
- There is no indication of serious difficulty functioning before problems appeared for the first time.
- Emotional responses are not suppressed or blunted.

Patients with two or fewer of these disease specifiers may have a poorer prognosis. About 33 percent of people who receive this diagnosis recover within six months. Most of the rest will ultimately be diagnosed with schizophrenia or schizoaffective disorder.

Sociocultural Influences

The American Psychiatric Association reports that schizophreniform disorder is not nearly as common as schizophrenia in developed countries, including the United States. The situation is markedly different in developing countries, where estimates suggest the number of people with this disorder may match the number with schizophrenia.

Sociocultural factors might have an influence on the recovery time from psychotic disorders. This makes sense if you accept the suggestion that environmental factors work in combination with genetic factors in the expression of psychotic disorders. The expectations of others and the manner in which an ill person is treated could conceivably influence the expression of such disorders in some individuals.

Schizoaffective Disorder

Schizoaffective disorder is a condition that includes symptoms of psychosis along with symptoms of mania or depression. It is not certain how many people have this disorder, but it may affect between 0.2 percent and 0.5 percent of the population. In contrast, schizophrenia affects approximately 1 percent of the population. Since the two conditions are so similar, some experts suggest that 25 percent to 33 percent of people with schizophrenia may have schizoaffective disorder. The illness can linger for years or decades, but recovery can be seen with individuals displaying no symptoms for extended periods of time.

Criteria for an Accurate Diagnosis of Schizoaffective Disorder

- Two or more psychotic symptoms
- A concurrent major depressive, manic, or mixed episode
- Delusions or hallucinations lasting at least fourteen days without prominent mood symptoms
- Symptoms of a mood episode must be present for a substantial portion of the active and residual periods of illness
- Drugs, medications, or medical condition must be ruled out as causes of the symptoms

Adapted from the *DSM-IV.*

It can be difficult for psychiatrists to establish the presence of both mood disorders and schizophrenia-like symptoms in a patient. It may require much observation to make a definitive diagnosis. The criteria are strict, and it is necessary to distinguish between the serious mood disorders of schizoaffective disorder and the disinterest and lack of pleasure that people with schizophrenia often develop.

Subtypes of Schizoaffective Disorder

Schizoaffective disorder is either bipolar type or depressive type. The bipolar type is applied if the patient experiences an episode of mania or a mixed episode of mania and depression at the same time. Major depressive episodes may also occur in this subtype. There are hints that younger adults are more prone this subtype than older adults. People with this subtype may tend to do better in the long run.

The presence of a major depressive episode with no prior history of a manic or mixed episode leads to a diagnosis of schizoaffective disorder, depressive type. Older patients may be affected more than young adults and women may be affected more than men. The increased number of women diagnosed with the depressive subtype probably explains the greater overall incidence of this disease among women.

Genetic Associations

Multiple studies indicate that children and siblings of people with schizoaffective disorder have an increased risk of developing schizophrenia. The incidence of mood disorders—depression and bipolar disorder—is also increased in relatives of people diagnosed with this psychotic disorder. This crossover between inherited susceptibility to schizophrenia, schizoaffective disorders, and mood disorders strengthens the argument that these diseases share at least some underlying root causes somewhere in the brain.

Delusional Disorder

The essential characteristic of this condition is the presence of non-bizarre delusions that last for at least a month. None of the other symptoms of schizophrenia are present. A diagnosis of delusional disorder may not be made if the patient is experiencing hallucinations unless they are hallucinations of only touch and/or smell that are directly related to the patient's dominant delusion. In addition, the delusion cannot be due to drug use or another disease such as Alzheimer's disease, dementia, or some other identifiable cause.

What psychiatrists consider non-bizarre delusions are often considered quite bizarre by non-psychiatrists. The *DSM-IV* provides two examples of non-bizarre delusions that might affect someone with delusional disorder:

1. A delusion of infestation related to a belief that the body is infested with insects; a tactile hallucination
2. A delusional belief that one is emitting a foul odor; an olfactory delusion

These are considered non-bizarre because they are possible, even if they are unlikely. Examples of bizarre delusions are the belief that others are controlling your thoughts or that you have been chosen by a supreme being to solve humankind's problems.

Criteria for an Accurate Diagnosis of Delusional Disorder

- The presence of non-bizarre delusions for at least one month
- No other symptoms of schizophrenia
- Hallucinations of touch and smell may be present if related to the theme of the delusion
- Aside from the direct consequences of the delusion, the patient's life is not affected in any way; in other words, intelligence and ability to function in society are normal
- Depression, if present, does not last as long as the delusion has been present
- The disorder cannot be traced to any medication, drug, or medical condition

Adapted from the *DSM-IV.*

Some people with delusional disorder do not function well, depending on the nature of their delusions. If the delusion is one that makes the patient afraid to leave his home for fear of his safety, he may not be able to work or maintain a social life. Again, this poor psychosocial functioning must be due to the delusion and not, for example, to unrelated social withdrawal and the apathy often seen in people with schizophrenia.

Most psychiatrists find that when delusional disorder is present, social relationships, including marriage, are more likely to suffer than is the patient's ability to work or reason. If the delusion does not figure closely into the subject of conversation or the task someone is working on, the person with delusional disorder can function well.

Prominent Types of Delusions

The subtype of delusional disorder is determined by the nature of the delusion. The erotomanic subtype, for example, is diagnosed when a person believes that someone else, often a person of higher social status, is in love with the patient. Lust often plays less of a role in the delusion than does the notion of intense romantic love, an unrealistic idealized connection between two souls. The object of desire is often someone the patient looks up to, such as a celebrity or someone who is obviously successful. It can be someone the patient doesn't know but believes has admirable traits and reciprocates the feeling of devotion.

If a female has an erotomanic delusion, you are likely to find her in a clinic. Men with this disorder more frequently come to the attention of police. While both sexes may try to contact the objects of their affection by repeatedly calling, writing, visiting, and stalking, males tend to be more aggressive in their pursuit.

There are exceptions to the generalized profile of this subtype, of course. For example, some patients may not tell anyone, not even the object of the delusion, about their obsession. The more aggressive pursuer who won't take no for an answer, however, is much more common.

There are several other types of delusions:

- A grandiose delusion elevates the importance of someone in his own estimation. This person is convinced he has special or unique knowledge, accomplishments, social connections, or talent. In an extreme case, a person may be convinced he is someone else, a person who is well-known. To explain the presence of the real celebrity, the patient insists that that person is a double or an imposter.
- A jealous delusion has as its key theme the imagined infidelity of a lover or spouse. This type of disorder can be traumatic for the partner, who can be subjected to unremitting and unfounded accusations based on innocuous evidence. The ill person may initiate investigations of the partner, follow her, or threaten her with violence.
- Persecutory delusions have several features in common with paranoid thinking. The DSM-IV defines this subtype as a person who believes he is "being conspired against, cheated, spied on, followed, poisoned or drugged, maliciously

maligned, harassed, or obstructed in the pursuit of long-term goals." The person with this disorder may repeatedly write to authorities seeking justice for imagined wrongs. When satisfaction fails to come, the patient's bitterness, anger, and frustration may cause him to attack his imagined enemies.

- Somatic delusions are fixated on the body. They can typically be divided into three general categories. The first is the most common: the belief that the patient's skin or a body orifice emits an unpleasant odor. The second imagines an infestation of insects or parasites somewhere in or on the body. The third group concerns the body's appearance or function. Despite the evidence in the mirror, people with this delusion are convinced that a body part is malformed, hideously unattractive, or not functioning properly.

- A patient will be diagnosed as having a mixed subtype if one subtype among the previous five categories is not dominant over the others.

- A diagnosis of an unspecified subtype is made if a patient's delusion doesn't fit any of the other subtypes.

Psychotic Disorder Due to a General Medical Condition

A patient's delusions and/or hallucinations can sometimes be traced to a medical condition other than schizophrenia. Dozens of medical conditions, ranging from neurological disorders to hormonal disruptions to metabolic diseases, can result in psychosis. Doctors must show that the symptoms are directly related to the physical abnormalities created by the medical condition. They can do this by using blood tests, a physical examination, and a detailed history of the patient's past health. Other psychiatric conditions that involve psychosis must also be eliminated. If a patient is aware that a hallucination is not real, this diagnosis is not applicable.

The *DSM-IV* implies that there may be more cases of psychotic disorder due to a general medical condition than doctors know about. It is difficult to know exactly how widespread it is because it occurs across so many medical specialties. Many of those affected may be treated by physicians who are not psychiatrists.

 Fact

Some studies indicate that psychotic disorder affects a significant percentage of patients with certain diseases: 15 percent of patients with the autoimmune disease lupus, 20 percent of patients with untreated disorders affecting the endocrine system, and 40 percent of patients with temporal lobe epilepsy, for example.

It is vital to seek an accurate diagnosis of and appropriate treatment for any instance of psychosis, including schizophrenia. Few causes of psychotic symptoms go away on their own, and it should never be assumed they will. Left untended, they can lead to years of suffering and mental decline.

Other Mental Disorders with Similarities to Schizophrenia

There are at least five other disorders whose symptoms superficially might look like schizophrenia. Two are psychotic disorders. The others belong to an entirely different classification of mental illness: personality disorders.

Other Psychotic Disorders

Substance-induced psychotic disorder is the result of exposure to a drug or a toxin. The drug can be legal or illegal, prescription or nonprescription. As long as it is directly responsible for delusions and/or hallucinations, it qualifies as a cause of this disorder.

Psychotic disorder not otherwise specified is a type of "remainder" diagnosis. Psychiatrists use it when psychotic symptoms do not satisfy the criteria for other types of psychotic disorders, when symptoms seem to contradict each other, or when there is simply not enough information to fit a person's illness into one of the diagnostic categories.

Personality Disorders

Personality disorders differ from psychotic disorders. While the dominant feature of psychotic disorders is the presence of hallucinations or delusions, the defining feature of the following personality disorders is the presence of inflexible personality traits that make it difficult for people to interact successfully with others. These individuals may appear odd to others and are often anxious and unhappy. The three personality disorders that might be related to schizophrenia or other psychotic disorders are paranoid, schizoid, and schizotypal.

Paranoid Personality Disorder

People with paranoid personalities are distrustful and suspicious of others. They routinely believe other people are trying to take advantage of them, deceive them, or harm them. These traits begin to appear in childhood, adolescence, or early adulthood and may affect more men than women.

Some studies hint at a link between this personality disorder and psychotic disorders, including schizophrenia and the persecutory type of delusional disorder. This type of personality disorder may appear more often in relatives of patients with these psychotic disorders.

Schizoid Personality Disorder

Social detachment is the most obvious feature of this relatively rare disorder. It is accompanied by a noticeable lack of emotional expression. Sex drive is absent or very weak.

There is some indication that this disorder shows up more often in relatives of people with schizophrenia. Its effect in children and teens is similar to that of paranoid personality disorder.

There are, of course, many people who prefer solitude and are considered loners by their peers, but these preferences alone do not qualify as a personality disorder. Only when traits such as these are rigidly maintained and cause problems for the person do they qualify as potential personality disorders.

Fact

People with schizoid personality disorder are cut off from companionship and make no effort to connect to others. The lack of interest in others can even extend to family members. Patients prefer solitude. Their work and hobbies often reflect this preference.

Schizotypal Personality Disorder

Like schizoid personality disorder, schizotypal personality disorder is not often seen in mental health clinics, although approximately 3 percent of the population is estimated to have the disorder—three times the number of people with schizophrenia. If this is accurate, many people with this disorder are able to function without coming to the attention of the mental health care community. Few go on to develop schizophrenia.

People with this disorder have trouble with personal relationships. They aren't comfortable with them and they aren't good at keeping them. Another symptom is what psychiatrists call "perceptual disturbances." These are not hallucinations as much as they are a sense that something is happening when in reality it is not.

People with schizoid personalities may have strange thought patterns that make them attribute significance to mundane occurrences. Another symptom of this disorder is belief in strange, paranormal, mystical, or magical phenomena. The disorder tends to run in families. It also occurs more often in relatives of people with schizophrenia.

CHAPTER 5

Symptoms of Schizophrenia

NO ONE SYMPTOM characterizes schizophrenia. In fact, proper diagnosis of the disease involves the presence of several symptoms that last for months. The American Psychiatric Association describes two general categories of symptoms: positive and negative. Other experts include additional categories, such as cognitive and psychomotor symptoms.

Positive Symptoms

Positive symptoms are not positive in the sense of being affirmative. They are positive in the sense of existing or being present as opposed to being absent or deficient. Positive symptoms are seen as additions to normal functions. These additional, unwanted contributions exaggerate or distort hearing, speaking, or thinking.

Positive symptoms include:

- Delusions, such as the patient's belief that others are plotting against him or that he is a great historical personality
- Hallucinations, which are usually auditory and involve hearing voices
- Strange, distorted, or larger-than-life ideas, behavior, or perceptions

Delusions

Delusions are firmly held beliefs in things that are not real but have great significance to the patient. They cannot be explained by a person's religion, philosophy, or cultural background. Instead, they are often strange ideas that most people who do not have schizophrenia would recognize as obviously unlikely or untrue.

A key feature of a delusion is that the patient will go on believing it even after he is presented with strong evidence that the belief is highly unlikely or obviously untrue. There are at least nine types of delusions seen in schizophrenia, and some patients may suffer from more than one.

Types of Delusions

- Grandeur. A patient may have a single, overriding delusion. He may believe, for example, that he has been chosen by God for a particular task or that he is extraordinarily powerful, creative, skilled, or otherwise exceptional.
- Thought control. A patient may believe that an outside force is putting thoughts into his mind.
- Passivity. A patient believes he is being controlled by an outside force or influence. He might be convinced that a space satellite or some form of electromagnetic radiation is controlling him.
- Reference. Anytime someone attributes a special, personal meaning to an unrelated event, thing, or occurrence, it is a delusion of reference.
- Poverty. A patient believes he has no money or security despite evidence to the contrary.
- Persecution. These paranoid-type delusions affect as many as one-third of schizophrenia patients. Patients may believe they are the subjects of highly elaborate plots.
- Guilt. People with delusions of guilt are convinced that they have done something unforgivable.
- Sickness. A physically healthy patient who is convinced he has a terrible disease has a delusion of sickness or ill health.
- Jealousy. An example of a delusion of jealousy would be an unshakable conviction, despite lack of plausible evidence, that one's spouse or partner has been unfaithful.

Adapted from the DSM-IV.

Hallucinations

While it may be an oversimplification, one way to understand hallucinations is to think of dreaming. When we dream, we see and hear people and things that are not there; our brains generate images from stores of memories. You can think of hallucinations as being similar to dreams except that they occur while a person is awake. Some people may experience hearing their name being called or a knock at the door as they are falling asleep (hypnagogic hallucinations) or as they are waking up (hypnopompic hallucinations). These are considered normal if they are transient and do not affect a person's behavior or cause them any emotional distress.

 Fact

Hallucinations are apparent perceptions that originate inside, instead of outside, a person's brain. Only the person experiencing the hallucination can sense it. Illusions are different. They have an outside source, but they are misinterpreted by the person who senses them.

The brain normally takes in information through sense organs. Nerves outside the brain coming from the eye, ear, nose, mouth, or skin pass information to cells in the brain. The brain processes the input and creates the conscious awareness of whatever sight, sound, smell, taste, or touch started the process. In a hallucination, cells in the brain that process information receive abnormal inputs from other parts of the brain rather than from cells that are outside the brain in close contact with the environment. The result is understandable: the brain thinks it senses something.

Alternatively, information-processing cells inside the brain may misinterpret input from outside the brain. The sound of a dog's barking, for example, might be misinterpreted as a human voice to create the hallucination that the dog is speaking.

Hallucinations associated with schizophrenia are most commonly auditory and involve hearing voices. The next most common are seeing things or people that are not there. Hallucinations may involve other senses, including touch, taste, and smell. Such non-auditory hallucinations, however, are rare in schizophrenia.

The voices that plague so many people with schizophrenia are very real to them, as real as the voices you hear in conversation every day. The voices may carry on conversations that the patient can over-hear, or they may speak directly to the patient.

Essential

Hallucinated voices may conduct a commentary on a person's actions or issue commands. Too often, they torment their victims, urging them to do unpleasant, disturbing things and threatening the person if they are not obeyed. Be aware of this when someone with schizophrenia seems unreachable, upset, anxious, or agitated. Voices may command a patient to hurt herself or others.

Visual hallucinations are more common when drug abuse or another identifiable medical condition is the cause. Other medical conditions are usually the source of hallucinations involving touch and smell.

Disorganized Thought and Speech

People with active schizophrenia symptoms often don't think logically. The exception might be those suffering from the paranoid form of the disease. Their delusion aside, they can sometimes function passably in society. Otherwise, people with schizophrenia may not be able to sort out what is relevant from what is not during a conversation or in a social situation.

Disordered thinking can result in very short attention spans, fleeting thoughts, and lack of focus. These symptoms may overlap with another class of symptoms associated with the disease: cognitive dysfunction.

Thought Disorder

Peculiar speech appears to reflect illogical thought patterns in some patients with schizophrenia. It is therefore one of the symptoms that most readily suggests to a layperson that a patient suffers from a mental disorder. The seemingly illogical train of reasoning and observation that accompanies formal thought disorder makes these patients very difficult, if not impossible, to understand at times. People who are unfamiliar with mental illness are baffled and often disturbed or frightened by such speech.

Thought disorder can take several forms. The patient may change topics rapidly, from sentence to sentence or even from the beginning to the end of a single sentence. Clinicians describe these seemingly unconnected shifts as loose associations. They refer to the symptom as derailment, as if the train of thought cannot stay on a straight, continuous track.

Negative Symptoms

Negative symptoms are "subtractions" from normal functions. They represent severely diminished or missing traits. Although most people think of delusions or auditory hallucinations when they think of schizophrenia, negative symptoms are just as much a part of the disease. In fact, three of the four negative symptoms discussed in this section are part of the definition of schizophrenia.

The Negative "A's"

Psychiatrists have four terms, all beginning with the letter "A," that they use to describe negative symptoms:

- Alogia refers to difficulty communicating; people with alogia don't speak much.
- Affective flattening, also known as blunted affect, reflects a lack of emotional expression displayed by many people suffering from schizophrenia.

- Avolition is a medical term used to describe the inability to form or initiate plans and to motivate oneself. It is pretty much the same as apathy.
- Anhedonia describes an impaired ability to enjoy life and find pleasure in previously interesting activities. While it is not part of the definition of the disorder, it is an important associated feature of it.

Compared to the more obvious, attention-getting displays of psychotic symptoms, negative symptoms naturally took a backseat for doctors in the years after the first effective antipsychotic medications such as chlorpromazine were introduced into the practice of psychiatry. The introduction of antipsychotic drugs was welcomed by physicians, but progress in treating negative symptoms has lagged. In fact, there is still no drug specifically approved by the U.S. Food and Drug Administration for the treatment of these persistent and troubling symptoms of the disease. Newer antipsychotic drugs, however, do show some effectiveness in some patients.

Lack of Emotional Response

Schizophrenia can produce a lack of emotional response in some people. Their facial expressions don't vary and they appear uninterested in what is going on around them. Psychiatrists call this a blunted or flat affect. This behavior is accompanied by withdrawal from other people. People with schizophrenia commonly won't leave home, preferring instead to remain alone for long periods. When pressed, the person will have little or nothing to say, a condition psychiatrists call impoverished thought.

Examples of Negative Symptoms
- Inability to enjoy books, music, celebrations, television, and hobbies
- A blank facial expression
- An inability to act, plan, and move toward a goal

- A disinclination to speak or having nothing to say about anything
- No interest in dating, attending parties, or socializing
- Lack of response or reaction to emotional events

Speech is uninflected and delivered in a monotone. Not surprisingly, a person in such a state will display little or no ambition, motivation, or interests. In extreme cases, this lack of motivation can result in near complete inactivity that extends even to personal cleanliness.

Alert

Some medications may have cognitive side effects. Familiarize yourself with side effects of medications and discuss them with your doctor if you suspect that one or more medications are impairing thinking ability or speed. An adjustment in dosage or choice of medication may solve the problem.

Some patients may use invented words, or neologisms, in their speech. The unique words may mean something to the inventor, but listeners are rarely able to follow their meaning. Other patients may speak in rhyme (a speech pattern called clang) when answering questions or making statements. Still others repeat the same thing over and over, a symptom called perseveration.

Social Isolation

Speaking to someone who is easily distracted and who apparently cannot distinguish relevant from irrelevant material is very disconcerting for people who do not understand the symptom. Consequently, the affected individual may be shunned by others. This obviously only adds to feelings of isolation.

Cognitive Problems

Many people who are not familiar with mental illness believe that difficulty thinking clearly, concentrating, and remembering are secondary problems in people with schizophrenia, the result of thought disorder, psychosis, or simply lack of ambition. In fact, cognitive problems appear to be true, primary symptoms of the disease and are included among the negative symptoms. They are also known as deficit symptoms. They can take the form of poor memory and an inability to pay attention or to make decisions. They can make it difficult for someone with schizophrenia to function easily in school, at work, and in his social life. Thought disorder is a strong impediment to maintaining an independent life.

Important Facts about Cognitive Problems in Schizophrenia
- They do not always disappear when hallucinations and delusions stop.
- They are not the result of laziness, indifference, or lack of effort.
- They are not always the result of antipsychotic medications.
- They do not result from long hospital stays.

Source: New York State Office of Mental Health

If symptoms such as difficulty thinking and performing mental tasks were secondary to schizophrenia, you would not expect them to persist after the worst periods of psychosis are over, but they often do. Nor would you expect them to appear before the first psychotic episode, which they do.

The idea that cognitive dysfunction can be a frontline symptom in schizophrenia is not surprising when you consider the results of functional brain imaging and neuroanatomical studies that show brain abnormalities in some patients.

The cerebral cortex, the prefrontal cortex, the hippocampus, and other brain regions closely associated with cognition are affected by the disease. Depending on the site examined, scientists report detecting signs of decreased activity, missing neurons, or smaller than average neurons. If key parts of the brain responsible for thinking, planning, and reasoning are compromised by the disease, it makes sense that these abnormalities underlie the cognitive problems so often observed in people with schizophrenia.

 Question

Do antipsychotic drugs fix cognitive problems?
Most antipsychotic medications don't do much to improve cognitive problems in a direct way. However, by relieving the distractions caused by hallucinations and delusions, antipsychotic medications allow most patients to improve their ability to think, concentrate, remember, and interact. They also make it easier to make progress in therapy sessions designed to improve cognitive skills.

Cognitive Problems Seen in Some People with Schizophrenia
- Difficulty paying attention
- Difficulty remembering and recalling information
- Difficulty processing information quickly
- Difficulty responding to information quickly
- Difficulty with critical thinking, planning, organizing, and problem solving
- Difficulty initiating speech

Adapted from Alice Medalia and Nadine Revheim's *Dealing with Cognitive Dysfunction Associated with Psychiatric Disabilities: A Handbook for Families and Friends of Individuals with Psychiatric Disorders.*

This does not mean that mental skills cannot be learned and improved in people with schizophrenia. Cognitive and other forms of therapy can provide useful skills that enable patients to improve their thinking abilities. Just as someone who has suffered an injury to a limb can improve his ability to function through physical therapy, someone who has schizophrenia has a chance of improving her ability to function through cognitive therapies. Consumers of mental health care can learn about the disease and learn how to participate in their own treatment. In many cases, they can even improve to the point at which they can function independently or with part-time assistance.

 ## Question

Do all people with schizophrenia have cognitive problems?
Most do. Neuropsychologists estimate that 85 percent or more will have some problem with intellectual tasks. The degree of impairment varies from person to person. Early in the course of the disease, cognitive problems may be particularly troublesome. In young people, cognitive impairment is a serious, early warning sign of schizophrenia even if it appears before psychotic symptoms.

It is not unusual for cognitive problems to be overlooked when far less subtle psychotic symptoms dominate the concerns of patient, family, and doctor. After hallucinations and delusions are under better control, problems with mental acuity may become more apparent.

Tips for Overcoming Memory Problems

- Repeat reminders and instructions often and dispassionately. Don't nag, dominate, accuse, or allow your frustration to show. Remember, the person with a memory problem may feel defensive and upset because of it. Try to be understanding.
- Work patiently with the person as you get him to repeat the instructions under consideration. Help him recall by offering clues and multiple choices. Expect errors, but concentrate on parts of the task he does remember.
- Write it down. Maintain lists of tasks, appointments, chores, and activities related to school, work, and home life. Write down plans, goals, and steps to achieve them. Work with the person to create the lists and review them regularly.

- Have a schedule for reviewing lists, plans, and routine chores or activities. Help the person learn through repetition.
- Experiment with memory aids.
- Try calendars, watch alarms, alarm clocks, journals, diaries, tape recorders, sticky pad note paper, and reminders taped to the refrigerator, front door, or in the car.
- Keep the techniques that work and abandon those that don't. Keep trying to find an approach that helps.

Adapted from Alice Medalia and Nadine Revheim's *Dealing with Cognitive Dysfunction Associated with Psychiatric Disabilities: A Handbook for Families and Friends of Individuals with Psychiatric Disorders.*

The delay in recognizing cognitive problems is one of the reasons they can be misinterpreted as signs of simple laziness, indifference, or even the result of treatment. Memory problems in people with schizophrenia can demand great patience on the part of the caregiver, but they are surmountable.

Variability of Symptoms

Listening to people with schizophrenia describe their illness and hearing accounts given by their relatives can give the impression that symptoms of the disorder are fairly uniform: hallucinations and delusions. It may take a closer look over a longer time to appreciate the diversity of symptoms and their changeable nature.

Clusters of Symptoms

Labeling someone with one of the five standard diagnoses of schizophrenia doesn't, unfortunately, provide much insight into how well she may respond to treatment or what course the disease is likely to follow. Psychiatrists have noted, however, that symptoms tend to change over time in groups.

The severity of one group of symptoms tends to change independently of other groups. Within a group, however, you are less likely to see changes.

Shifting Patterns of Symptoms

Hallucinations and delusions, psychotic symptoms, tend to increase or decrease in severity together. The same is true for negative symptoms and for disorganized behaviors and speech. Each of these three categories of symptoms can change from absent to mild to moderate to severe.

Gender Differences

Just as there are differences in the characteristics of heart disease in men and women, there are significant differences in how schizophrenia strikes the two sexes. Perhaps these sex differences might be traced to different effects of male and female hormones during brain development and/or to their effects on the disease process around the time of puberty. At this time, no one knows exactly why they exist.

Differences in Age of Onset

Schizophrenia usually appears early in the lives of both sexes, but some studies indicate that it may appear slightly earlier in males than in females. The median age is in the early twenties for males. This means half of men showing symptoms for the first time are less than twenty-three years of age.

For women, the median age of onset is in the late twenties. Thus, while many males show obvious signs of the disease in their early twenties, many women tend to develop obvious symptoms in their late twenties to early thirties. Women also seem to experience a faster onset of the disease than men do. Most adults over the age of forty who develop late onset schizophrenia are female.

Differences in Disease Severity

Schizophrenia seems to develop more rapidly in women than in men. When the disease is at its worst, females tend to suffer from its positive symptoms such as hallucinations, delusions, and disorganized or bizarre behavior. But these symptoms are more likely to come and go rather than persist in females. During the remissions, women are more likely to do better than men. They can often function quite well without much impairment. As a group, females also have fewer cognitive problems. Not surprisingly, these features of schizophrenia in women contribute to their generally better chances for recovery.

Question

Is schizophrenia "nicer" to women than to men?
No. It is a serious disease for both sexes. Women are more likely than men to have had a higher level of functioning in their social, school, and work life before becoming ill. Schizophrenia may also take less of a toll on women. Observations like these are based on a very large sample of patients and vary depending on the individual.

A gender difference has also been reported in the incidence of schizoaffective disorder. More women than men are diagnosed with this disorder, particularly its depressive variety.

The Threat of Suicide

The National Alliance for Research on Schizophrenia and Depression estimates that as many as 40 percent of schizophrenia patients will attempt suicide. The Schizophrenia Society of Canada suggests as many as half will make an attempt. Claiming an estimated 10 percent to 15 percent of the lives of schizophrenia patients, the suicide rate is much higher than in the general population. It is the major cause of premature death in people with schizophrenia.

Severe depression can occur when patients are free of psychosis. Understanding and struggling with such a serious illness can be very demoralizing. Patients may lose hope of ever recovering. It is under these psychological burdens that most suicide attempts occur.

Younger adult males with schizophrenia are most at risk, but any mention of the subject by any patient must be taken very seriously—and people with schizophrenia are very likely to bring up the subject. Not everyone who talks about suicide attempts it, but it is very difficult to predict who will attempt to take his own life and who won't. Seek professional help immediately if someone you care for talks about suicide or indicates to you that he may be at risk. These patients should be under the care of a psychiatrist, who should be informed that the patient is discussing suicide.

Alert

Many people assume suicide is the result of psychosis or severe delusions. The torment of voices and other psychotic symptoms can contribute to the risk of suicide, but these symptoms are responsible for fewer suicides than most people believe. Despair and depression are more often the reason people with schizophrenia attempt suicide.

If, in an emergency, you cannot find a psychiatrist right away, immediately seek help at a hospital emergency room or by calling a crisis or suicide hotline. Psychiatrists can prescribe an antidepressant medication and antipsychotic drugs to help counter the effects of depression.

CHAPTER 6

Warning Signs of Schizophrenia

IT IS NOT unusual for a patient developing a mental illness to go to a general practitioner's office complaining of vague symptoms of physical discomfort as well as sleeplessness, fatigue, and even headache. Some patients first see a psychiatrist only after symptoms have been present for years. This is something you should avoid. Incipient mental illness calls for quick treatment.

Onset: The Early Warning Signs

The earliest symptoms of schizophrenia, such as apathy and withdrawal from others, often are overlooked by family and friends. Later, after a diagnosis is made, a psychiatrist may refer to this as the prodromal phase of the disease. Since patients may start avoiding social situations during this stage, it is easy to see how this could be interpreted as simply needing or wanting time alone. At this point in the development of the disease, there may be no way to know that a young person is not experiencing a phase of moodiness unless you are familiar with the early warning signs of mental illness and the first signs of schizophrenia in particular.

Possible Hints of Trouble to Come

The American Psychiatric Association provides a list of some changes that could indicate the beginning of a potentially serious mental illness. Not all of these signs have to be present. You might notice just one sign at first or you might see several.

Warning Signs of Mental Illness

- Marked personality change
- Inability to cope with problems and daily activities
- Strange ideas or delusions
- Irrational fears
- Prolonged feelings of sadness
- Marked changes in eating or sleeping patterns
- Thinking or talking about suicide
- Extreme highs and lows
- Abuse of alcohol or drugs
- Excessive anger, hostility, or anxiety
- Violent behavior

Source: The American Psychiatric Association

Becoming aware of a pattern of potential warning signs may help you guide someone to much-needed psychiatric care. You also should not hesitate to seek help if you suspect trouble. It is better to be reassured than to miss early signs of mental illness. The stakes are very high.

Prodromal Symptoms of Psychotic Disorders

Prodromal symptoms are traits, behaviors, and preferences appearing in children or young adults that may indicate developing psychosis. For some, the symptoms subside or remain subtle and no treatment is necessary. For others, they are the first signs of a developing, potentially serious disease. Recognized and treated early, these symptoms can lead to more effective treatment and better outcome.

Changes in Behavior or Performance that Might Signal Schizophrenia

- Social withdrawal or isolation. Little interest in speaking or being with others. Preference for spending time alone.
- Sleep disturbance.
- Little motivation, energy, or ambition. Little interest in previously enjoyable pastimes, hobbies, sports, or other activities.
- Easily distracted. Reduced concentration, difficulty paying attention or remembering things.
- Deterioration of grooming, self-care, or personal hygiene habits.
- Problems performing or functioning in school, at work, or at home. Difficulty understanding what others say or what one is reading.
- Lack of emotional display. Little facial expression. Flat, monotone speech.
- Inability to organize speech.
- Conversation includes statements irrelevant to the topic, inappropriate choice of words, unconnected flow of speech.

Adapted from the CARE program at the University of San Diego, California; the Center of Prevention and Evaluation, Columbia University Department of Psychiatry/New York State Psychiatric Institute; and the Centre for Addiction and Mental Health, University of Toronto.

Children in the process of developing the disease also undergo changes in the way they see and think about things. Some of these changes will be obvious to someone who knows the child. Other changes, such as unusual perceptions, are not apparent to others.

Changes in Feelings or Thoughts that Might Signal Schizophrenia

- Unusual perceptions. Strange sensations: Things look or sound different. Hearing voices, seeing things that are not there, or imagining things. A feeling that something strange is happening even with familiar events and objects. Misinterpreting sounds for voices. The perception of objects is exaggerated, dulled, or otherwise changed. Greater sensitivity to taste, sounds, smells, or sights.

- Unwarranted suspiciousness. Misinterpretation of events. Uncertain if being followed, watched, or the subject of plots.
- Developing unusual pattern of thinking with odd, strange, or eccentric behavior, ideas, or beliefs. Seeing special meaning or threats in commonplace events. Difficulty telling the real from the imaginary. Déjà vu experiences more often than usual. Suspicion that others can hear thoughts, read minds, or control behavior. Preoccupation with mystical ideas, religion, or superstitions.
- Grandiose ideas leading to feelings of superiority. Exaggerated belief in talent, fame, power, importance, status, or abilities.
- Anxiety or irritability.
- Muddled or disorganized thinking. Mental confusion. Thoughts seem sped up or slowed down.

Adapted from the CARE program at the University of San Diego, California; the Center of Prevention and Evaluation, Columbia University Department of Psychiatry/New York State Psychiatric Institute; and the Centre for Addiction and Mental Health, University of Toronto.

Trust Your Intuition

If your gut feeling indicates that something is not right with someone you know, investigate the source of these feelings. Keep on the case until you are convinced the changes you sensed or observed were fleeting and you can no longer see any evidence of change. Ask other people if they detect any changes. Take their impressions into consideration, but rely on your intuition so you don't ignore any warning signs you think might be significant. The sooner a person gets help for a mental disorder, the better chances she has of experiencing a less severe illness that responds better to medication and psychotherapy.

When secondary features of schizophrenia such as agitation, disturbed sleep, and a disinclination to socialize is combined with a decline in cognitive abilities or a loss in intellectual sharpness, you have a clear indication that something potentially very serious is developing.

 Question

Are there any signs that someone is about to become psychotic?
Sometimes, early symptoms of schizophrenia produce significant changes in behavior that can be very disturbing for family members and friends. In other cases, changes may be subtle. Some secondary problems related to the onset of schizophrenia can provide a hint that psychosis may be present or developing. Look for evidence of disturbed sleep, anxious behavior or agitation, and avoidance of social situations.

Some Indicators in Early Childhood Behavior

What we know about the pathology of schizophrenia indicates no outstanding difference between the illness that strikes in adolescence and the illness that strikes in adulthood.

There may, however, be a difference in severity of symptoms. When the disease strikes early, patients tend to have:

- More severe brain abnormalities present before diagnosis
- More abnormalities in brain cells
- Poorer future outcome
- Possibly a greater genetic burden based on their relatives who have or have had psychiatric illnesses

If symptoms are present early, they may not appear particularly startling on their own. Not all children who go on to develop schizophrenia stand out as different in their behavior.

When considered in retrospect, the behavior of children later diagnosed with schizophrenia, may seem "different." From a very early age, they may have been less social and more emotionally distant than other children. Looking back after full-blown schizophrenia has developed, these symptoms are often recognized as the beginning of a decline in functioning.

Danger! Decline in Intellectual Functioning

Adolescence is often a challenging time for young people and their parents. Passage through normal adjustment periods can be frustrating and aggravating for both parent and child.

While some early warning signs of mental illness and prodromal signs of schizophrenia may have alternative explanations, there is one that usually does not. When a young person shows a decline in his intellectual or thinking abilities, a psychiatrist will begin to suspect schizophrenia. A loss in cognitive ability in a young adult is rare unless schizophrenia is involved.

This doesn't mean one or two bad grades. It means a pattern of problems that indicate a young person cannot understand, read, write, or think as well as she once could. You should seek professional advice if you detect such cognitive dysfunction in a young person.

School Problems Due to Cognitive Problems

A 2008 study of more than 900,000 Swedish children born between 1973 and 1983 found that students who received the lowest scores on standard tests had double the risk of being diagnosed with schizophrenia later in life. Those with the worst performance records in all areas of schoolwork had four times the normal risk of developing the disorder. The medical records of the children, who were fifteen or sixteen years old when they took the tests, were examined when the subjects were seventeen or older.

The researchers who conducted the study do not believe that lack of intelligence explains the observation. For these children, the researchers believe, it is likely that their poor performance was a consequence of cognitive problems.

Fact

Cognitive dysfunction is known to develop before more obvious symptoms such as full-blown or florid psychosis. Problems with memory, concentration, attendance, self-discipline, organizational abilities, and even social skills can contribute to poor school performance in a child who previously showed normal or above normal ability and intelligence.

One of the authors of the Swedish study, Dr. James MacCabe of the Institute of Psychiatry at King's College London, was quoted by the BBC: "Doing badly at school is not a cause of schizophrenia, but it is a marker for something not being quite right several years prior to diagnosis."

Developing Schizophrenia Before and After Adolescence

In the vast majority of cases, this brain disease does not become apparent until well into adolescence. At the other end of the age spectrum, it does not commonly appear in adults past age forty or so. When it does appear in an unusually young or old individual, one thing seems clear: it is similar to the disease that usually strikes young adults or adolescents. It is not clear what might accelerate or delay the appearance of symptoms in cases that develop in the very young or in those who are middle-aged.

Childhood Schizophrenia

It is extremely rare, but children as young as five can develop schizophrenia. In these unusual cases, the disease tends to follow a more chronic course with persistent symptoms and few if any periods of relief from them. It would be quite unusual, however, to detect psychotic symptoms such as hearing voices or other hallucinations or delusions in such very young children.

Although childhood schizophrenia appears to be similar to the disease that more commonly affects adolescents or young adults, it is often associated with other brain-related problems, including behavioral and learning problems, and neurological symptoms, including seizures and slight or mild mental retardation.

 Fact

Just as brain abnormalities have been detected in adults with schizophrenia, they have also been detected in children with the disease. Brain imaging studies reveal decreased gray matter in the cerebral cortex and decreased brain size, a feature that progresses with time.

Some children may display indications that suggest they are not mentally healthy. These children often suffer from abnormal language development, and they may go on to develop schizophrenia or another mental disorder when they are in their teens, twenties, or early thirties.

Late Onset Schizophrenia

When schizophrenia first appears in an individual after the age of forty, it is called late onset schizophrenia. This subclassification of the disease is distinguished from very-late-onset schizophrenia-like psychosis in which symptoms appear after age sixty. Estimates of the number of cases developing after age forty run as high as 10 percent to 23.5 percent of all schizophrenia cases. It is possible that the late onset condition is the result of underlying pathologies distinct from the disease that strikes young people, but no one knows for sure. It has been suggested, however, that symptoms accompanying very-late-onset disease might be traced to the social isolation and impaired senses that can affect older people.

In 2000, a group of seventeen international specialists in the treatment of late onset schizophrenia published a consensus in the *American Journal of Psychiatry.* They agreed to the following points about schizophrenia when it strikes after age forty:

Some Features of Late Onset Schizophrenia and Very-Late-Onset Schizophrenia-like Psychosis

- Women tend to show symptoms later than men.
- There are more similarities than differences in early- and late-onset disease. This is particularly true for positive symptoms. However, visual, tactile, and olfactory hallucinations may be more common in late onset schizophrenia.
- Cognitive deficits generally appear to be similar in early- and late-onset disease, but learning and the ability to abstract information may be less impaired with later onset disease. There is no evidence that dementia plays a role.
- Negative symptoms and formal thought disorder are rare in very-late-onset schizophrenia-like psychosis.
- Seniors affected by very-late-onset schizophrenia are less likely to have other family members affected by schizophrenia than are people with earlier and middle-age onset.

As with all forms of schizophrenia, treatment relies heavily on antipsychotic drugs. A major difference in pharmaceutical therapy in late onset disease, however, is dose. Older individuals seem to be more sensitive to the effects of antipsychotic medication and should initially receive much lower doses than young patients. For most people affected by late onset disease, the dose might be only 25 percent to 50 percent of the dose a younger person would receive. And a person with very late onset disease might respond favorably to a dose just 10 percent of that given to a younger patient.

Can Schizophrenia Be Prevented?

While we do not yet know how to prevent schizophrenia altogether, we are indeed able to intercept its early development in some people and significantly lessen its impact. This is an active and promising area of research that may represent the next significant advance in schizophrenia therapy. One of the challenges this approach presents is the need to identify and direct at-risk people to the mental health care system before symptoms develop.

Starting Before the Disease Strikes

Preventive care can be invaluable in conditions such as schizophrenia. As a caretaker, you are best placed to determine whether you or someone you know is at risk. You can seek preventive care even before symptoms appear. You can tap into the expertise of those who are investigating, treating, and trying to prevent schizophrenia in its earliest detectable form or forms.

Some Risk Factors for Schizophrenia

- Family history
- Having older parents
- Maternal infections during pregnancy
- Complications during pregnancy and delivery
- Social adjustment problems in children and adolescents
- Velo-cardio-facial syndrome (a genetic condition affecting facial appearance, heart function, and some gland development)

Adapted from "Considering Schizophrenia from a Prevention Perspective," M.T. Compton. Published in the *American Journal of Preventive Medicine*, February 2004.

Medical researchers have already identified a likely biological basis for schizophrenia believing it may be possible to halt or slow mental deterioration produced by schizophrenia. The structural abnormalities present in the brains of some people with schizophrenia may change over time or may even be affected by treatment. It had been assumed that these abnormalities were established early in a patient's life, but recent long-term neuroimaging studies indicate that the brain changes may progress over time. This means it may be possible someday to intercede and slow—or even stop—the progressive changes with preventive and early care.

Advice for Someone at Risk of Developing Schizophrenia

Having a close relative with schizophrenia is a risk factor for developing the disease. Genetics, however, is not the same thing as fate. If one identical twin can be free of schizophrenia while the other has it, it is likely the twins have undergone significantly different experiences or environmental interactions. Some of these factors may have been encountered in the womb or shortly after birth, while others may have been encountered in childhood. Consequently, parents and future parents should practice the best prenatal and infant care they can.

 Alert

If you have a family history of schizophrenia, you can take action to reduce your chances of being incapacitated by the disease. If you are worried, contact a mental health care clinic or early treatment center and get some advice. Read about steps you can take on sites such as *www.schizophrenia.com*.

Many programs across the country are actively seeking young people with an elevated risk of developing schizophrenia to participate in innovative research programs aimed at preventing the emergence of the disease. Adolescents with a family history of schizophrenia can lower their risk by not using illegal drugs or abusing alcohol. People with a predisposition toward mental illness may be particularly susceptible to bad reactions to recreational drugs. Use of marijuana, cocaine, methamphetamines, hallucinogens, and other street drugs can accelerate or precipitate mental problems.

Other precautions include taking steps to counter the signs of negative symptoms of schizophrenia such as social withdrawal, lack of interests and ambition, and slow thought processes. Work at getting and keeping a network of healthy friendships. Try to be socially active, even more so than you are normally inclined to be. Read about different personalities and social interactions. Direct your attention outward toward others as much as you direct it inward toward yourself. If you find yourself spending a lot of time alone, change the pattern. Get out. Join clubs. Call someone you know.

 Fact

Participating in different pastimes, hobbies, and other interests that stimulate your mind may help preserve mental function and foster social interaction. Consciously seek out positive events, milestones, and accomplishments that are not featured at the top of the news hour or on the front page.

Mastering stress will benefit you. Use physical activity, meditation, yoga, and recreation to reduce stress. Competitive sports are fine, and you don't need to be a good athlete to participate. You can also be athletic without competing by participating in individual sports in which you try to improve your past performance rather than try to defeat an opponent. Exercise eases stress. If you feel anxious, learn about anxiety and how to offset its effects on you.

Seek help at the first sign of mental distress, including depression and anxiety. If you ever feel that life is getting to be too much or things are piling up on you, talk to a competent professional. It is not a sign of weakness; it is a sign of intelligence and a sign that you are in control.

Psychotic Symptoms Are an Emergency

It is not unusual for a person to become psychotic in such a way that it goes undetected or unrecognized for weeks, months, or even longer. The length of these unnecessary delays can vary, but researchers at the University of British Columbia estimate that, in many cases, a year or more passes between the first appearance of psychotic symptoms and the start of proper treatment. Other estimates place the delay at up to seven or even nine years on average.

Better Outcomes

Long delays between the appearance of psychotic thoughts and the initiation of therapy may make it more difficult to overcome disease symptoms. When signs of schizophrenia are spotted early and treatment is sought sooner, patients start therapy with fewer and less severe symptoms than if psychosis is allowed to run untreated. Researchers have also found that patients who received treatment with less delay had a better response.

Alert

Do not pretend that changes in behavior or warning signs will be temporary. If you see symptoms of psychosis, don't assume it is a phase someone is going through. A crisis requires medical treatment that can comfort the patient and decrease the duration and severity of a psychotic episode.

Fast treatment can also help preserve self-confidence and self-esteem. This, in turn, can improve a patient's ability to function successfully in school, at work, and as part of a family or other social group. It may decrease the severity of depression that often strikes patients as they face the realization that they must struggle with a mental illness as serious as schizophrenia.

Treating Initial Psychotic Episodes

Young people experiencing their first psychotic episode can be very sensitive to the effects of antipsychotic drugs. Although the use of these medications can help suppress delusions and minimize their destructive impact on a person's life and thoughts, it is a good idea to ease into their use if they are required. Low doses given over longer time periods can minimize side effects. It may take up to a few weeks for the patient to respond, but if her symptoms were caught early, they may be controlled effectively by the medications.

Explanations and Therapy

The emergence of mental illness is confusing and upsetting for the patient and her family. Following a psychotic episode, a person may feel confused and demoralized, and lack a sense of worth and confidence. You can help by explaining to her that, like millions of other people, she has been ill but is receiving treatment and will improve. Without lecturing, make it clear that illness is not something to be ashamed of.

To help establish rapport with a person being treated for schizophrenia, assure her that, as with her doctor, her conversations with you will be confidential. Tell her you will not discuss anything she confides to you with anyone else. If she is not comfortable disclosing something to her doctor, try to find out why. Offer to help find a doctor she will feel comfortable talking to.

Psychoeducation classes help first-time patients by teaching them and their families about the illness and what is likely to happen next. Cognitive therapy may sometimes help correct delusions, while other therapeutic approaches can improve the patient's ability to handle stress.

Early Warning Clinics

If you are at high risk or if you see symptoms that might be related to schizophrenia or other mental illness in someone you know, you have several options for seeking help. You can contact a local psychiatrist experienced in treating schizophrenia or a nearby psychiatric treatment facility. Hospitals associated with research universities often offer state-of-the-art care. Another option is an early diagnostic clinic. These facilities can be found all over the United States and

Canada. You can find them listed under "Mental Health Services" in the Yellow Pages of the phone book or by using the services locator at *http://mentalhealth.samhsa.gov.* Appendix C also has a list of early treatment clinics.

Consider calling a clinic close to you. A trained staff member will tell you about the programs they offer and arrange an appointment, if appropriate, for you to visit for an interview and an evaluation.

 Question

Who can benefit from early treatment clinics?
Usually someone who has had one or a few psychotic episodes or who has been receiving treatment for less than six months to a year is considered to have an early psychotic disorder. Some clinics also evaluate and treat young people at high risk of developing psychotic symptoms.

Most of these clinics are interested in treating people around the teenage years, but the range varies widely. They tend to accept residents of the counties or provinces in which they are located. Most conduct research studies that involve their patients. The treatment and services they provide are extensive and often include family therapy.

Some clinics provide services on a sliding fee scale, making them affordable to many people regardless of their level of income. A few of them charge nothing except the cost of any medications. Call, write, or e-mail to determine if you are eligible and to learn details about a clinic that interests you.

If you cannot find a clinic near you, call local hospitals and mental health care providers to find out what programs are available in your area. Make use of all possible resources to find the facility and treatment that are best for you. You might be able to find a local therapist or doctor who is willing to work with you to try to prevent further development or progression of the disease.

CHAPTER 7

Schizophrenia-like Symptoms in Other Medical Conditions

ONE OF THE reasons the criteria for diagnosing schizophrenia are stringent, inclusive, and detailed is the need to make sure some other completely unrelated medical condition is not causing similar symptoms. Many medical conditions, psychiatric and otherwise, produce symptoms such as psychosis that can be confused with schizophrenia unless a careful examination of the patient is conducted.

Bipolar Disease

This fairly common mental illness used to be called manic depression or manic-depressive illness. The two poles indicated in the name refer to depression and mania. It is much more common than schizophrenia. Some patients with bipolar disorder experience psychotic symptoms such as hallucinations or delusions that may sometimes be mistaken for schizophrenia. However, the prominent mood symptoms, mania or depression, help distinguish it from schizophrenia.

Depression

When depressed, a patient with bipolar disease may lack energy and be sad, joyless, and uninterested in the world. She may not eat or sleep well. The depressive state can take a different form, with despair leading to tension, anxiety, restlessness, and fears that reach a delusional level.

Mania

When she is manic, a patient is overly, abnormally excited. She may also be irrationally enthusiastic, talkative, easily distracted, impatient, or irritated. Ideas speed through the mind. Concentration is poor. Constantly in motion, overly confident and sure of her ability to accomplish whatever pops into her mind, a patient in a manic state may spend money indiscriminately and make unrealistic plans.

Alternation in Mood

For some people, these extreme moods may alternate with one another in a cyclical fashion. In other cases, the patient may have symptoms that combine features of both depression and mania, or one may be dominant over the other. The different moods may come and go quickly or slowly.

 Fact

Three percent of the population will experience psychosis at some point during their lives. Around two-thirds of these people will not develop schizophrenia. While some may have only one or few psychotic episodes in their lifetime, it is very important that everyone experiencing psychosis be evaluated.

Depression often dominates the disorder. For some, extreme manic states don't play a very large role, although patients may experience periods of elevated mood as they come out of a period of depression. Whichever mood dominates, some patients with the disorder may have psychotic symptoms, including delusions and hallucinations.

Drug-Induced Psychosis

A fairly wide variety of chemical substances can produce psychosis. These include prescription medications, legal over-the-counter medicines, and illegal drugs. Not all of these substances will induce psychosis in everyone who uses or abuses them. Some people are more susceptible to this side effect than are others. Obviously, people with a predisposition to or a history of psychosis are at elevated risk of experiencing drug-induced psychosis. Be sure you are familiar with the medications the person you care for takes and seek drug counseling for him if you see signs of drug abuse.

Legal Drugs

Some drugs prescribed for legitimate medical reasons can produce psychosis in some people. Steroids and levodopa (in Sinemet), a drug commonly prescribed to counter the symptoms of the movement disorder Parkinson's disease, are two examples. Patients with schizophrenia are especially sensitive to the psychosis-inducing side effect of levodopa, which works by increasing levels of dopamine in the brain. Many antipsychotic drugs prescribed to treat schizophrenia decrease the activity of dopamine. It is not difficult to see how people with schizophrenia would be especially sensitive to levodopa's psychosis-inducing side effect.

Two legal drugs, alcohol and nicotine, are as dangerous as some illegal drugs. Besides contributing to the deaths of millions of people worldwide, they pose particular threats to people with schizophrenia.

Schizophrenia and Smoking

According to the National Institute of Mental Health, the majority of people with schizophrenia smoke tobacco. This high rate of smoking may be an attempt by patients to medicate themselves. Nicotine, the active ingredient in cigarettes, may help people with schizophrenia focus by stimulating a specific set of brain receptors called alpha-7 nicotinic receptors. Smokers find nicotine's effects soothing. People with schizophrenia may be getting a response that somehow relieves some aspect of the disease. More research is needed before this phenomenon can be explained satisfactorily.

Unfortunately, smoking can lessen the effectiveness of medications prescribed to counter the most disturbing effects of schizophrenia, making higher doses of antipsychotic drugs necessary. Higher doses, of course, raise the risk of side effects, which, in turn, increase the likelihood that a patient will not take his medicine. In most cases, a person's chances of relapsing increase significantly when he doesn't take his medication.

 Question

Can drinking produce psychotic symptoms?
It is not uncommon to see psychotic symptoms in a victim of chronic alcoholism. Patients who are dependent on alcohol may experience hallucinations after binge drinking. They also may experience delusions and/or hallucinations when they go through a state of withdrawal from alcohol.

While starting smoking is obviously not recommended for a person with schizophrenia, quitting smoking presents complications of its own. Nicotine is a highly addictive drug. For many people, breaking an addiction to it is as difficult as breaking an addiction to harder drugs.

Nicotine withdrawal is uncomfortable, but it can be especially troublesome for people with schizophrenia. It may make their schizophrenia symptoms worse as long as the withdrawal period lasts.

The best option is to persuade someone not to start smoking, if possible. If the person already smokes, encourage him to quit with a doctor's guidance. The doctor may want to adjust the patient's medication during the nicotine withdrawal period and will be able to offer advice in the use of nicotine patches or other replacement remedies that may help patients stop smoking.

Illegal Drugs
There is no doubt that many street drugs can produce psychotic symptoms in otherwise mentally healthy people. In some cases, the

psychotic episode caused by these drugs is indistinguishable from schizophrenia. These effects may be particularly damaging in people prone to mental illness.

Use of street drugs is risky for anyone, but this is especially true for people with severe mental illness. People with schizophrenia, for example, may turn to illegal substances to distract them from their symptoms. This form of self-medication is obviously self-defeating. Patients who self-medicate may stop treatment and experience even worse disease symptoms.

Alzheimer's Disease and Other Dementias

Alzheimer's disease is the most common form of dementia. It produces a gradual but continuous decline in memory and intellectual abilities. Victims have trouble performing once familiar tasks, learning new things, paying attention, and generally understanding events.

Alzheimer's disease is linked to the appearance of dense, plaque-like material in the brain, tangles of cellular proteins, and the death of neurons in parts of the cerebral cortex responsible for higher mental functions.

Although patients with this form of dementia may show psychotic symptoms, Alzheimer's disease is distinguished from schizophrenia by loss of memory and other basic brain functions. These losses follow a very evident decline in short-term memory over a span of several months. Furthermore, it is a disease that occurs after the age of sixty-five in the vast majority of patients.

 Fact

Besides memory loss and confusion, people with Alzheimer's disease may also develop paranoia, other delusions, or hallucinations and behavioral changes. When these changes result in disorganized behavior, they appear similar to some of the behaviors that are seen in schizophrenia.

Dementia can also be caused by hardening of the arteries in the brain (cerebral arteriosclerosis) and repeated mini-strokes, both of which deprive key brain regions of their essential blood supply. In some patients, this damage can produce psychotic-like symptoms.

It is not unusual for patients who suffer from Huntington disease, an inherited, neurological condition characterized by involuntary muscle movements, to be mistakenly diagnosed first with schizophrenia. The mental deterioration and psychotic behavior that can accompany Huntington disease is responsible for the confusion.

Psychosis Resulting from Other Medical Conditions

Other disease processes that affect the brain can produce psychotic symptoms. These include strokes, some seizure disorders such as epilepsy, brain infections, or conditions that affect the body and its blood vessels and may spread to the brain in some cases.

Sometimes It Isn't Really Schizophrenia

Problems with the thyroid gland, which regulates metabolism, can cause psychoses unrelated to schizophrenia. This can take the form of hypo- or hyperthyroidism—too little or too much production of the thyroid hormone. Other medical conditions that produce psychotic symptoms are the autoimmune disease systemic lupus erythematosus, the viral infection AIDS, and vitamin B12 deficiency.

Brain Damage

It is possible that damage to the brain following falls, wounds, and other forms of trauma can produce psychotic symptoms in some people. They can certainly cause dramatic changes in personality. It is also possible that such injuries may be associated with the onset of schizophrenia in some vulnerable people.

Brain tumors present a less complicated situation: they, as well as some forms of epilepsy, can definitely produce psychotic symptoms.

The tumors may be located in the frontal, parietal, or occipital lobes. Tumors that affect a master gland in the brain called the pituitary are also associated with the production of schizophrenia-like symptoms.

Infection

Before antibiotics became available, infection by the bacterium that causes syphilis, *Treponema pallidum*, was more common than it is today. In the final stage of the disease, the microbe attacks the brain. This condition, which is called neurosyphilis, was one of the most common reasons patients were admitted to psychiatric facilities in the late nineteenth and early twentieth centuries. The damage the bacterium does to the brain may cause dementia and psychosis. A blood test and examination of cerebrospinal fluid reveals the presence of the bacterium, which is readily treatable with antibiotics. The disease process can be stopped and symptoms may be relieved depending on the damage already done.

If HIV, which is the virus that causes AIDS, gets into the brain, it can produce symptoms that mimic severe mental disorders, including schizophrenia. The fact that *T. pallidum* and HIV can produce schizophrenia-like symptoms underlines the importance of having a complete physical exam, including specialized testing for these infections.

Other Psychotic Disorders

Even a thousand psychiatrists contributing to the *DSM–IV* cannot fit some instances of psychosis into neat categories. The solution is to lump them into a category of their own called "Psychotic Disorder Not Otherwise Specified."

Postpartum Psychosis

It is common knowledge that mild depression after giving birth affects some new mothers. As many as 30 percent of these patients suffer enough to be considered clinically ill with postpartum depression. Unfortunately, one out of every 1,000 new mothers is also at risk of developing postpartum psychosis.

Alert

Postpartum psychosis can be successfully treated with antipsychotic medications just as postpartum depression can be successfully treated with antidepressant medications. It is possible, however, that psychosis could recur after giving birth again. A woman at risk for postpartum psychosis should discuss with her doctor whether there is a risk if she gives birth again.

If a woman develops psychotic symptoms after giving birth, she will first be examined to determine whether she is suffering from any of the defined psychotic disorders. If none of those fit, her diagnosis will be postpartum psychosis. It usually strikes within four weeks of delivery and has all the features of schizophrenic psychosis, but it is brief in duration and is therefore technically called, according to *DSM–IV*, brief psychotic disorder with postpartum onset.

Other Psychosis of Unknown Causes

Sometimes psychoses occur for reasons that seem more mysterious than schizophrenia or other major mental illnesses. It is possible, for example, for a person to begin hearing voices or experience auditory hallucinations but have no other features of disease or mental disorder. These may include so-called musical hallucinations, in which a person most often is aware that these are indeed hallucinations generated by her brain and not something real in the environment. They tend to occur in older individuals who have some hearing problems and are becoming somewhat deaf.

CHAPTER 8

Impressions of Schizophrenia

PEOPLE WHO DISPLAY psychotic symptoms can puzzle and frighten those around them. If you can get a sense of what a person with schizophrenia is experiencing, his behavior may make much more sense to you. Of course, a healthy person could never experience the full shock of psychosis, but with descriptions provided by patients and former patients, you can gain an intellectual understanding. This comprehension destroys stereotypes and misconceptions about schizophrenia.

Hallucinations

Many people describe experiencing increased sensitivity to sensations such as sight and sound long before their illness incapacitated them. This can be pleasant on a limited scale for a short time. When the sensations become very intense, the resulting distractions make it impossible to perform routine functions.

Imagine if the room around you became many times brighter, the colors so shimmering, startling, and intense that you had trouble looking away from them. Everywhere you turned, you saw the same extreme intensity of sights and colors. How easy would it be for you to function in such a world?

Auditory hallucinations can create the same effect. This is one of the reasons some people with schizophrenia have trouble concentrating on a task or subject, paying attention to someone who is trying to talk to them, maintaining a line of thought, or perceiving what is going on around them.

It is clear, for example, that people with schizophrenia often hear internal voices that no one else can hear. This alone can be disorienting and terrifying. Imagine living with voices originating inside your head. Whose voices are they? Why do they say such demeaning, disturbing, and demoralizing things? Why won't they stop?

Delusions

If a young person is just beginning to develop early symptoms of schizophrenia, it may be possible to reach her and alter her thought processes before delusions become fixed. Once a delusion is fixed in a patient with long-term schizophrenia, however, you cannot talk her out of believing it.

Like hallucinations, delusions have credibility for people with schizophrenia because there they have no obvious reason to doubt their validity. For example, a person's brain convinces him that he is cold in winter without a coat. There is no doubt the person feels cold. When the same, previously reliable brain tells the person that others are plotting against him, this internally generated misinformation seems just as valid as information about the outside temperature.

The same thought processes that have served a person well for twenty or so years appear to the person to continue to provide reliable information. The delusion seems just as real as valid information provided by the brain. Nothing distinguishes the delusional beliefs from the valid beliefs generated by the brain. There is no reason to doubt one and not the other.

If the person can be reached by positive outside influences, such as therapy, before the "evidence" supporting the delusion becomes overwhelming, it is possible to weaken the basis of the delusion much more easily than if the "evidence" is allowed to accumulate over years of unchallenged illness.

Proof Is Everywhere

A key feature of delusional thinking in a person with paranoid schizophrenia is connectedness. Events that are truly random and unconnected for most people will assume great significance for the patient. If the dominant delusion is that a person is being spied on, then all sorts of random occurrences are incorporated into the delusion. Leave for work and find your tire is flat? It must have been sabotaged by the people who are doing the spying. Hear a noise outside your window? It must be one of "them" moving around out there. Meaningless, random events can be encompassed into other delusions. These events can be unending and only tend to confirm the underlying delusion.

Conviction

Choose a part of your life that is important. It could be your job, a pet, your apartment, or the food you eat. Now imagine someone trying to convince you that that thing does not exist. You know it exists. You interact with it or participate in it every day. Every memory and sense you have attests to its existence. It is important that you understand that the experience of schizophrenia convinces people that their hallucinations and delusions are as real to them as the familiar things in your life are to you.

 Fact

Therapy, talk, and reasoning will no more change a person's mind about the reality of her fixed delusion than it could change your conviction that you have a heart. Antipsychotic medication can and does weaken delusional convictions, allowing many patients to begin to examine their thinking processes.

Now imagine that you are absolutely certain other people are controlling you. The prospect is frightening. If you are convinced that someone can read your mind or control your most private thoughts, your reaction is likely to be one of panic. And what if you saw and heard messages delivered just for you in television news broadcasts or in signs in shop windows? It doesn't seem real and you know it is outrageous, but you cannot deny it is happening. To you it is a fact, as real as everything else in your life.

Fright is too weak a description of the feeling you would have if you began to lose touch with reality and you could tell it was slipping away. Most people experience such stresses only by watching horror movies or reading horror stories. For many people with untreated schizophrenia, these experiences are horrible realities. For some, they can happen at any time; for others, they never end.

Paranoia Exercise

Try to remember a time when you misplaced something valuable or something that was important to you. It might have been a favorite pen, a piece of jewelry, your wallet, a watch, or even your keys. Did it ever occur to you, however fleetingly, that someone must have taken it? After all, it was right there where you thought you left it and now it is gone. Try to recall that feeling that someone might have taken it. Usually, you find the item or accept the fact that you misplaced it.

Now imagine that things like this begin happening frequently, routinely. Your brain tells you that weird things are happening to you. This is the same brain that has served you well all your life. It has never betrayed you before. You know those people across the street are talking about you. It is obvious to all your senses that it is happening. What else can you conclude but that something is causing this to happen to you?

You can increase your level of anxiety by realizing that there exist elaborate conspiracies, all directed against you personally. People you see on the street are actually plotting against you. Your life might be in danger because of them. You are 100 percent convinced that the threats are real because your brain tells you it is really happening.

Loss of Control

Schizophrenia often is characterized by a feeling that one is losing control. Thoughts may race so quickly that it becomes impossible for untreated patients to focus on a single subject or topic. In Ronald J. Comer's *Fundamentals of Abnormal Psychology,* one patient describes his thought process.

"My thoughts get all jumbled up. I start thinking or talking about something but I never get there. Instead, I wander off in the wrong direction and get caught up with all sorts of different things that may be connected with the thing I want to say but in a way I can't explain. . . . My trouble is that I've got too many thoughts. You might think about something, let's say that ashtray and just think, oh! Yes, that's for putting my cigarette in, but I would think of it and then I would think of a dozen different things connected with it at the same time."

It is easy to understand how difficult it would be to organize your thoughts and use them to be productive when you are handicapped in this way.

This loss of control is not like attention-deficit/hyperactivity disorder, which involves the persistent inability to pay inattention or focus on a task or issue and/or excessive physical activity and a tendency to active impulsively. The loss of control in schizophrenia is more a loss of control of mental processes including thoughts, impressions, feelings and associations. Thoughts flash into consciousness in a helter-skelter manner. One thought is replaced by another before the person has time to analyze it.

A Maze of Experiences

Another patient quoted in Comer's text and in E. Fuller Torrey's book *Surviving Schizophrenia* describes a similar challenge. For her, schizophrenia means "trying to think straight when there is a maze of experiences getting in the way, and when thoughts are continually being sucked out of your head so that you become embarrassed to speak at meetings." It is easy to understand how difficult it would be to organize your thoughts and use them to be productive when you are handicapped in this way.

The same woman provides an overview of her experience. For her, schizophrenia means "fatigue and confusion, it means trying to separate every experience into the real and the unreal and sometimes not being aware of where the edges overlap. . . . It means feeling sometimes that you are inside your head and visualizing yourself walking over your brain, or watching another girl wearing your clothes and carrying out actions as you think them. It means knowing that you are continually 'watched,' that you can never succeed in life because the laws are against you and knowing that your ultimate destruction is never far away."

A consumer quoted by the Canadian Mental Health Association recalled: "It was like I was having a million thoughts all at once and yet I was so disorganized, nothing was getting done. I was frightened and anxious because I felt someone was trying to harm me. Increasingly, I spent most of my time alone in my room doing nothing. I didn't want to be bothered with friends or family. The television started having special messages meant only for me and I was hearing voices commenting on what I was doing. Looking back, I realize things just weren't making sense anymore. At the time though, it seemed normal and I didn't mention what was happening with me to anyone."

Sense of Self and Emotions

People with schizophrenia may be confused about where they stop and objects and people in the world around them begin. Understandably, they also experience emotional changes that have a major effect on their lives. The changes can range from overemotional states to an apparent lack of emotional responses.

Distorted or lost sense of self

It is not unusual for people with schizophrenia to experience strange sensations concerning the relationship of their bodies—and sometimes their identities—to things and people in their surroundings. Placing a hand on a table may raise uncertainty in a person's mind about where the hand stops and the table begins. Limbs may appear to change in size. A person may feel disconnected from parts of their body.

These sensations might be related to the abnormal processing of sensory information that is responsible for the exaggerated, intense, and distorted sights and sounds people with schizophrenia frequently experience. They share some similarities with hallucinations and delusions and undoubtedly can overlap with these positive symptoms. They differ, however, by affecting the person's identity and sense of self. A person with a delusion may be convinced he is being hunted by government agents, but he may still retain his sense of self, which feels threatened. Another person may hear tormenting voices but still retain her identity; after all, she can still distinguish between the voices and herself.

A person experiencing an altered sense of self, however, may feel inanimate or cut off from "who he was" before his illness. He may feel like a robot, an automaton, a machine, or something under the control of an outside force.

Other people report that they become convinced they are someone else whom they are watching. It is not clear what aspect or aspects of the schizophrenic disease processes accounts for these feelings or sensations, but it clearly reflects changes in higher brain function.

Emotions Here and Gone

People with schizophrenia undergo a range of emotions as their illness develops, including shame, embarrassment, fear, and guilt. It is not unusual for a person to be depressed after experiencing a psychotic episode but many individuals develop clinical depression before they show any positive signs of schizophrenia. Depression may be present at other times during the course of the illness caused, at times, by the person's realization that they have a serious illness. If it becomes very serious, a doctor may prescribe an antidepressant, a step that can not only relieve emotional suffering but save the person's life since the risk of suicide is higher than average in people with schizophrenia.

Emotional expressions may change quickly in some people and exaggerated feelings may also occur; fear may become paralyzing, guilt incapacitating and happiness euphoric. Dr. E. Fuller Torrey cautions in *Surviving Scizophrenia* that while exaggerated emotions are common in the early stages of the illness, they are rarely seen beyond that period. In fact, he warns that "if the person retains exaggerated feelings to a prominent degree beyond the early stages of the disease, it is much more likely that the correct diagnosis will turn out to be manic-depressive illness." The following list details some of the emotional changes that may be triggered by schizophrenia. It is adapted from Torrey's *Surviving Schizophrenia.*

 Question

What is inappropriate affect?
For a psychologist or psychiatrist, affect refers to the expression of emotions. Inappropriate affect is an unusual emotional response seen in some patients with schizophrenia. It causes them to respond to news or to an event in a manner opposite the way most people would respond. Informed of good news, a person with inappropriate affect might show signs of sorrow. Informed of bad news, a person might laugh.

Some Aspects of Emotional Changes in Schizophrenia
- Depression
- Exaggerated feelings
- Fear
- Guilt
- Rapidly changing emotions
- Inappropriate affect
- Lack of emotions

At the other extreme is a near total lack of emotional expression. It seems as if emotional feelings are turned off in many people who have struggled with the disease for years. This might be related to the commonly observed inability to appreciate what other people are feeling. This seeming self-centeredness appears to be another consequence of the disease process.

CHAPTER 9

Treating Schizophrenia with Drugs

CURRENTLY AVAILABLE ANTIPSYCHOTIC drugs do not cure schizophrenia, but they do offer hope to many patients by lessening or suppressing the disease's most severe symptoms. These medications allow many people a chance to loosen the grip of an otherwise debilitating disease, take back control of their lives, and return to a much better level of daily function. They are the best treatment now available for treating schizophrenia and the psychotic symptoms of other psychiatric conditions.

Finding the Right Medication

The response to treatment varies from one person to another. One medication may help one person but not another. One medication may cause unbearable side effects for one person while another may tolerate it very well. This is an area in medical science where we still have much to learn.

Trial and Error

Doctors have to rely on trial and error as they try to make educated guesses when choosing the best medication for each patient.

This trial and error method is used in most medical specialties. This is how doctors treat blood pressure, diabetes, asthma, and many other conditions. The key to the success of this process is effective and open communication among the doctor, the patient, and the family. Letting the doctor know which symptoms improve and which do not, and which side effects are troubling you and which are not, is the best way to help the doctor help you find the right medication and the right dose.

Knowing What and How to Prescribe

Prescribing antipsychotic drugs requires expertise. Ideally, it should be done by a psychiatrist or a physician who has received special training in these treatments. It is not enough to know only the different medications and their characteristics; it is also necessary for the prescriber to have global medical knowledge about the body in general, about its different organs and their functions. This is because medications affect all parts of the body. After they do their job, most medications are broken down by the liver and other organs and are filtered out of the body by the kidneys. It is therefore essential for the prescriber to understand how the body's organs react to various medications, how other diseases and their treatments may change the treatment of schizophrenia, and how potential side effects of the drugs should be monitored, prevented, or minimized.

Essential

Initial doses of antipsychotic medications should be low and increased slowly until the target symptoms are suppressed. As little medication as possible should be prescribed. The dose should be just enough to avoid recurrences of psychotic symptoms while avoiding side effects, which should be monitored closely.

The prescriber must have up-to-date knowledge of conditions that may be associated with antipsychotic medications, such as diabetes, high blood pressure, and high cholesterol. Whoever takes the responsibility for prescribing these medications should follow certain minimum guidelines: Generally, only one medication should be used at a time, and its side effect profile should be carefully considered with regard to the person taking it.

 Fact

In the last fifty years, dozens of effective antipsychotic drugs have been synthesized, studied, and introduced into clinical therapy. These medications remain vital components of most schizophrenia treatment plans. They continue to provide the majority of patients the opportunity to live better lives, something the patients once had little or no chance of achieving.

It is sometimes necessary to change either the type or the dose of a patient's medication. The goal is always to reach the best balance between the benefits and the side effects. A newly diagnosed patient may require different treatment than does someone who has had the disease for months or years.

How Do Antipsychotic Medications Work?

Drugs that relieve symptoms of schizophrenia alter the activity of specific chemicals, called neurotransmitters, in the brain. These chemicals transmit signals from one brain cell to specific receptors on the next brain cell. Neurotransmitters play a crucial role in the processes responsible for communication between different brain cells.

Interactions with Chemical Messengers

We don't know exactly how it happens, but we do know that mental functions can be altered and adjusted through the use of drugs that affect brain cell function, either by exciting or by inhibiting them, by speeding up or slowing down some of their activity. All psychoactive substances, from socially acceptable drugs such as caffeine to antipsychotic drugs such as clozapine, affect the activity of neurons, although each has its own potency, target in the brain, and psychoactive effect.

Side Effects and Medication Targets

Antipsychotic drugs in general interfere in the functioning of several neurotransmitters and receptors, notably dopamine. Many of the older antipsychotic drugs show strong correlations between their ability to block dopamine receptors in the brain—particularly receptor subtype D-2—and their ability to relieve psychotic symptoms.

Clozapine targets serotonin receptors more than it does dopamine receptors. Dopamine receptors, like serotonin and other neurotransmitter receptors, are found in different parts of the brain and body. These receptors have different subtypes that are given numbers, such as D-1, D-2, D-3, D-4, and so on. Each of the subtypes has a different function. Dopamine D-2 receptors control body movements; if they are blocked, the tremors associated with Parkinson's disease can result. Since clozapine has less of an effect on the D-2 receptors, it does not cause symptoms like Parkinson's disease, but it does have very strong antipsychotic actions. It also interacts with other receptors, not only those specific to dopamine and serotonin. These interactions seem to account for some of the side effects that may occur with clozapine, including drowsiness, constipation, difficulty urinating, and possible weight gain.

As in other medical specialties, we still do not fully understand how these medications work. Some research, however, suggests they block dopamine receptors in one area of the brain that causes psychotic symptoms without blocking them in other areas. This may explain why some newer antipsychotic medications do not cause some of the undesirable side effects that older medications do.

Ziprasidone is an example of a second generation or atypical antipsychotic that blocks serotonin receptors as well as dopamine receptors. This compound has other interesting pharmacological properties that give it additional therapeutic value: it is fairly good at preventing norepinephrine and serotonin, two neurotransmitters linked to depression, from being taken up into neurons after they have been released.

Ziprasidone thus prolongs the action of these two neurotransmitters by extending their stay in the gap between neurons, where they continue to stimulate their respective receptors. Consequently, some newer medications like Ziprasidone are useful for patients who have symptoms of depression in addition to their symptoms of schizophrenia.

This is only a small example of the many chemical activities these drugs have, and it is an oversimplification of the chemical imbalance that appears to be present in schizophrenia. Nevertheless, it is a basis for beginning to understand the actions of antipsychotic medications.

Two Main Types of Antipsychotic Drugs

Antipsychotic drugs are divided into two general groups. The older first generation drugs are called typical, traditional, or conventional antipsychotic medications. They were once referred to as neuroleptics, a term derived from the neurological features of their side effects. Neuroleptic means "grabbing or taking hold of neurons."

Their use is limited to only 10 percent of the market today. The more commonly prescribed, newer medications are called atypical or novel antipsychotic drugs or second generation antipsychotics. These newer drugs have shown treatment benefits beyond their antipsychotic effects, including treatment of bipolar disorder. Consequently, some doctors refer to them as broad spectrum psychotropics. Psychotropics are drugs that affect the mind. This term more accurately reflects the ability of newer medications to serve as more than just antipsychotics.

Typical Antipsychotic Drugs

The first antipsychotic drugs, now more than half a century old, brought about a revolution in psychiatry due to their ability to decrease the severity of schizophrenia's symptoms. Early studies compared the drugs to already available sedatives. Despite the presence of some unwanted side effects, they represented a real breakthrough in treatment. For the first time, patients could realistically look forward to the hope of escaping from their delusions and hallucinations. These typical antipsychotics could also control disorders of thought that plagued patients with schizophrenia.

Effectiveness of Older Antipsychotic Medications

The American Psychiatric Association's Guidelines for treatment of patients with schizophrenia summarized several studies on the efficacy of first generation antipsychotics in the acute phase of treatment. These studies found that approximately 60 percent of patients treated for six weeks improved to the extent of complete remission or experienced only mild symptoms, compared to only 20 percent of patients treated with a placebo.

Table 9-1: Typical or Conventional Antipsychotic Medications

Trade or Brand Name	Generic Name
Haldol	haloperidol
Loxitane	loxapine
Mellaril	thioridazine
Moban, Lidone	molindone
Navane	thiothixene
Orap	pimozide
Serentil	mesoridazine
Thorazine	chlorpromazine
Trilafon	perphenazine
Permitil, Prolixin	fluphenazine
Stelazine	trifluoperazine
Taractan	chlorprothixene
Vesprin	triflupromazine

Sources: *Medications for Mental Illness, The Essential Guide to Psychiatric Drugs,* and *The Complete Family Guide to Schizophrenia.*

Forty percent of patients treated with typical antipsychotic medications continued to show moderate to severe symptoms, compared to 80 percent of patients treated with a placebo. Only 8 percent of patients treated with these medications showed no improvement or a worsening of symptoms, compared to nearly 50 percent of placebo-treated patients.

It appears that all first-generation antipsychotics are equally effective. If a patient had responded to a given medication in the past, he was likely to respond to the same medication again.

Like all medications, older antipsychotic drugs have side effects. The more serious ones will be discussed later in this chapter, but the following list should give you a basic idea of what to expect.

Some Common Side Effects of Conventional or Older Antipsychotic Drugs

- Muscle stiffness or spasms
- Tremors
- Dry mouth
- Jumpiness
- Sedation
- Weight gain
- Constipation
- Loss of motivation
- Sensitivity to sunlight
- Dizziness

Atypical Antipsychotic Drugs (Second Generation Antipsychotics)

Atypical antipsychotic medications were introduced into the marketplace in the 1990s. Initially they were hailed as major advances in schizophrenia psychopharmacology. Pharmaceutical companies highlighted the lack of the neurological side effects that so often affected people taking the older antipsychotic drugs. Furthermore, clozapine, the first atypical antipsychotic, demonstrated the ability to effectively treat patients who did not respond to typical antipsychotic medications.

Table 9-2: Newer or Atypical Antipsychotic Medications

Trade or Brand Name	Generic Name
Abilify	aripiprazole
Clozaril, FazaClo	clozapine
Geodon	ziprasidone
Invega	paliperidone
Risperdal	risperidone
Seroquel	quetiapine
Zyprexa, Zydis	olanzapine

Sources: *Medications for Mental Illness, The Essential Guide to Psychiatric Drugs,* and *The Complete Family Guide to Schizophrenia.*

The newer antipsychotic drugs have been more popular among psychiatrists than were the older drugs. One of the most important features of the second generation antipsychotics is their potential ability to block dopamine in the area of the brain that is associated with psychosis but not in brain pathways (called extrapyramidal pathways) which are responsible for movement coordination. This is possibly why newer medications cause fewer extrapyramidal symptoms—side effects involving movement—than do the first generation antipsychotics. This has made them more appealing to doctors and patients alike. These medications, however, have some significant side effects of their own, which will be discussed later.

It was initially thought that all the second generation antipsychotics that became available after clozapine would show the same level of efficacy in patients who did not respond to the typical antipsychotics. However, this did not turn out to be true for most of the newer medications.

What's in a Name?

Medications often have at least three names. The most basic name is the one given to it by chemists. This chemical name is often long and difficult to pronounce and can include numbers that indicate where certain atoms or groups of atoms are bound to each other. Hearing the chemical name, a chemist can draw the molecular structure of the compound without hesitation. Haldol, for instance, is the trade or brand name of a drug whose chemical name is 4-(4-(p-chlorophenyl)-4-hydroxy-piperidino)-4'-fluorobutyrophenone.

The generic name is easier to remember than the chemical name and is often linked to it in some way. The generic name of Haldol is haloperidol. If the drug is no longer under patent or exclusive ownership by a pharmaceutical company, any generic drug manufacturer can manufacture the drug and sell it, but only under its generic name. The trade or brand name is a medication's "commercial" name, the copyrighted name under which the company that has rights to the drug sells it. No other company can sell the drug under that name.

Chemically, a molecule is a molecule and the label it has is irrelevant to its ability to do its job. The only difference between a drug sold under its brand name and its generic name will be price, assuming both manufacturers have the same standards of quality control when making the drug. The FDA monitors these drugs and their manufacturers to make sure that these standards are met. Nevertheless, there have been reports of patients losing the benefits of a certain medication when they change from a brand to a generic or from one generic to another. While this is uncommon and its reasons are not always well understood, if you notice worsening in symptoms after you switch to a generic drug, speak to your doctor to consider the possibility that this was due to a different manufacturer or a variation among generic drugs.

If you change doctors, be sure you keep careful records of prior treatments. The new doctors may get a copy of your old records, but you should not rely on paperwork that is handled out of your control. Keep a record of treatments and changes in treatments. This is particularly important if you change doctors while in the middle of changing medications. Use a journal so you don't lose track of all details about the medications in use. Note their effectiveness, side effects, dosages, starting and stopping dates, and past adjustments. Share this information with the new doctor.

Know Your Medication

Make sure you have the right drug. Two groups responsible for drug safety, the U.S. Food and Drug Administration and U.S. Pharmacopeia, warn that it is becoming easier to confuse medications because of similar sounding names. It is one of the most common medical errors.

There are at least 3,170 confusing pairs of drugs with similar names. Close to 1,500 medications have names that look or sound much like those of other medications. Confusing one drug for another with a similar name happens to an estimated 375,000 people every year. This can happen when prescriptions are written sloppily, words are smudged on faxes, names are not pronounced clearly, a pharmacist grabs the wrong drug container, or when a patient mistakenly tells a doctor he has been taking a drug that sounds like one he should be taking.

Alert

When you get prescriptions filled, write a note to tell the pharmacist what the medication is for. Use a paper clip to attach a small piece of paper to the written prescription; do not write on the prescription itself. Write on the paper, for example, "Olanzapine for schizophrenia." You can also ask your doctor to write what the medication is for directly on the prescription.

The antipsychotic clozapine has been confused with clofazimine and clonazepam. Zyprexa has been confused with Zyrtec and Zaroxolyn. Sometimes these incorrect substitutions will be quickly spotted and corrected, but it is important to be cautious and learn the names and dosages of your medications well. The U.S. Pharmacopeia's Drug Error Finder website (*www.usp.org/hqi/similarProd ucts/choosy.html*) tracks drugs with similar names.

APA Groups

The American Psychiatric Association divides antipsychotic medications into four groups. Group 1 includes the typical antipsychotic agents, while Group 2 is made up of the atypical antipsychotic agents. Clozapine makes up Group 3, and Group 4 includes long-acting, injectable antipsychotic drugs.

Features of Some Popular Antipsychotic Medications

Although they are more popular, the newer antipsychotic drugs may not always be better than the older ones. In fact, one government-financed study—which was not sponsored in any way by pharmaceutical companies—concluded there was little difference between four atypical antipsychotic drugs (Risperdal, Seroquel, Geodon, and Zyprexa) and one older drug, perphenazine. The report in the New England Journal of Medicine found that all of the drugs were effective at decreasing debilitating symptoms of schizophrenia.

Zyprexa surpassed the others in controlling symptoms for a longer time, but one of its side effects—weight gain—was a serious drawback. In fact, side effects had a large impact on the study. Nearly three out of every four patients participating in the study stopped taking their first assigned drug. They blamed side effects or other sources of discomfort. Those patients, however, went on to take other medications that they tolerated better and that produced better results for them.

An important lesson from this study is that you should persevere in the search until you find the medication that works best for you with the lowest side effect profile. Follow your physician's recommendations, but don't rule out any drug candidate, old or new, in your joint effort to find a medication that will help.

The First of the Atypical Drugs

Clozapine (Clozaril) was the first of the antipsychotic medications to be called an atypical drug because it did not produce the neurological side effects associated with the older drugs. It has the striking advantage of being effective in the 10 to 30 percent of patients who do not respond to other medications. Some psychiatrists think it is often overlooked and underused as a treatment option.

When other drugs fail to help a patient, clozapine often does help, although it may take longer than other antipsychotic medications to prove its effectiveness. One advantage is that it does not seem to raise prolactin levels, which are linked to lack of sexual drive, breast enlargement, and milk production and disruption of the menstrual cycle in women. In one out of 100 people, clozapine may cause agranulocytosis, towering the number of white blood cells that the body uses to fight infection. Besides this potentially serious side effect, it can also produce sedation, excess salivation, and seizures in a small number of people. With proper monitoring, however, clozapine remains a useful option for patients who cannot tolerate other medications or do not respond to them. It was also found to be more effective in getting rid of suicidal thoughts, and for that reason may be a good option for a patient who is chronically struggling with suicidal thoughts or behavior.

Risperidone (Risperidal)
Risperidone is another atypical antipsychotic and is less likely to produce extrapyramidal symptoms in lower doses than are the first generation drugs. It may cause drowsiness or insomnia and it may increase prolactin production.

Olanzapine (Zyprexa)
Olanzapine is also an atypical antipsychotic. While it can produce significant weight gain, blurry vision, problems with excretion, and drowsiness, it rarely causes neurological problems. Prolactin levels may increase in patients using olanzapine, but to a lesser degree than is observed with the typical antipsychotics.

Quetiapine (Seroquel)
Quetiapine has an even lower risk of producing extrapyramidal side effects or elevated prolactin levels. It can cause dizziness, dry mouth, stomach upset, and drowsiness in some users.

Ziprasidone (Geodon)

Ziprasidone is another atypical antipsychotic agent that is less likely to cause extrapyramidal side effects, but it may raise prolactin levels like other drugs in its class. According to an FDA warning about Geodon, it should not be taken by patients with certain heart conditions. Because Geodon may affect heart function in some people, it is important not to mix it with other medicines that do the same. Patients who are susceptible to dehydration or electrolyte imbalances may be at greater risk for this side effect. Be sure to let your doctor know about all the medications you are taking.

If you develop an infection that requires antibiotics, make sure your doctor knows that you are taking Geodon in order to avoid any serious drug interaction. Like other medications in this group, it can also cause weight gain in some people, although this side effect may be milder and less frequent for Geodon than it is for some of the other drugs, like Zyprexa.

Aripiprazole (Abilify)

This drug might produce restlessness, nervousness, anxiety, sleeplessness, and nausea, among other side effects, in some people.

Is There a "Right" Medicine for Everyone?

The large majority of people with schizophrenia experience substantial improvement when treated with antipsychotic agents, but finding the best medications may take time. Drug therapy for schizophrenia often falls into two stages: the initial or acute phase and the long-term or maintenance phase. The acute phase is often brought about by a psychotic episode and sometimes requires higher doses of antipsychotic drugs to relieve the symptoms.

If possible, it is preferable to treat a patient experiencing a first psychotic episode with as low an effective dose of antipsychotic medication as possible to limit chances of side effects. If a person experiences the stress of a psychotic episode and soon after comes to associate an unpleasant side effect with treatment, he will be more likely to avoid treatment in the future.

Doctors may prescribe an anti-anxiety medication or minor tranquilizer, such as Ativan (lorazepam), Xanax (alprazolam), Klonopin (clonazepam), or Valium (diazepam) for a few weeks after starting antipsychotic drug therapy. Until the antipsychotic drug becomes fully effective, anti-anxiety medications can reduce agitation and calm the patient as he recovers from the trauma of his psychotic experience.

 Question

What are minor tranquilizers?
Also called anxiolytics, or anti-anxiety agents, minor tranquilizers are medications that reduce tension and relieve anxiety. The best known belong to a group of chemicals called benzodiazepines. They are useful for calming people under physical and psychological stress. They reduce feelings of fear and agitation at least in part by increasing the activity of a chemical messenger in the brain called GABA (gamma-Aminobutyric acid).

Other adjunct medications, such as Cogentin (benztropine) or Artane (trihexyphenidyl), are used to reduce problems with extrapyramidal side effects. These medications, however, may sometimes cause side effects of their own, including constipation, difficulty urinating, and blurry vision. Older patients may be particularly vulnerable to these side effects. If side effects don't present a problem, both benzodiazepine and Cogentin or Artane can be dropped from the drug lineup as the antipsychotic medicine exerts its full therapeutic effect.

Newer, atypical antipsychotic medications are also prescribed for treating initial psychotic episodes. Many doctors believe they are preferable because they have few or no extrapyramidal side effects, and adjunctive treatment with benztropine may not be required.

Once symptoms are under control, the patient enters the maintenance phase, in which doses are reduced as much as possible to minimize the side effects while continuing to prevent the recurrence of acute psychotic episodes. The maintenance phase may be lifelong for many individuals.

Essential

Medications can interact in dangerous ways. Avoid harmful drug combinations by making a list of all prescribed drugs, over-the-counter medicines, herbal remedies, vitamins, and supplements that someone with schizophrenia is taking. Show the list to your doctor and your pharmacist. They can determine if there is a danger of harmful interactions.

Finding a good match between a patient and a particular medication for the maintenance phase is a trial-and-error process. Different individuals often respond differently to the same drug.

Example of a Treatment Plan

Antipsychotic medications typically start working in the first week of treatment, but they may require up to three months to be fully effective. It may take considerable effort to hit on the right treatment, but try not to get discouraged.

Adjunctive agents such as diazepam or lorazepam may be prescribed if the patient experiences restlessness due to the antipsychotic therapy. This side effect may also be effectively treated with propranolol (Inderal), a medication known as a heart and blood pressure medicine, or Benadryl (phenhydramine), a well-known antihistamine or anti-allergy medicine.

In *The Essential Guide to Psychiatric Drugs*, Jack M. Gorman, MD, advises continuing the antipsychotic medication for one year after the initial stabilization of symptoms if the patient has a history of one psychotic episode, and for several years if he has had two or more episodes. If a patient forgets, refuses, or is unable to take daily medication, a long-lasting injectable version of Haldol (Haldol Decanoate), Prolixin Decanoate, or Risperdal (Risperdal Consta) may be tried. The American Psychiatric Association's guidelines for initial treatment of schizophrenia suggest starting with atypical antipsychotic agents. For treatment of the first psychotic episode, the APA guidelines suggest trying risperidone, olanzapine, quetiapine, ziprasidone, or aripiprazole (one of the new or second generation drugs). It recommends considering clozapine in patients who do not respond to other treatments or have persistent, chronic, and unrelenting suicidal thoughts or behavior. Some of the atypical antipsychotics might also benefit patients with tardive dyskinesia, a side effect involving involuntary movements.

The Group 2 drugs could be considered if the patient has a history of extrapyramidal side effects, but they should avoid high doses of risperidone. Patients who gain weight easily, have high blood sugar, or show high cholesterol in the blood might respond better to ziprasidone or aripiprazole. Again, patients who repeatedly fail to take their medications can be treated with long-lasting injectable formulations of antipsychotic drugs that may be given once every two to four weeks. Of course, regular monthly visits to the doctor will help spot side effects such as tardive dyskinesia, weight gain, or diabetes.

Realizing the Benefits

The decision to take a particular medicine is a balancing act between its benefits and its side effects. Aspirin, for example, has the potential to kill in large enough doses and to cause bleeding in the stomach lining with long-term use. Its ability to treat headache and decrease inflammation at lower doses nevertheless makes it a popular and widely used drug. Cancer medications have a much narrower safety factor than aspirin. That is, their effective doses are close to their dangerous doses. When the stakes are high, greater risk is taken in treatments. Side effects that would not be acceptable for treating a mild headache often are readily accepted when a life is at stake.

Taking Antipsychotic Medications

Antipsychotic medications are usually taken in tablet or liquid form once or several times a day, depending on the specific medication. Depot formulations, which require injections only once every two to four weeks, are available if patients cannot or do not take their daily medications. Some medications are available in formulations that make them disintegrate and dissolve in the mouth within seconds. These are good for people who have problems with swallowing pills or who may hide and not swallow their medication. These medications are also available in injectable formulations that may be given in emergency situations if a patient is acutely upset, hostile, aggressive, paranoid, angry, or severely distressed by acute worsening in their psychotic symptoms. Check with your doctor if you have questions about how and when to take any prescribed medications.

 Fact

The potencies of drugs vary. A low dose of one medication may be enough to produce a positive effect, while a second drug requires a much higher dose to be as effective. It takes roughly twenty times as much Thorazine, for example, to match the effect produced by Haldol.

The drugs available to treat psychosis have serious side effects. Still, the consensus of the medical community is that the risk of side effects is worth taking if the right drug is found.

Antipsychotics effectively treat psychotic episodes and reduce the chance of recurrence. The Schizophrenia Society of Canada reports that 80 percent of patients will have a relapse within two years without treatment. This drops to less than 45 percent with regular use of antipsychotics. Adding therapy and training classes is believed to reduce the two-year relapse rate even more.

Early Warning Signs of Relapse
- Increased agitation
- Increased sense of unease or discussion of troubling delusions
- Change in sleep patterns
- Avoidance of other people

Consistent use of medication results in a 50 percent reduction of the chances of rehospitalization. Also, by eliminating the tormenting symptoms of the disease, the risk of suicide can be reduced.

Although these medications may not make psychotic episodes disappear entirely from every patient's life, they are very effective at reducing the number and severity of such episodes. Dosages used for long-term maintenance are typically lower than those used to treat severe, active psychotic symptoms. If a psychotic episode appears to be starting, doses can be increased temporarily under the doctor's supervision.

Antipsychotic Medications in Perspective

The development of antipsychotics was one of psychiatry's most significant advances. Before their introduction, the back wards of state psychiatric hospitals were filled with thousands of patients who had little hope of ever leaving these institutions.

Although the harshest treatments of earlier centuries—including chains and physical abuse—had long been abandoned as "treatment" for the mentally ill, restraints and locked cells were still used routinely before the discovery of antipsychotic medications. That began to change for many patients after chlorpromazine was introduced in 1952.

The introduction of the next generation of antipsychotic drugs further improved the situation. The effectiveness of drug therapy for schizophrenia can be variable, like the symptoms and course of the disease itself. Some people can't tolerate most antipsychotic drugs but are able in time to find one that works well. A few rare individuals get better without medication. Most find significant to satisfactory improvement by using them.

Deciding on a Medication

While there is overlap, side effects produced by the older and newer antipsychotic drugs differ considerably. Today, older antipsychotic medications are prescribed much less than they were prior to the mid-1990s. However, they may still be recommended for patients who, for some reason, cannot tolerate the newer drugs. It is therefore very important that you familiarize yourself with the pros and cons of these traditional drugs if they are prescribed.

While the descriptions of the side effects can be discouraging and even alarming, keep in mind that the same drugs that cause them can also eliminate some of the worst and most distressing symptoms of schizophrenia. With effort, the benefits of antipsychotic medication can be realized while the side effects are minimized. But it may take effort and perseverance, depending on the patient's unique metabolism and illness.

Side Effects of First-Generation Versus Second-Generation Drugs

Older medications carry a greater risk of a movement disorder called tardive dyskinesia. While several of the side effects that were mentioned previously stop once the medication is stopped, tardive dyskinesia may sometimes be irreversible even if the medication is stopped.

Although newer medications may cause tardive dyskinesia much less frequently than the older, first generation drugs, they have their own risks, including weight gain, diabetes, high blood pressure, heart disease, and other complications. As more medications are developed, more options become available for finding one that minimizes or counters side effects for individual patients.

The word "antipsychotic" refers to the symptoms these medications relieve best: positive symptoms, including hallucinations and delusions. Negative symptoms are not controlled by typical antipsychotic medications. Furthermore, in some cases they may be made worse by these medications.

The brain and the body have different cells that are responsible for different functions. Different cells are targets of different drugs. The interaction between antipsychotic medications and one type of cell may bring about the intended benefits, while the interaction between these drugs and other cells may cause unwanted side effects.

Alert

Antipsychotic side effects are a complicated medical issue and require an experienced physician to negotiate. If you suspect a medication is causing a troublesome side effect, the safest thing to do is stop taking the medication and call your doctor immediately. Always tell the doctor if someone stops taking prescribed medication for any reason.

Side effects involving the brain may also involve changes in certain hormone secretions. The majority of antipsychotic medications can raise levels of prolactin, which stimulates breast cells and causes the secretion of milk in women. Prolactin also maintains a part of the ovary that provides progesterone, a female sex hormone.

Side Effects of Older or Typical Antipsychotic Drugs
- Restlessness, muscle spasms, Parkinsonian symptoms (extrapyramidal side effects, EPS)
- Involuntary, rhythmical muscle movements (tardive dyskinesia)
- Dry mouth, constipation, blurred vision (anticholinergic effects)
- Elevated prolactin
- Sedation
- Neuromalignant syndrome (a rare neurological disorder)

Too much prolactin may suppress menstruation. Excess amounts of this hormone can produce brittle bones (osteoporosis) and decrease interest in sex. Elevated levels of the hormone can cause men to experience impotence.

Essential

It is important to remember that different people have different experiences with side effects. The selection of a medication should take into account its side effect profile and the patient's past and current medical history. All or most of the side effects are expected to go away once the medication is stopped.

Recognizing the Side Effects

Some side effects of antipsychotic medications tend to show up soon after the medication is started and tend to get better with time as the person's body and brain adjust to the medication. While side effects vary from one medication to the next and from one individual to another, they may include blurred vision, dry mouth, restlessness, drowsiness, muscle spasms, and tremor. Adjusting the dosage, changing medications, or taking additional medication are the usual approaches to dealing with these side effects.

Other, often more serious side effects may show up later. Again, this depends on the medication and the individual.

Sedation

Drowsiness or sedation can occur to a greater or lesser degree with all drugs used to treat psychosis. Among the first generation drugs, this side effect is more common in drugs with lower potency, that is, drugs that require higher doses to attain an antipsychotic effect. Drowsiness often fades with time as patients adapt or develop a tolerance to the drug.

Drowsiness can be a problem if it affects daytime functioning, but when treatment is first started it can be helpful. Sedation can control the agitation many patients feel after experiencing their first psychotic episodes.

A doctor has several options to try to free a patient from this unacceptable side effect. These include adjusting the dose, instructing the patient to take the drug before bed, or changing the medication.

Seizures

More than 99 percent of people taking antipsychotic medication have no problem with seizures, which are the abnormal, uncontrolled firing of brain cells. The remaining few, including those who had seizures in the past, find that these medications can lower their seizure threshold. High doses of many antipsychotic medications increase the risk, as does the use of the atypical antipsychotic clozapine. If a patient's psychotic symptoms respond well to a drug that causes seizures, her doctor may prescribe an anticonvulsant drug to control them.

Anticholinergic Side Effects

Anticholinergic effects involve a neurotransmitter called acetylcholine. This is the neurotransmitter that communicates between nerves and skeletal muscles. It also plays a key role in controlling other important functions in the brain and body. These side effects may occur with any antipsychotic, but they are more severe with some of the older, lower potency antipsychotics such as Thorazine.

Antipsychotic drugs interfere with acetylcholine's control of vision and excretion. Thus, anticholinergic side effects include blurry vision, constipation, and difficulty urinating; they may also cause rapid heartbeat.

Neuroleptic Malignant Syndrome

This rare side effect presents an urgent medical emergency. The patient becomes very rigid, so much so that she cannot move. The heart beats very fast, breathing becomes difficult, and the body heats up and develops a fever. The patient may become disoriented or incoherent. The patient should be taken to a hospital immediately if these symptoms appear. The doctors can administer drugs to help

control the symptoms, and they will discontinue use of the antipsychotic drug that produced this potentially life-threatening side effect.
All antipsychotics may cause this side effect, although it is important
to stress that it is very rare. The second generation drugs are less
likely to cause it than are the first generation drugs. It is important to
note that Abilify may be an exception; to date, there have not been
any reports of neuroleptic malignant syndrome caused by Abilify.

Effects of Conventional Antipsychotic Drugs on the Extrapyramidal System

The serious side effects of older antipsychotic medications such as
Haldol and Thorazine can be traced to their effects in parts of the
brain collectively called the extrapyramidal system. This interconnected system of sites in the brain influences motor or movement
functions of the body. The side effects produced by the actions of
antipsychotic drugs on these brain regions are referred to as extrapyramidal signs (EPS). These are symptoms that are similar to Parkinson's disease; the only difference is that EPS disappear once the
medication is stopped. There are three categories of EPS symptoms:

- Akathisia is an intense feeling of restlessness and being
  unable to sit still or even stand still. Patients describe the
  feeling as wanting to climb the walls. A person ends up pac-
  ing the floors or fidgeting constantly. This tends to happen
  when the treatment is first started and gradually improves
  on its own or with dose adjustment. Sometimes it becomes
  necessary to treat it with another medication to allow the
  patient to become more comfortable and better able to tolerate the antipsychotic treatment.

- Dystonia is an intense contraction or severe tensing up of a
  muscle that lasts for several minutes. While it is not a dangerous side effect, it may be very painful and scary, especially
  if it involves the muscles of the eye or the tongue. This may

be an emergency only because it is severely uncomfortable, and it is frequently relieved with an injection.

• Parkinsonism produces symptoms similar to those of Parkinson's disease. They can consist of tremors, most frequently involving the fingers or hands. Other symptoms are slow movements; decreased frequency of blinking, which makes the person appear as if she is staring into space; walking stiffly without swinging the arms; and a stooped posture.

The latter symptoms are responsible for some of the images that were associated with mental illness in the past. It has been called the zombie effect. It is important to realize that this is not a desirable outcome of treatment and your doctor should do all he can to get rid of these side effects and minimize their influence.

Table 9-3: Medications for Treating Antipsychotic-Induced Extrapyramidal Side Effects

Side Effect	Generic Medications
Akathisia	Benztropine, Trihexyphenidyl, Diazepam, Lorazepam, Propranolol
Acute dystonia	Benztropine, Biperiden, Diphenhydramine, Trihexyphenidyl
Parkinsonism	Benztropine, Trihexyphenidyl, Amantadine

Sources: *The Essential Guide to Psychiatric Drugs* and *The Physician's Desk Reference*

Tardive Dyskinesia

Another serious side effect involving movement is tardive dyskinesia, which affects approximately 15 to 20 percent of patients taking older antipsychotic medications. The symptoms of this neurological condition include involuntary movements of the lips, tongue, hands, and feet. Sometimes the trunk and limbs are affected. It usually shows up after years of treatment with conventional antipsychotic medication, although it can appear sooner. If it is recognized early, tardive dyskinesia may disappear with a change of dose or medication. Sometimes the condition is mild and the patient is not bothered by it, but it can also become a permanent condition. Again, the key is for patients to have regular medical exams.

Side Effects of Atypical Antipsychotic Drugs

While some atypical drugs can produce side effects similar to those produced by the older medications, particularly at high doses, overall they are less of a problem in this group. A major advantage of new antipsychotic medications over the older ones is their general tendency to cause milder extrapyramidal side effects, if they produce any at all. Tardive dyskinesia is also rare with the newer generation of medicines. High doses of the newer medications, however, can also produce Parkinsonian symptoms and social withdrawal.

Atypical drugs have their own characteristic side effect profile, and some of the side effects are just as serious as those associated with older drugs. These complications can be traced to changes in the body's metabolism. The result can be significant weight gain. An obvious counter to this side effect is regular exercise and a good diet. If the patient can be encouraged to follow these recommendations, her health will improve.

Essential

Weight gain associated with the use of newer antipsychotic medications may level off with time, but it should not be allowed to go untreated. This symptom appears to be the result of changes in the way the body processes and regulates sugar and lipids (fats) in the blood. These changes, in turn, increase the chances of developing diabetes and coronary heart disease.

The FDA has required that this group of medications be labeled with a warning about the possibility that they may increase blood sugar and may cause or worsen diabetes. They have been associated with increased levels of cholesterol, significant weight gain, and high blood pressure. There is some variability from one medication to another and from one individual to the next, so we do not have enough knowledge to predict whether any given patient will have a particular side effect from a particular medication. We also can't predict how severe a side effect will be for a particular person. For this reason it is important that every patient be closely monitored for these potential side effects. Patient, doctor, and family should have plans for prevention of side effects such as weight gain and early intervention if they develop.

Common Side Effects of Atypical Antipsychotic Drugs

- Insomnia
- Anxiety
- Weight gain
- Runny nose
- Sedation
- Headache
- Constipation
- Agitation
- Dizziness

Adapted from *The Physician's Desk Reference*

The risk of developing diabetes is increased in patients with a family history of diabetes and in those with glucose intolerance. Obesity also increases a patient's chances of developing treatment-emergent diabetes when taking these medications. Regular physical activity and a good diet can decrease the risk.

Precautions

It often takes time and patience to find a drug or combination of drugs that work for an individual. Some patients may stop taking their medications because they feel they no longer are ill, they don't like the side effects, or their behavior is too disorganized. It is important not to stop taking medication abruptly without a doctor's knowledge. Antipsychotic drugs should be discontinued under a doctor's supervision to avoid the return of symptoms.

Frustration and Suicidal Thoughts

You may have to fight discouragement in yourself and in the patient you are helping. There is no need to rely on antipsychotic drugs alone. Combine drug therapy with counseling and self-help groups for caregivers and patients during your search for the best treatments. Continue seeking assistance until you have found the best drug or combination of drugs, the best therapist, and the most helpful support group.

Alert

A patient should have only one or two days' worth of medication in his possession, and a caretaker should keep the remainder of the medication in a safe and secure place. Do not be afraid to ask someone you care for if he is thinking of harming himself. If you think he is, seek help immediately.

Don't believe the myth that you may plant suicidal thoughts in someone's head by addressing the subject. People with suicidal thoughts frequently welcome the opportunity to discuss them. That is why they call suicide hotline phone numbers. They may be open to discussing ways to make themselves feel better and to implement some safety measures.

Are Antipsychotic Medications Safe During Pregnancy?

The real question is not whether a given medication is safe during pregnancy. The more appropriate question is this: Which is worse for the baby and the mother, the medication or the untreated illness? In

April 2008, the American College of Obstetricians and Gynecologists issued updated guidelines for the treatment of certain psychiatric illnesses during pregnancy and breastfeeding. The authors suggested that while the exposure of the fetus to a certain medication may not be totally safe, leaving a mother untreated may cause poor prenatal nutrition; lack of compliance with care; potential increase in alcohol, tobacco, or other drug use; deficits in mother-infant bonding; and disruptions of the family environment.

In the United States, it is estimated that more than 500,000 women suffer from various psychiatric illnesses before or during their pregnancy and that one-third of pregnant women are exposed to psychiatric medications. All psychiatric medications that have been studied are believed to cross to the fetus in the womb and are also excreted in the milk. Typical antipsychotic drugs have a more extensive and better known safety profile in pregnancy than do the second-generation antipsychotic medications.

While none of these medications are believed to be totally safe in pregnancy, chlorpromazine, haloperidol, and perphenazine have not been found to cause any birth defects or any complications with delivery or during the baby's first few weeks of life. Furthermore, the second-generation antipsychotic drugs have not been associated with any birth defect or a significant risk for toxicity to the newborn. Discuss your situation with your psychiatrist and your obstetrician in order to make the best informed decision for yourself or for your loved one.

Combination Treatments

Some research, most of which concerns first generation drugs, suggests there may be some added benefits in treating the symptoms of schizophrenia when antipsychotic medications are combined with other medications. The studies are ongoing, but the results have been somewhat inconsistent and remain inconclusive. Some of the drugs used in combinations include lithium, valproic acid (Depakote), antidepressants, glycine, D-cycloserine, D-serine, clonidine, and polyunsaturated fatty acids such as eicosapentaenoic acid (EPA) or docosahexaenoic acid.

According to the APA Guidelines, some research indicates that electroconvulsive therapy (also known as ECT or shock treatment) was not effective for treating schizophrenia by itself. For some patients, however, the combination of ECT and antipsychotics worked better than either treatment alone. This was especially true for patients who suffer from catatonia that does not respond to standard treatments.

It is important to note that ECT is an effective and safe treatment when needed. It is a brief procedure that is usually done in a hospital setting and may take ten to fifteen minutes. The patient receives anesthesia and does not experience any pain or discomfort during the procedure. Like all other treatments, it has possible side effects that are important for you to discuss in detail with the treating doctor.

CHAPTER 10

Therapy for Schizophrenia

BEFORE 1955, PSYCHIATRISTS and psychologists had no effective means for controlling runaway hallucinations and delusions in people with schizophrenia. Patients who are distracted by psychotic thoughts are not open to rational discussions about their condition, nor are they able to express their needs. They are too absorbed by their symptoms. Today, improved antipsychotic drugs in many cases dampen psychotic symptoms enough to allow people with schizophrenia to benefit from therapy.

Why Therapy?

Therapy may give a person a better understanding of her illness and provide insights into her emotions and her response to stress. This, in turn, can lead to improved relationships with family, friends, and other people in her life. It also can improve her ability to meet the challenges of daily living imposed by the disease.

Occupational therapy offers people with schizophrenia a chance to improve their hands-on, practical skills for day-to-day tasks. Activity therapy can benefit patients by establishing and improving existing positive social contacts in the community. The ability to actively participate in therapy sessions gives people an opportunity to make decisions and exert more control over their situation.

Improved Social and Personal Skills

Although medications are a major breakthrough in the treatment of schizophrenia, different types of therapy are often needed to improve the remaining behavioral and cognitive symptoms of this brain disease. Patients can learn practical skills that will help them improve aspects of their daily lives that might otherwise suffer because of the disease. People dealing with, and recovering from, schizophrenia also can benefit from training that teaches them about the disease and its implications.

Less Hospital Time

Speaking regularly to a skilled, empathetic therapist, counselor, or adviser can help keep consumers of mental health care out of the hospital. Studies have shown that therapy works best in combination with medication. In one study, nearly three-quarters of the patients who stopped taking antipsychotic medicines were rehospitalized in the following year.

 Fact

Researchers such as the late Gerard Hogarty at the University of Pittsburgh School of Medicine have shown that therapy in combination with antipsychotic medication is better than medication alone in reducing the number of relapses and in helping patients adjust to the challenges of schizophrenia.

Two-thirds of the people who attended practical therapy sessions without taking medications ended up back in the hospital, but only one-third of those who took antipsychotic medications without therapy had to be readmitted. The group that did best received both medication and therapy: only one-quarter of this group needed to go back to the hospital. If you want to have the best chance of avoiding hospitalization, encourage the use of medication in conjunction with therapies designed to improve living and coping skills.

Modern Therapies versus Older Therapies

Many people still think of Sigmund Freud's couch when they think of therapy. Actually, therapeutic approaches developed over the last sixty years are very different from the older psychoanalytic therapy developed by Freud and his followers in the late nineteenth and early twentieth centuries. The therapies used today to help people develop their ability to cope with the challenges of schizophrenia are based on entirely different premises.

Less Emphasis on the Past

Freud believed that uncovering unconscious mental processes was crucial to making progress and that human psychology followed certain set paths or patterns. He stressed the dominance of past experiences as major influences on behavior.

Question

Why is Sigmund Freud so closely associated with psychiatry?
Freud's development of psychoanalysis was an intellectual accomplishment that greatly stimulated interest in mental processes. A trained neurologist, he believed the functioning of the human psyche had a biological basis. Before modern biological psychiatry, Freud's method of talking to uncover the hidden roots of psychological problems dominated the public's image of psychiatry.

Some therapists began advocating and teaching a different kind of therapy around the 1960s. This movement, which stressed treating people more as unique individuals who possessed significant potential to change their behavior, was based on the premise that people can gain self-insight and change without starting from childhood experiences.

Modern approaches are more practical. They teach patients how to handle and avoid everyday problems. Psychoanalysis, by contrast, requires years of delving into a person's childhood. Most important, it does not help patients with schizophrenia, and research has demonstrated that it might cause some patients to get even worse and have more symptoms.

Individual Psychotherapy

After a patient's psychotic symptoms are under control, she may benefit from private meetings with a mental health care professional. This therapist may be a psychiatrist with a medical degree, a psychologist with a doctorate, a psychiatric social worker or psychiatric nurse with a master's degree, or a licensed counselor with a master's degree. Whoever it is, it is important that the therapist is well-trained and sensitive to the patient's psychological state.

Individual therapy offered in a supportive environment that stresses pragmatic, reality-based insights can be of tremendous benefit to many individuals affected by mental illnesses, including schizophrenia. It is important that the consumer trusts the therapist and feels comfortable talking to him.

Sharing thoughts and concerns with a trusted outsider can help a person with schizophrenia gain understanding and perspective about the feelings and events affecting her life. In time, these sessions can lead to greater insight and self-confidence. With the help of a skilled therapist, a person can improve her ability to distinguish between reality and the distorted thoughts of schizophrenia.

Behavioral Therapy

Another movement that has influenced current therapies is behavioral or conditioning therapy. It is based on experimental principles of learning. It seeks to change undesirable behavior and replace it with desirable habits. It seems coldly scientific to some people, but it includes techniques that are very useful for improving behavior, coping skills, and the ability to function day-to-day.

The best therapists know enough to tailor therapy to an individual's needs and ability to respond. They can use techniques from a variety of therapeutic approaches to solve problems and improve coping skills. The format and goal of therapy may change over time to adjust to the changes in and the needs of the patient.

One area where therapy is demonstrating great potential for improving lives is in the treatment of young people at risk of developing mental illnesses. Employing therapy as a means of primary prevention in children and adolescents is an important goal of the mental health community.

Supportive or Rehabilitative Therapies

These programs can help people with drug dependency problems, poor social skills, and limited qualifications for obtaining employment or volunteer positions in the community. Rehabilitation therapies are nonmedical programs designed to help people with schizophrenia live independent, productive, rewarding lives outside of mental hospitals.

 Fact

Rehabilitation offers opportunities to improve skills that are needed in school, during social interactions, and at work. These programs can include advice in areas such as use of public transportation, job training, money management skills, motivation, and establishing and maintaining social relationships. Their aim is to help the patient live a more normal and independent life.

A type of beefed-up outpatient service called long-term assisted outpatient treatment does a better job improving the outcome for people with severe mental illness compared to standard outpatient care. It includes routine outpatient services and at least three outpatient visits per month. In short, better outcome seems to be correlated with more follow-up treatment.

Psychosocial Therapy

This therapy trains people to improve their social skills. Relatives of people with schizophrenia also benefit from psychosocial programs by increasing their social contacts. Group services include education and/or treatment groups, peer support/activity groups, family psychoeducation groups, and family support groups.

Psychoeducation

Psychoeducation teaches consumers and their close relatives about schizophrenia. It presents accurate facts about a very severe mental illness without discouraging hope. Well-conducted psychoeducation programs are able to provide useful information about the nature of the disease and its characteristics. This information should help dispel some of the worry and confusion that accompanies a diagnosis of schizophrenia.

Some Benefits of Psychoeducation for Patients

- Better personal functioning skills for patients
- Improved social relationships
- Increased interest in finding a job
- More social interests
- Increased ability to handle social conflicts

Adapted from "Patient functioning and family burden in a controlled real-world trial of family psychoeducation for schizophrenia," L. Magliano, et. al. Published in *Psychiatric Services*, December 2006.

The therapist can explore the patient's ideas about what is happening to him and try to reconcile these explanations with what modern science has learned. Psychoeducation can also demonstrate how and to what degree the disorder can be treated. Finally, it should take into account the need for every consumer to maintain a good sense of self-esteem.

Occupational Therapy

Occupational training teaches people how to be more independent in daily life. This training is essential if someone wants to live independently but lacks domestic skills needed for managing money, shopping, cooking, cleaning, dressing, and tending to personal hygiene. Other programs can help a person acquire skills that will enable him to take a full-time, part-time, or volunteer job, whichever one the person's abilities and interests qualify him for.

⌐ Essential

Don't neglect therapy just because someone's hallucinations or delusions are no longer overwhelming her. Therapy can aid patients, whether they are in a hospital or receiving outpatient care. The goal for the family and for therapists is to guide, encourage, and support a patient's efforts to recover as many living skills and gain as much insight into her own condition as possible.

Another important factor in a patient's life is his physical well-being. Physical health, as well as mental health, contributes to quality of life. If possible, efforts to maintain or improve a person's physical well-being should be incorporated into his therapy program.

Family Therapy and Education

Along with doctors, family members often have the most influential role in the life of a person with schizophrenia. Depending on the individual's personal circumstances, however, non-family members may play a big part in a patient's life.

A professional care manager, a friend, someone who runs a shelter, a social worker, or a rabbi, priest, minister, or other religious figure can make a big difference in the life of someone affected by this illness.

It is easier for people to handle some of the cognitive problems associated with schizophrenia if they have the support of family or others in a safe, stimulating environment. The more information family members know about the mental illness, the better they will be able to handle challenges. From a therapist's standpoint, working with a patient and her family together can maximize a person's chances of making significant progress against the disease.

Cognitive Therapy

The goal of cognitive therapy is to change the distorted thinking and behavior that hinders a person's ability to function. It uses a structured approach to modify a patient's thought processes. It strives to improve a person's mood and actions. A patient is given a chance to think about her illness and early psychotic symptoms in new ways, ways she probably would not discover on her own.

 Fact

> If therapy helps a person examine his psychotic symptoms in realistic ways, delusions may not have a chance to become permanent fixtures in his brain. Cognitive therapy, in effect, has the potential to challenge abnormal and bizarre ideas before they become fixed in a patient's thought processes.

Cognitive-behavioral therapy helps people deal with other problems related to developing psychosis, such as worry, stress, and depression. It provides practical, problem-solving skills and techniques for dealing with stressful challenges.

Finding Good Therapists

Depending on where you live, you may have to work to find the right health care for yourself or a loved one. Begin with recommendations from people you trust and respect. If that doesn't yield satisfactory results, consult online resources and your local library. Remember that a name turned up by referral or by research is still only a candidate for you. Keep trying until you find someone you are comfortable working with as a partner.

Community Mental Health Centers (CMHCs)

There are hundreds of CMHCs across the country that provide outpatient services. These state and federally funded programs have services directed at helping people with severe mental illnesses, including schizophrenia. The following contact information can help you locate one near you.

Substance Abuse and Mental Health Service Administration's Mental Health Information Center

P.O. Box 42557
Washington, DC 20015
(800) 789-2647
(240) 747-5470
nmhic-info@samhsa.hhs.gov
http://mentalhealth.samhsa.gov/databases

You can also call SAMHSA's 24-hour toll-free telephone referral helpline: (800) 662-HELP (662-4357).

Ŀ., Essential

It is important for the patient to feel comfortable working with a particular therapist, but this doesn't always happen right away. It takes time to get to know a therapist. It is a good idea to attend several sessions before making the decision to quit and try another therapist.

A therapist should not become a friend, but good therapy does take two—that is, the patient and the therapist have to have a good rapport to develop trust and respect.

After getting several referrals from doctors, social workers, friends, or a professional organization, choose one you think you and the patient will feel comfortable with. Call the office and ask some questions. If you like the answers you receive, make an appointment.

Questions to Ask When Choosing a Therapist

- What do you charge? Do you accept my health insurance?
- Do you accept payment based on income (a sliding-scale fee)?
- Do you have experience working with people with schizophrenia?
- How long have you been practicing? Where were you trained?
- Will you coordinate the therapy you offer with my doctor or my other health care provider(s)?
- Will the therapy you offer me be geared to my situation, or is your approach pretty much the same for everyone you treat?

Source: the National Mental Health Information Center

The ultimate goal of all therapies is to assist the patient and the family with all aspects of life affected by schizophrenia. It has been shown that the best results are obtained with an approach that integrates all of the therapies that address the patient's and family's needs. These cover four general areas.

There are clinical needs that focus on treating symptoms and helping the person come to terms with them. Rehabilitative needs can be met by improving socialization and job-training skills. There is also the need to assist with what is sometimes called humanitarian matters. These may involve quality of life issues and a patient's sense of well-being. Patients can also benefit from programs that address issues that help them understand and balance their individual rights with the welfare of the community.

CHAPTER 11

What if Nothing Works?

A MINORITY OF patients do not respond well to treatment. Ineffective medications, missed appointments, and use of illegal drugs may be contributing factors. It is important that you consult a doctor if the person you care for is not receiving or accepting treatment. The goal is to get the person to resume treatment voluntarily. In some cases, the next best step is to legally force the patient to accept treatment. This step must be approved by a court of law.

Are Alternative Therapies Right for You?

At this time, no alternative therapy has been shown to work against schizophrenia. This does not mean an alternative therapy will not someday be shown to be effective. All it would take for this to occur would be the demonstration of positive results from a reproducible, well-controlled research study conducted with a large enough group of people. Unfortunately, for many therapies, that is a big hurdle.

Why Do People Think Alternative Approaches Work?

The fact that some people still recommend untested treatments can be explained in several ways. A minority of patients recover from schizophrenia or experience periods of relative improvement on their own. This is possible because disease symptoms can wax and wane in some individuals and some even recover.

In addition, some companies may promote alternative treatments for profit, and some individuals who truly believe in the effectiveness of their theory or favored treatment promote it prematurely. The only way for medical science to progress and benefit the most people is for it to use scientifically proven treatments. So far, no alternative therapies have passed this test as well as standard treatments have.

Special Diets

Diet is a crucial part of good health. Poor nutrition can contribute to both physical and mental problems. Anyone dealing with schizophrenia, both patients and caregivers, will benefit from a healthy diet.

This does not mean anyone has yet identified a diet that will cure schizophrenia. People have tried taking large doses of vitamins, which is advocated by those practicing orthomolecular psychiatry or megavitamin therapy, but there is no reproducible, convincing evidence it works.

Lack of Compliance or Failure of Medical Care

Lack of medical compliance by patients is a problem for physicians in many medical practices, not just psychiatry. It is seen by doctors treating diabetes, heart disease, lung disease, and even cancer. It refers to the fact that many people won't take their medications or follow through with other prescribed treatments such as physical or psychological therapy. When people with schizophrenia stop taking medications, the results can be disastrous.

Anosognosia: Denying Illness

There are several reasons why some people refuse treatment. In the case of schizophrenia, a major reason is called anosognosia, the lack of insight by the patient into the nature of her disease. Anosognosia is not a psychological denial or refusal to accept the notion of illness by a person who, on a deeper level, may very well be aware that something is wrong. It is instead a symptom of schizophrenia that prevents the patient from realizing she is ill.

 Question

What if someone does not want my help?
Someone experiencing symptoms of schizophrenia may not recognize she is ill. This can be true even if she hears voices or has other psychotic symptoms. Another person may know she is not well, but the fear, confusion, and embarrassment caused by her symptoms may lead her to deny she needs help.

Some studies estimate that as many as one in four people with schizophrenia have anosognosia. Other studies suggest that as many as half lack insight into the extent of their illness.

You have at least two options if you face this challenge. You and perhaps other mental health care providers might be able to persuade the patient to take a medication at least once every two to four weeks. There are injectable, long-acting antipsychotic drug formulations that effectively treat psychotic symptoms in some patients and eliminate the need to take daily medications.

Medications are the best way to keep psychotic symptoms under control and allow a patient to develop insight into the nature of her illness. If the antipsychotic medications are successful, the patient may become more amenable to discussion and realize that she is ill and could benefit from therapy.

Willing but Forgetful or Unorganized

A psychiatrist may be able to help you simplify the medication routine, again by prescribing long-acting injections or single daily doses. These options are subject to the patient's responsiveness to the medications available in these formulations. Three possibilities you can discuss with a psychiatrist are intramuscular injections such as haloperidol (Haldol Decanoate); fluphenazine (Prolixin Decanoate); and risperidone (Consta).

For some families, simple organizing routines can help. Taking medications with meals or at other predetermined times increases the chances of sticking to a schedule. Check with your doctor for the best time to take particular medications. This can make it easier for you to observe the patient swallowing the pill or pills. You can use compartmentalized pill containers labeled with the days of the week and/or medical calendars to keep track of what pills should be taken at what times. You also can set timers or alarms to remind you and the consumer when it is time to medicate.

Assisted Treatment

Assisted treatment is a euphemism for obtaining the legal means to ensure that an ill person receives medical care even if he otherwise refuses it. This subject presents a dilemma. Every person has the right to make important decisions, such as whether or not to take medicine with potentially serious side effects. On the other hand, what is to be done if the very illness a person suffers from prevents him from seeking treatment? A would-be caretaker could actually be negligent if she did not insist on treatment under those circumstances.

Essential

According to U.S. law, the potential benefit of treatment on the patient overrides her objections to it if the disease in question prevents her from using logical, rational thought to make her decision concerning medical care. Schizophrenia is one such condition that distorts patients' thinking processes.

As a caregiver, you can assure that a patient receives treatment by becoming his guardian or conservator. You may also seek to have the patient committed either as an outpatient or to a psychiatric in-patient hospital. Outpatient commitment laws vary from state to state. The Treatment Advocacy Center in Arlington, Virginia (*www.treatmentadvocacycenter.org*), provides excellent background information on the topic of assisted treatment. It is the source of much of the information in this section.

Advance Directives

In some states, a patient who is free of symptoms of schizophrenia may be able to sign a legal document directing others how he wishes to be treated if he relapses. This document may spell out who can direct his care and what kind of assisted treatment he expects, if any.

The Treatment Advocacy Center points out that there are potential problems with this option. First, it is not clear how well it works in practice. Second, patients have no way of knowing whether new symptoms of schizophrenia or another mental illness will be present if they relapse. Deciding on treatment options in advance can be counterproductive because they may not adequately anticipate future needs in the event of a relapse.

 Question

What is a Ulysses contract?
It's another name for an advance directive. Ulysses is the hero of Homer's epic poem "The Odyssey." Ulysses sailed close to the isle of the seductive Sirens, who lured sailors to their deaths. Ulysses had his men plug their ears but had himself tied to the mast of his ship so he could hear the Sirens' call. He instructed his men not to untie him, no matter what he said, until they were past the threat.

If you are interested in pursuing an advance directive, you will first need to find out if your state recognizes them. Then you will need to consult both a lawyer and psychiatrist.

Assertive Case Management

Assertive case management programs track down patients and bring treatment to them. The National Alliance on Mental Illness (NAMI) is dedicated to promoting these programs, also known as assertive community treatment (ACT) and program of assertive community treatment (PACT) services. These programs even help those whose illnesses prevent them from showing up for treatment at traditional mental health care facilities.

Unlike agencies that direct patients to mental health care treatment centers and services, successful delivery of care under these programs does not depend on the discipline of the patient, whose illness may hinder medical compliance. This results in a better level of care for the patient.

Fact

NAMI uses PACT and ACT interchangeably to refer to assertive case management programs.

Several studies have found that ACT teams, which are composed of doctors, nurses, therapists, and other professionals, significantly reduce rehospitalization days. In one study of homeless individuals, the reduction was greater than 50 percent. During the following year, those treated by the ACT team also spent less time in the hospital, living on the streets, and locked up in jail. The ACT patients received more medical treatment overall than those in outpatient care. Nevertheless, at any given time, one in three were not taking their medicine, a finding that led the Treatment Advocacy Center to conclude that ACTs are a valuable tool but are not effective for all patients.

This might be expected for homeless people suffering from schizophrenia since they are more difficult to treat than are patients living with their families, in their own homes, or in group residences. For these patients, ACTs bring well-documented advantages over less consumer-friendly treatment scenarios, including involuntary outpatient care.

Representative Payee

It is possible to have a patient's social security insurance, disability insurance, or veteran's administration payments sent to a family member, a mental health care facility, a clinic, or a case manager if the patient is unable to handle his own financial affairs. The person who takes responsibility for the patient's finances is called a representative payee.

This practice has been shown to have several benefits, including reduced rates of hospitalizations, homelessness, and substance abuse. There have not been any long-term studies to track the efficiency of this method, but the center suggests it may be useful to make the patient's access to the monthly payments contingent upon maintaining a treatment plan.

Conditional Release

A court can order the release of someone committed to a psychiatric hospital and impose conditions on the patient. For example, the patient may be allowed to receive treatment outside the hospital so long as he takes his medication and attends therapy sessions. If he stops treatment, he can be rehospitalized. The majority of states have laws allowing conditional release. It is up to the hospital director to determine whether the patient should be treated in or out of the hospital.

Although conditional release is commonly used for patients who have committed crimes, it sometimes is employed for others. The Treatment Advocacy Center cites data showing that in the state of New Hampshire, 27 percent of non-criminal patients committed to hospitals were released conditionally in 1998. A follow-up study of twenty-six seriously ill psychiatric patients in that state showed impressive improvements in medical compliance after one and two years on conditional release compared to the year before hospitalization.

Mandated Community Treatment

This type of outpatient commitment differs from conditional release in that it involves a court ordering a patient to receive treatment outside the hospital if he wishes to reside in the community. Failure to comply can result in rehospitalization. Mandated commitment helps people living with schizophrenia get better care by increasing the chances they will stick to their treatment plans.

⊑, Essential

Mandated community treatment is also called outpatient commitment, assisted outpatient treatment, or involuntary outpatient commitment. It is a form of assisted treatment in which a court orders someone with a serious mental disease such as schizophrenia to obtain treatment without being committed to a hospital or other institution.

Most states have laws that allow their courts to order patients to receive outpatient care. Check with your mental health care provider or lawyer to find out if this a good option for your situation.

The Treatment Advocacy Center refers to several studies supporting the value of court-ordered community treatment. In one, 60 percent of patients ordered into treatment programs agreed, after receiving treatment, that it was a good idea.

A separate study conducted in New York by the New York State Psychiatric Institute and Columbia University found that initially about 50 percent of those ordered to accept treatment were embarrassed or angered by it. But the study found the following results after treatment:

- 75 percent attributed a gain in their ability to better control their lives to the enforced treatment
- 81 percent credited mandated treatment with helping them "to get and stay well"
- 90 percent said the experience increased the chances they would accept treatment, including taking medications and keeping appointments
- 87 percent were confident their case manager could help them
- 88 percent agreed on their therapeutic priorities

Studies in at least half a dozen states indicate that mandated outpatient treatment improves lives. Multiple studies document significantly reduced cases of homelessness, psychiatric hospitalization, and trouble with the law among patients ordered to undergo outpatient treatment.

Fact

> More than one assisted treatment approach can, and in many cases should, be applied to a patient, depending on her needs. An assertive case management program, for example, can be combined with a guardianship, appointment of an assertive case manager, and/or a representative payee.

Conservatorship

A person appointed by a court to make decisions for someone who has been judged mentally incompetent is called a conservator or guardian. Conservatorships and guardianships are commonly established in cases of mental retardation or dementia, but they can also be useful for patients with mental illnesses. A California study of the effectiveness of conservatorships in California found that mental health consumers who had conservators had significantly longer periods of mental health stability.

Benevolent Coercion

Benevolent coercion is a euphemism for a well-meant threat. Basically, a patient who won't submit to treatment is told he will be committed unless he accepts treatment. The Treatment Advocacy Center estimates that this approach is used but is generally not discussed.

It is difficult to assess the effectiveness of this approach because it is an informal practice with no regulation. It might be used by caregivers, family members, judges, or anyone who has the potential to influence the care and treatment of a person with schizophrenia. It would not be surprising, however, if its effectiveness depended on the individual patient's history, medical condition, and ability to exert self-control.

Treatment or Jail

In some communities, informal arrangements may be agreed upon between local authorities and mental health care providers according to TAC. The police arrest seriously ill patients on minor charges if they refuse to accept treatment and pose a safety risk. A judge then suspends their sentences as long as they return to treatment. The problem with this approach is that the judge's only option is to jail the patient if he continues to avoid or refuse treatment. Psychiatric care in jail is often minimal if it is available at all.

What Is a Clinical Trial?

One option for someone who can't hit on the right medication is participation in a test of a medication still in the development stage. Clinical trials are experiments that are designed to find out how safe and effective new treatments are in humans. They are sponsored by private parties such as medical researchers, drug developers, and medical institutions. Government agencies such as the National Institutes of Health also run clinical trials. Some are conducted in just one location and some are conducted in multiple hospitals, universities, or clinics. Some studies don't test new treatments but instead observe and document changes in a population of people. Patients who participate are closely monitored and guided by a team of researchers and health care workers.

Benefits and Risks

Why do people participate in clinical trials? One reason is to help others. By participating, subjects provide valuable scientific information that can improve medical treatments for many people. Another reason is to seek benefits that are not available from current, approved medical care.

Reasons to Join a Clinical Trial

- To allow the patient to assume a different type of active role in her own treatment
- To receive potentially cutting-edge treatments long before they become generally available
- To help advance medical progress for others
- To benefit from expert medical care at little or no cost

Sources: The National Institutes of Health and ClinicalTrials.gov

A patient who cannot take or benefit from any available antipsychotic drugs, for example, may want to volunteer to test a new experimental drug to see if it can help her. In this way, she may receive treatment that she would not otherwise be able to obtain.

You should consider the potential downside of clinical trials before you sign up for one. Because new and unapproved drugs are experimental, they may have unknown side effects that were not seen when they were tested on animals. In very rare cases, they have been fatal.

Of course, the experimental treatment may be perfectly safe, but it may not work for everyone. Finally, participation in a clinical trial might be less convenient than a traditional treatment that is available at a home clinic or from a psychiatrist. There is a good chance it will take more of your time. Instead of taking pills once a day and attending therapy, treatment might be more involved and require more on-site observation.

These factors vary depending on the nature and design of individual clinical trials. Be sure to know exactly what is required before agreeing to participate. Patients who participate in clinical trials adhere to treatment that is spelled out in a protocol. This is another name for the action plan the researchers developed and must follow as they conduct the trial. It states the trial's purpose and details concerning the design of the study.

Types of Clinical Trials

Clinical studies have different goals depending on what is being tested. Some trials compare two approaches for treating a disease to determine which is better. Other trials aim to identify or prevent disease in a certain population.

Many clinical trials test experimental drugs, drug combinations, or new therapies. Not all studies are treatment trials, however. Screening trials, for example, try out different ways to spot diseases in an appropriate group of people. Diagnostic trials look for improved ways to diagnose a health problem. Prevention trials seek clues that may help people avoid getting a disease or prevent it from striking again.

Clinical Trial Phases

Clinical trials are divided into four steps or levels, called phases, based on how advanced an experimental drug is in its development. You should know the phase of any trial you apply for. It may influence the benefit you can derive from the study.

- Phase I trials are the first step in the long road toward approval of a new drug or treatment. These studies are designed to learn how the body handles the drug. They look for side effects at different doses and for signs of effectiveness in twenty to eighty subjects. Some Phase I trials study only people without disease, while others include patients as well.
- Phase II trials look more closely at the ability of the new drug's effectiveness in 100 to 300 patients. They also track any side effects.
- Phase III trials follow only if Phase II results are encouraging. They are larger trials with up to 3,000 subjects and are designed to learn more about the benefits and side effects. The results help determine what will be included on the drug's label.
- Phase IV trials are conducted after the drug has been approved and marketed. Once it is released to all patients, the number of subjects who are exposed to a new drug increases far beyond the number that could be tested in the clinic. Monitoring the drug's effect in so many patients can help determine the most effective and safest doses and identify previously unseen or rarely seen side effects.

Interventional versus Observational Studies

Some clinical trials observe patients. The participants are not treated with any new or experimental drugs or procedures. They often continue to take any standard, already approved medications they normally use. The purpose of observational studies is to watch for and measure changes in medical conditions of the participants.

Investigational trials are different. They compare the effects of new drugs or treatments with either standard treatments or with placebo treatments. The control group, about half of the total number of participants, receive a placebo or their usual medication. Their outcomes are compared to those of the experimental group, which receives the new drug or treatment.

 Question

What are placebos?
Placebos, sometimes called sugar pills, are look-alike medications designed to prevent subjects from knowing whether they are taking real or inactive medications. Their use is an effective way to eliminate psychological factors that can confuse results. Many people may believe they are being affected by a treatment even when the treatment has no biological action.

The well-documented placebo effect can make people react differently simply because they believe they are being treated. Placebos can make someone feel better for a while, but most of the time they don't cure or treat severe disease for long. In double-blind studies, neither the patients nor the researchers are supposed to know who receives the placebo and who gets the test substance. Only the institutional review board, a committee consisting of independent researchers, physicians, and other overseers, has the key that reveals who is getting what.

A review board is established for each trial to approve and monitor its progress. The board evaluates the purpose of the study and decides whether its potential benefits outweigh potential risks. It is charged with

149

maximizing the safety of all participants and will step in and stop the trial if it detects any health threats. It may also stop a trial if a new drug is working so well it would be unethical to deprive the other patients in the study, the control group, who are not being treated with it.

Essential

Signing an informed consent document does not mean you are obligated to participate in a study. It simply means that you have read it and acknowledge that you know the purpose, potential benefits, and risks that come with participating in the trial. It will weaken the study if you quit without a good reason, but can leave any time you like.

Before you sign up for a study, you will get a detailed explanation of the clinical trial. A member of the clinical trial staff will go over an informed consent document with you. This is not a contract. It is a document that spells out the trial's purpose, the impact of your participation on your treatment, and the potential side effects, if any. Patient confidentiality applies in a clinical trial as it does in a standard medical practice; your name can never be released to anyone outside the staff conducting the study.

Finding Clinical Trials

In the United States, it is not unusual for there to be hundreds of clinical trials at a time actively recruiting people across the country to help evaluate treatments for schizophrenia or schizoaffective disorder. New trials are planned, approved, and begin recruiting volunteers regularly.

Their objectives are wide-ranging. Some seek to find out why patients stop taking existing antipsychotic medications. Others determine the safety and effectiveness of new antipsychotics, combinations of old and new drugs, or medications designed to treat side effects.

CenterWatch (*www.centerwatch.com*) maintains a frequently updated website that lists ongoing clinical trials. It helps patients find trials that match their interests and needs. The company neither promotes nor is involved in the trials, but it does provide information that makes it easy for users to learn about and apply for them.

The U.S. National Institutes of Health maintains the website *www.clinicaltrials.gov*, which enables consumers to locate clinical trials by location, sponsor, drug intervention, or condition. It also provides a useful glossary and background information.

In any clinical trial some of the results are due to chance. At the end of the trial, researchers use a formula to establish the statistical significance or the results.

Question

What is statistical significance?
It is a mathematically based method for determining how likely it is that a result—for instance, a good drug effect—is real instead of being a result of chance. In a clinical trial, for example, statistical significance indicates whether a drug has a beneficial effect. It depends on how many people are studied and how big the effect is.

Try to coordinate your choice of clinical trial with the advice of your personal doctor, if possible. Participation in a study does not replace treatment by your regular doctor. Most trials do take over all of your medical care. Your doctor and the sponsors of the trial will coordinate their activities so neither the study nor your needed treatment is compromised.

Applying to Take Part in a Clinical Trial

Your eligibility to take part in a clinical trial depends on the guidelines spelled out in its protocol. Different studies have different criteria for selecting eligible participants or subjects. In clinical trials involving schizophrenia, trial protocols will specify the age range, previous medical history, previous treatment history, and current health of a prospective participant. The rules for allowing particular people to participate in a given trial are written to allow investigators to answer specific questions in a scientifically valid manner.

What to Consider

Before you call a hospital or research facility to ask about a specific clinical study, talk to your doctor, other advisers, and other family members if they also act as caregivers. Learn all you need to feel comfortable about joining a study. Consider interviewing a clinical study staff member. Jot down your concerns and questions. The U.S. National Institutes of Health offers some useful questions to get you started:

- What is the purpose of the study? Who will participate?
- Why do researchers believe the experimental treatment being tested may be effective?
- Has it been tested before?
- How do the possible risks, side effects, and benefits in the study compare with my current treatment?
- How might this trial affect my daily life?
- How long will the trial last? Will hospitalization be required?
- Who will pay for the experimental treatment? Will I be reimbursed for other expenses?
- What type of long-term follow-up care is part of this study?
- How will I know that the experimental treatment is working? Will results of the trials be provided to me?
- Who will be in charge of my care?

Sources: the National Institutes of Health and ClinicalTrial.gov

When you go to ask your questions, it helps if a friend or relative comes along to hear the answers and offer support to you. You can also ask to record the conversation so you can replay it for yourself later.

CHAPTER 12

Other Views of Schizophrenia and Current Treatments

FOR THE MAJORITY of patients, medical reviews and experience have shown that properly prescribed and used antipsychotic medications combined with education and therapy go a long way toward lessening—and in many cases controlling—psychotic symptoms. A small number of individuals appear to improve without treatment or with selected, unconventional treatment. Critics may cite these instances as proof that conventional psychiatric treatments don't work. It is important to distinguish between claims based on one or a few anecdotes and scientific proof obtained from controlled experiments.

Public Perception of Schizophrenia

The National Alliance on Mental Illness reports that 85 percent of the people it surveyed know that schizophrenia is an illness. Seventy-nine percent believe treatment can enable people with the disease to live independently. Unfortunately, fewer than one in four know much about the disease. In too many cases, ignorance is replaced by misinformation.

Word Confusion

One of the most common misconceptions is that schizophrenia means having a split personality, that people with the disease simultaneously hold two contradictory viewpoints or have two separate personalities.

This confusion is firmly part of the language. There are two definitions for the word "schizophrenia." The primary definition refers to the disease. The secondary definition refers to a more general situation in which there are two opposing or contradictory views. Unfortunately, the secondary definition contributes to the misconception of schizophrenia as a disease of split personalities.

Fear of Violence

Another common misconception is promoted by the news and entertainment media who publicize instances of violent acts by people with mental illnesses. Positive nonviolent acts and accomplishments by consumers of mental health care largely are ignored. As a result, people equate mental illness with violence.

Schizophrenia Onscreen

In extreme cases of media ignorance or lack of concern, schizophrenia is equated with serial or spree killers. By contrast, the successful movie *A Beautiful Mind* was free of much of the misunderstanding and even nonsense that is often presented in depictions of schizophrenia in films and fiction. Some significant details of the main character's illness were not accurately portrayed in the film, but the director and screenwriter did not abuse the subject.

 Fact

Nobel Prize-winning mathematician John Forbes Nash Jr. struggled with schizophrenia. His discoveries are well known and highly regarded by economists and mathematicians. Nash became more widely famous following the publication of a biography by Sylvia Nasar, *A Beautiful Mind*, and later, an Oscar-winning movie of the same name staring Russell Crowe.

For example, in real life, the protagonist heard voices. He did not have visual hallucinations as the character in the movie did. Also, in real life John Nash was able to discontinue antipsychotic medications after twelve years of illness, while the movie character began taking an atypical antipsychotic later in the film.

Schizophrenia in Literature

Several outstanding novelists have written insightful accounts of characters with believable psychotic illnesses, including schizophrenia and schizophreniform disorder. Some of the symptoms of Nikolai Gogol's character Axenty Ivanovich Poprishchin in the short story "Diary of a Madman" are consistent with schizophrenia. Gogol's novel is a skillful depiction of a person who might be descending into disorganized schizophrenia experiencing a delusion of grandeur.

The nineteenth-century novelist Honoré de Balzac accurately captured many features of schizophrenia in his depiction of the title character in his novel *Louis Lambert*. Cognitive problems, social withdrawal, a preoccupation with mystical ideas, a lack of interest in communicating, and thought disorder are important elements of Balzac's characterization of his fictional character.

In the twentieth century, one of the best-known literary figures to deal with schizophrenia in both his personal and professional life was F. Scott Fitzgerald. Fitzgerald's wife, Zelda, experienced severe psychotic episodes in the early 1930s. Diagnosed with schizophrenia, she lived for most of the rest of her life in a sanitarium.

Fitzgerald relied heavily on Zelda's experience of schizophrenia when he wrote *Tender Is the Night*. This novel explores the effects of the disease on the life of his character Nicole, who experienced acute symptoms at age sixteen.

Schizophrenia in Reality

The majority of people with schizophrenia do not live on the street, they are not confined for years in mental hospitals, and they are not violent. Most people with the disease live with their families, in group homes, or on their own.

Another misconception is that people with schizophrenia are crazy geniuses who alternate between brilliant insights and psychosis. In fact, they are people just like everyone else except they have a condition that can affect their ability to function. To regain enough of that ability, they have to work hard and use the assistance of others to regain skills lost to the disease. If they don't succeed, they can be mentally incapacitated by the disorder.

Anti-Psychiatry

Psychiatry has some very vocal critics. They are in the minority and come from widely different social groups. A few are professionals—therapists, psychologists, and psychiatrists—who disagree with the majority of their colleagues about the causes, treatments, and even the existence of mental illness.

For example, in *Toxic Psychiatry*, psychiatrist Peter R. Breggin, MD, claims that psychiatric drugs produce long-term brain damage. He also suggests that instead of using pharmacotherapy, doctors should listen to patients more and offer understanding and help.

A Tenet of Faith?

Other critics belong to religious organizations or are followers of organizations whose beliefs include dogmatic condemnations of psychiatry. Followers are taught that psychiatry amounts to little more than a sham or an attempt to control others.

They Just Don't Trust It

Others who have a low opinion of psychiatry are former patients who disliked their treatment and are convinced they were treated poorly or were never really ill. Unpleasant experiences with the side effects of antipsychotic medications and unsuccessful interactions with therapists and other mental health care professionals might contribute to the complaints of this group of critics.

more than $5,000 would not have influenced their decision to write prescriptions for certain drugs, because they were already doing so. This is a tricky problem because psychiatrists can help pharmaceutical companies design better drugs and judge their effectiveness. However, to avoid the appearance of conflict of interest, and to rule out any chance of conscious or unconscious bias or favoritism, the physician-consultants should not benefit financially from the success of the product.

Are Nontraditional Treatments Effective?

Nontraditional or alternative treatments cover a wide range of therapies, techniques, and healing philosophies. They are effective for some conditions, but nobody has shown they can relieve the symptoms of schizophrenia. However, some alternative and complementary treatments might provide positive ancillary or side benefits.

One example is stress reduction. Stress is known to trigger problems in people with schizophrenia. Yoga, massage, meditation, and acupuncture may have some positive physical and/or psychological effects, but they do not treat the core symptoms of serious diseases. Anything that can effectively counter the effects of stress, however, may have health benefits for consumers of mental health care. Many alternative treatments may have calming effects on people, although this is difficult to measure. As long as such treatments do no harm and are not used as replacements for proven therapies, there is no reason to avoid them.

Help from the Plant World

Some plants and plant extracts can affect the body in good ways and bad, but none have been shown to be as effective against schizophrenia as antipsychotic drugs. In addition, some herbal supplements may interact with conventional drugs. This is an active area of research partly because of the appeal of natural products. Scientists should learn more about these interactions in coming years.

Homeopathy, naturopathy, shamanism, therapeutic touch, and Ayurveda are other alternative therapies that have not been proven to be effective in treating schizophrenia. Finally, insurance companies will not pay for most alternative therapies.

 Question

What natural substance did ancient medicine offer as a treatment for schizophrenia?
The root of the tropical plant Rauwolfia serpentina, found in India and other parts of Asia, contains a substance called reserpine. The root was ground to a powder and used to treat high blood pressure, sleeplessness, and mental illness because it is a very potent tranquilizer. Reserpine was first extracted from the plant in 1952, just before the first antipsychotic drugs were introduced.

Some alternative treatments may provide a placebo effect. That is, if they make a person feel better psychologically and produce no harm, there might be no reason to avoid them. Any form of treatment, however, that involves the administration of plants, herbs, chemicals, or other substances should be considered very carefully before use by a person with a mental disorder.

Generally, scientists and medical experts agree that patients with psychiatric disorders should not rely on alternative treatments in place of established psychiatric therapies. If they don't interfere with standard treatments and don't harm patients, some might be useful as adjunctive therapy if they safely raise morale.

Useful Lessons from Alternative Approaches

Nontraditional therapies may not be proven to be effective against mental disorders, but many offer a holistic approach. This means they attempt to consider all aspects of a person's life; not just the physical and the mental, but the emotional and spiritual as well. Modern biological psychiatry has its hands full treating the worst symptoms of schizophrenia. Therapists, relatives, religious advisers, and other counselors can contribute a great deal to a patient's sense of well-being by addressing concerns many physicians can't.

The Proof Is in the Study

The only way to tell if a proposed nontraditional treatment is effective is to treat one group of patients with it and see how well they do compared to a group that does not receive the same treatment. The first group is called the experimental group and the second is called the control group.

No matter how often you hear that someone knows someone who benefited from an alternative treatment, this hearsay does not constitute scientific proof. Even if you watched it happen to someone close to you, it would be necessary to rule out other factors that might have influenced or even explained the effect you witnessed before you could claim that the alternative treatment worked. Without a controlled test, it is merely an anecdote.

If you are making treatment decisions affecting someone you care about, learn to ask this question when you hear a claim that something works: Is this an anecdote or is it scientifically proven? It often seems as if anecdotes that contradict standard practice receive more publicity than do anecdotes confirming standard practice.

There are plenty of physicians and scientists who would like nothing more than to find a better treatment for schizophrenia. These researchers would leap at the opportunity to identify something that could aid recovery from this serious brain disease. So far only the typical and atypical antipsychotic drugs have passed that test.

It is not difficult to design a study of a new treatment, but there are potential complications. One important factor is the length of time patients will receive the experimental treatment and the control treatment. It often takes time to see the effects of medications. A short-lasting experiment might not show any results only because they never had a chance to become apparent. Conducting a longer study raises the question of how fairly one is treating the patients who receive only the placebo, that is, no treatment at all.

Testing a New Treatment

On paper, it is possible to design a study that compares an experimental group receiving a nontraditional treatment and a control group receiving only a placebo. In reality, such a simple design might not be approved by an ethical review board that must approve all studies or experiments involving humans or animals.

 Alert

> It is very important that you keep the doctor informed about all treatments a patient with schizophrenia is receiving, both prescribed and unprescribed. Some alternative approaches might interfere with traditional treatment and have adverse physical or psychological effects on susceptible individuals.

It might not be approved because schizophrenia is such a serious disease. It is unethical not to treat patients for an extended period if even partially effective treatments are available. Not treating the control group at all would knowingly endanger their health. Since it is also possible that the nontraditional treatment might be ineffective, the experimental group might also be entitled to receive current, standard antipsychotic treatment instead of facing months without proven effective treatment. Thus, the actual experimental design of a long-term study might involve an experimental group receiving antipsychotic medications and nontraditional treatment compared to controls receiving antipsychotic medications and a placebo. It can get complicated, but it is doable and is done in tests of potential new treatments every year.

CHAPTER 13

Ensuring Good Psychiatric Care

PSYCHIATRISTS ARE THE specialists most closely associated with care for people with schizophrenia. They are medical doctors and doctors of osteopathy who specialize in diagnosing and treating people with psychiatric disorders. There are 36,000 psychiatrists who are members of the American Psychiatric Association (APA), and some of them specialize in treating patients with schizophrenia. Clinical psychologists who earned a doctorate degree and became licensed in clinical psychology are also active in this field, as are various mental health care workers who specialize in different types of therapy.

Diagnosing a Mental Illness

Sometimes, the first physician a patient with psychiatric problems sees is a family doctor. These general practitioners may not witness the first psychotic episode a patient experiences, but they see people with subtle psychological changes that may precede psychosis. These doctors should be aware of the basic warning signs and symptoms of schizophrenia and other psychiatric disorders. They should know how to conduct a preliminary psychiatric exam and, if appropriate, immediately refer the patient to a psychiatrist or other mental health care specialist who can perform a thorough exam and start a treatment program.

You should find a psychiatrist who specializes in, or has a lot of experience treating, patients with schizophrenia. Treating a person with this complex condition requires individualized attention. The psychiatrist should have up-to-date knowledge about the best possible medications to try, correct dosages, and approaches for monitoring the benefits and possible side effects of the medication. Additionally, the psychiatrist must provide you with referrals for other treatment resources such as psychotherapy, vocational therapy, and other therapies, so you receive comprehensive care and maximize the benefits and outcome of your treatment.

Avoiding Missed Diagnoses

Symptoms should not be brushed aside as "typical teenage problems" or "a bit of depression." A good family doctor will be suspicious of the psychological deterioration or cognitive decline of a patient and should direct you toward specialized help as soon as possible. Early detection allows early intervention and can prevent some very destructive consequences, some of which may be irreparable.

Schizophrenia is sometimes misdiagnosed as depression, especially in cases of young people in the early stages of schizophrenia. Unfortunately, the patient will suffer from the delay. It is crucial that a proper psychiatric examination be performed for individuals showing early signs of schizophrenia. Some patients may be too embarrassed to tell the doctor about the strange experiences and thoughts they are having, and input from the patient's family can help the psychiatrist reach the correct diagnosis sooner and more accurately.

Alert

Never accept a cautious wait-and-see attitude if you suspect someone you care for is developing a psychotic disorder such as schizophrenia or a related illness. Rapid, accurate assessment and proper therapy are important for the future health of the patient.

It is also possible that a patient may not be totally forthcoming with the doctor if she is paranoid or afraid of being "put away." Sharing observations by other family members is almost always an essential part of making the right diagnosis. If a doctor does not make time to meet with the family, find another doctor. A doctor should talk to family members to acquire more information about the patient's condition and answer the family's questions about how they can help in the management of this disease. This should be the minimum standard for treating schizophrenia. If any doctor dismisses serious, persistent, negative changes you observe in the personality or behavior of a young adult or adolescent, find another doctor.

Physicians may err by not working closely enough with a patient. Make sure your doctor does the following:

1. Ensures that the person is continuing to get her recommended treatment
2. Accommodates the person by adjusting doses or changing medications in response to her concerns
3. Gives the person clear instructions in a straightforward treatment plan

The Comfort Factor

It is important that you and your loved one feel comfortable with the doctor. Many patients stop treatment because they do not like their doctors. Rapport between doctor and patient may not be immediate. One session is not enough to determine if you have found a compatible physician, but if after several sessions or weeks the patient feels no trust or willingness to confide in one doctor, look for another.

Locating Good Care Near You

Personal referrals are the best way to find a good doctor. Ideally, you should seek out someone who has experience with schizophrenia.

Get a recommendation from your primary care doctor and ask her the reasons behind her judgment.

Ask everyone you trust if they can refer you to a good psychiatrist. This may include friends, family, members of social clubs and religious groups, or colleagues.

Professional Recommendations

Call the closest Community Mental Health Centers (CMHCs) and ask to speak to someone about your interest in consulting a psychiatrist or other professional mental health care provider. CMHCs have a twenty-four-hour toll-free telephone referral helpline: (800) 662-HELP (662-4357). You can also consult the nearest medical school or teaching hospital, particularly if it has a large, well-regarded faculty.

Next-in-Line Recommendations

You can also check with a professional organization such as the American Psychiatric Association (APA; *www.psych.org*). The APA will be able to tell you where you can find one or more qualified psychiatrists near you. However, the APA and other professional services will not be able to gauge the quality of care. These referrals are based on whether a doctor is affiliated with a particular organization.

You can write to the APA Answer Center at the American Psychiatric Association, 1000 Wilson Boulevard, Suite 1825, Arlington, VA 22209. To phone the APA free of charge dial (888) 35-PSYCH (350-7924); from outside the United States, including Canada, call (703) 907-7300. E-mail the organization at *apa@psych.org*. Tell the association how to contact you by providing a complete mailing address, e-mail address, or fax number.

Researching a Doctor's Background

For emergency treatment, you won't have the option of researching a doctor's background. Calming, stabilizing, and evaluating a person in the midst of a psychotic crisis will take precedence over finding the perfect doctor. During periods of hospitalization or long-term outpatient care, however, you have the option of learning about the background of the physician who will be overseeing care.

Doctors have varying degrees of experience and training. You should inquire about a doctor's education, years in practice, and past and pending disciplinary proceedings.

What to Look For

Start with your doctor and her staff. Politely ask her about herself. There is no reason to be intimidated. As long as you respect her and her professionalism, you as a medical consumer have the right to inquire about anything that could have an impact on the type and quality of care the patient will receive.

Areas of Interest
- Medical school that awarded the degree
- Internship, residency, post-doctoral, or fellowship training
- Medical licensing information
- Board certification
- Years of experience
- Experience treating schizophrenia
- Hospital affiliations and privileges
- Evidence of ongoing training, education, publications, and lectures
- Teaching experience or academic appointments
- Any special citations, awards, or recognition by colleagues, professional organizations, advocacy groups, or community organizations

Nothing you discover in a background search will assure you of top notch psychiatric care. But such a search can increase your chances of finding a competent, experienced professional.

Warning Signs
- Disciplinary actions or board suspensions
- Evidence of criminal behavior or convictions

- Multiple instances of being sued
- Malpractice judgments
- Hidden or unadvertised partnership or ownership in any for-profit special clinics, in-house treatment facilities, or other commercial interests the doctor may recommend or prescribe.

If your questions evoke a haughty, arrogant, or indignant response, find a doctor who is more self-confident. A good doctor will not be insulted if you ask about her experience and record. On the other hand, this conversation may be enough to reassure you. Based on the answers you receive, you may decide not to investigate any further.

Finding More Information

You have the option of confirming what you learn from public records. There are two ways to do this: on your own and by paying a company that specializes in collecting and selling background information on professionals. You can determine whether your doctor is board certified by contacting the American Board of Medical Specialties (ABMS). The service is free and can be found online at *www.abms .org*. You can also call the ABMS Certification Verification Service at (866) ASK-ABMS (275-2267). The call is free. The ABMS does not provide other background information or offer advice on finding a doctor.

Other potential sources for your do-it-yourself background check include the Food and Drug Administration, Drug Enforcement Administration, and the Department of Health and Human Services. These agencies could provide information about individuals who have been investigated for either criminal or unethical behavior.

You might also receive some basic information concerning an individual physician's background from the American Psychiatric Association, the American Medical Association, and state or other local medical societies.

The American Medical Association (AMA) provides contact information for all of the state medical societies on the "Patients" page of its website (*www.ama-assn.org*). The same page offers a "Doctor Finder" service. The psychiatrists and other specialists whose names and information are provided include both AMA members and non-members. More information, including educational background, office hours, and insurance companies accepted by the doctor's practice, is provided for doctors who belong to the AMA.

Fact

Your state medical board can provide some useful information at no cost. Visit the website of the Federation of State Medical Boards (*www.fsmb.org*) to find contact information for medical boards in your state. Click the Public Services tab.

Uncovering . . .

You will probably have to do some research to determine if a doctor has been disciplined by a medical society. You can do this by conducting a background check using the resources described in the following sections. Even if you find such evidence, remember that few stories can be completely evaluated until both sides are heard. If something in your doctor's past concerns you, ask him about it. It is up to you to decide the significance of the information you uncover.

Question

What does it mean if a physician has no record of disciplinary action?
It means he has not been convicted of breaking the rules and regulations of any state medical agency, medical organization, or federal regulatory agency. There is also no evidence he has any impairments that could interfere with his ability to provide good care.

A lawsuit against a doctor may mean nothing. Many doctors are sued at some point in their careers by former patients who do not have legitimate cases. If, however, you find that a physician or therapist has been sued repeatedly, you should evaluate that information especially carefully.

Professional Physician Background Checks

Several companies maintain up-to-date records of physician contact information, education, qualifications, certification, specialties, and disciplinary rulings. These businesses sell this information for fees starting at around $20. As with all online sources, be careful with both free and for-profit sources of information. Make sure you know who is offering information and where they get it. Get the phone number from any website you are considering and speak to a representative to get answers to any questions you want to ask. Make sure you are confident that you can trust the information you pay for.

The State Medical Board

The Federation of State Medical Boards (FSMB) itself will give you an instant Online Physician Profile (*www.docinfo.org*) of any doctor for $9.95. The federation has information about medical professionals licensed in the United States, including disciplinary actions, education, and other background material. If there is a record of disciplinary action, the FSMB report will include details, such as the nature of the punishment, when the action took place, and the reason for the action.

The profile will not include information about lawsuits or medical malpractice claims or settlements. This information is available from some public sources, such as court records, and from private companies that provide background checks for a fee.

For-Profit Investigators

MDNationwide (*www.mdnationwide.org* or 1-877-242-8556) has been in business since 2002. The company charges $19.95 for background information, including past or pending disciplinary investigations. As a separate service, MDNationwide maintains a list of medical specialists it considers worthy of recommendation. A search based on state, city, and medical specialty costs $9.99. If you are new to an area and can't get any good referrals, this is an option to consider.

Another business offering background information is USA Records Search (*www.investigateyourdoctor.com*). In business since

1999, the company employs both attorney and private investigator associates to find information. It charges $35 for a full physician background report.

Working with Your Doctor

A competent doctor will ask you many questions in order to learn as much about the patient's background as possible. Be prepared to discuss the patient's life, personality, behavior, and ability to function before the illness led to a visit to the doctor.

Find out if any relatives suffered from a mental illness. This includes schizophrenia, other psychotic disorders, bipolar disease, and depression. Ask your relatives about this if you are not familiar with the medical history of other family members.

Don't be surprised if the psychiatrist wants to meet with the patient alone before meeting together with both of you. The doctor needs to establish a rapport with the patient, and seeing him alone helps accomplish that goal. It may take several sessions for the patient to feel comfortable enough to confide in the doctor. Some patients can hide their most troubling symptoms, such as hearing voices. But if the patient begins to trust the physician, the physician will be able to approach the topic of psychotic symptoms without threatening the patient. Longer conversations are more likely to reveal thoughts, delusions, and other problems the patient may want to hide from others.

When Did This Start?

Try to determine exactly when the patient's behavior became noticeably different. Using specific examples of unusual behaviors may help you date the onset of symptoms, something that could be very helpful in making a correct diagnosis. Describe all the symptoms you have observed, as well as details of the behavior associated with any delusions, hallucinations, or bizarre thoughts. Your impressions about the changes you have observed and sensed in the patient are important too.

Keep records during treatment. Note what symptoms were present and the dose of medication the patient was taking at the time they appeared. These observations can help the doctor and patient find the most effective medication.

Your records also may help you spot troublesome episodes earlier, when medical intervention might be more effective. Stopping an episode in its early stages is much less traumatic and stressful for everyone. Since early indicators of relapse differ for each individual patient, your observations and notes may be useful in the future.

The Mind Has a Body

A recent National Alliance on Mental Illness survey found that 49 percent of people living with schizophrenia believed their doctors did not consider a patient's medical problems as seriously as they should. This perception is especially troubling since people with mental illness are two or even three times more likely than the rest of the population to die from ailments such as diabetes and heart disease.

Fact

A study of more than 97,000 people in Taiwan found that patients with schizophrenia had a higher risk of suffering a ruptured appendix than patients who did not have schizophrenia. Patients with schizophrenia were 2.83 times more likely to suffer from a burst appendix than were other patients with acute appendicitis.

There are several reasons people with schizophrenia do not receive medical treatment as quickly as others. First, schizophrenia's symptoms may hinder a person's ability to recognize and/or tell anyone about physical ailments at an early stage. Cognitive, psychotic, and negative symptoms may all act to prevent a person with mental illness from reporting the symptoms of a physical problem. It is also possible that some physicians unfamiliar with mental illness may discount or overlook physical symptoms, dismissing them as part of a patient's delusions.

If a patient experiences a physical problem while receiving inpatient psychiatric care, make sure he is evaluated by an internist. All free-standing psychiatric facilities are required to have internists and other medical specialists available.

If the problem is urgent, it may be better if the patient is transferred to a general hospital at which psychiatric specialists may continue to provide psychiatric care. It is common for patients admitted for inpatient psychiatric care to be hospitalized on specialty psychiatric floors of general hospitals, where other specialty care is readily available if required.

The Caregiver's Role

There are many ways you can assist the doctor as you help yourself and the person you care for, including the following:

- Show the patient there is someone he can trust no matter what happens.
- Decrease chance of relapse by encouraging the patient to take prescribed medication and attend therapy. Alert the doctor if the patient goes off his medications.
- Summon help in the event of a psychotic episode or other crisis.
- Communicate with the patient's physician about problems, medical compliance, and progress.
- Monitor quality of medical care.
- Provide support, encouragement, and understanding.
- Seek out additional mental health resources in the community.
- Educate people close to the patient.

Encouraging Treatment in Reluctant Individuals

A major challenge for you may be persuading the person you care about to take his medicine and attend therapy. It is not unusual for people with schizophrenia to discontinue treatment. There are many reasons, one of which is the nature of the disease itself. It often prevents the patient from realizing he is ill, a condition psychiatrists call anosognosia, a lack of insight or awareness about their condition.

"There Is Nothing Wrong with Me!"

If someone you know is clearly suffering from a psychiatric illness but is unable to realize it, consult Xavier Amadors's book *I Am Not Sick, I Don't Need Help!* for useful advice on what to try. Also get advice from mental health care practitioners in your area.

Table 13-1: Reasons Patients Stop or Won't Accept Treatment

Reason	Possible Solution
Lacks knowledge of illness (anosognosia)	Education, therapy
Denies illness	Education, therapy
Medical side effects	Adjust dose, change medications
Irrational fear of medicine	Education, therapy
Fear of medicine dependency	Education, therapy
Dislike of doctor	Find new doctor
Confused, disorganized, cognitively impaired	Therapy, training

Adapted from E. Fuller Torrey's *Surviving Schizophrenia*.

Other patients may realize something is wrong but may deny it to themselves and others. The disease can disrupt rational thought so much that a patient may not possess the discipline required to stick to a treatment plan. In this case, you or another caregiver will have to take action to ensure treatment is provided. In extreme cases, it may require getting the courts to order the person to undergo treatment.

Other Reasons for Medical Noncompliance

If a person with schizophrenia is convinced that the side effects of medication are worse than the disease, it is unlikely he will take his medication. Abuse of drugs and alcohol can also contribute to medical noncompliance by lessening the effectiveness of medications and therapy. The patient's friends and even other members of your family who know little about the disease may hinder recovery by giving bad advice or even encouraging the patient to stop treatment "because it does more harm than good." This is not true; in the majority of cases, stopping treatment leads to renewed psychotic symptoms.

Essential

It can be very challenging to treat the patient as an independent, self-directed adult, but it is important to try. Respect for the person is not only her basic right; it can be very useful in building a basis for a joint collaboration for managing this disease.

In the face of these and other difficulties, helping someone resume or stick to a treatment plan requires flexibility. There is no failure in having to change treatment, whether pharmacological, psychological, or both. The only failure is in abandoning treatment completely. If you are doing your best to maintain continuous care, you are doing a tremendous service to someone who needs it very much.

Confidentiality

By law, you have the right to keep your medical history secret. The best medical and psychiatric care demands it if a patient is to reveal intimate details about her life and illness.

Certain realities of modern life make it vital that your medical history remains confidential. The lack of understanding and fear of mental illness that still exists in today's society can result in loss of jobs, promotions, health care benefits, and insurance coverage for a person whose private medical history is not protected.

If you care for someone who is being treated for schizophrenia or another mental illness, ask your psychiatrist and other mental health care providers how they protect your confidentiality. Find out what they disclose to insurance companies and others when they share information.

If a present or prospective employer or an insurance company requests information from your doctor, it can only be released if you sign an authorization form. The American Psychiatric Association Guidelines on Confidentiality state that you should be told clearly who wants to see your medical records and why. The guidelines also say you should not be forced or threatened in any way to give permission for others to see your records; your permission should be given freely. Nevertheless, there is an unavoidable implied threat in such requests: unless you sign the form, there is a good chance you might not get the job or the money from the insurance company.

If you are looking after the interests of someone with schizophrenia, make sure you know the identity of the third party asking for medical records, why it wants them, and what it is going to do with them. Find out how the third party is going to protect your privacy and whether or not it intends to share the records with any fourth parties.

Affordability of Mental Health Care

Until new federal legislation goes into effect in January 2010, many health insurance policies are likely to exclude nondiscriminatory coverage for mental illness. Call your insurance provider or HMO to find out what kind of coverage it offers. It is also important that you have the power to choose your own psychiatrist. If you can afford it, it may be worth it to pay to see one who is not approved by your insurance company. Compare plans and, if you have the option, switch to one with the coverage that best meets your needs. Ask the following questions before you sign up for a health plan:

- Is the coverage for mental illnesses the same as that for other medical illnesses?
- Will it pay for all the medical services and treatments you might need?
- Will you be able to appeal if the insurance company decides you don't need a certain treatment?
- Do you have to go through a general care physician before you can see a psychiatrist or the mental health care provider you want to see?
- If a favorite psychiatrist is not approved by your health insurance company, can she sign up to be included on the list of approved providers?

Source: the American Psychiatric Association

If hospitalization of the patient seems necessary, you will have to get your insurance company to agree to the hospitalization before it will pay for it. Employees of the insurance company may go over the patient's case with the psychiatrist. If they agree that the patient's symptoms are so severe that she cannot be treated effectively in an outpatient setting, the insurance company will agree to pay for a short hospital stay.

The patient's mental state will be re-evaluated before the patient is released, and hospitalization may be continued if the doctor and the insurance company agree it is needed.

If you disagree with the insurance company's decision to deny payment for either first-time hospitalization or continuation of in-patient care, you and the patient's doctor have the right to appeal the company's decision.

CHAPTER 14

Should a Person with Schizophrenia Live at Home?

IF CERTAIN CRITERIA are met, a person with schizophrenia certainly should consider living in her own place or in a family home with relatives. The living arrangements should not impede treatment or contribute to an inability to cope. The patient, for example, should be able to function without being a threat to herself or to others. Her behavior should not disrupt life for those around her so much that they cannot work or otherwise complete activities required for daily living.

When Living at Home Is a Good Idea

Someone starting to make progress against the challenges of schizophrenia should consider living at home if she benefits from the support of relatives. A supportive home environment will aid progress.

Treatment Options for People with Schizophrenia
- Twenty-four-hour inpatient care in a general hospital psychiatric unit
- Private, public, or state psychiatric hospital
- Federal psychiatric hospital
- Veterans Administration hospital
- Partial hospitalization or day care

- Residential care, supported housing
- Community mental health center
- Psychiatrist or other mental health practitioner office
- Support group

Source: the American Psychiatric Association

A Base for Treatment with Moral Support

If the home offers a safe haven from which the patient can maintain a treatment regimen and make progress regaining social and cognitive skills, then living at home is ideal. In addition, if continuing to live at home eases financial burdens on the patient and her family, both parties can benefit from working out a suitable domestic living arrangement.

Table 14-1: Benefits of Living at Home

The Relatives	The Patient
Allows close health monitoring	Assured care at all times
Opportunities to help recovery	Encouragement, family available to help
Less expensive	Possibility of saving money
Less worry about consumer's safety	Less time spent alone
Companionship	Familiar companion(s)

Adapted from Mueser and Gingerich, *The Complete Family Guide to Schizophrenia.*

With new antipsychotic medication, better therapies, and a treatment team, living at home has become the norm. It is important that the patient is able help to around the house after a treatment program is agreed upon and implemented. She should have assigned chores that she agrees to complete. She should be able to agree to, and abide by, the rules of the house. The home should not be turned into an asylum. It should be a base for recovery.

Patients who live at home may have an increased chance of success if they are female, function at a high level, have social contacts outside the home, do not share the home with siblings, and have a family capable of providing the support and love needed to make the arrangement work, according to Rebecca Woolis in *When Someone You Love Has a Mental Illness.*

Living Independently

The question of whether or not someone should move from a family home into her own place is a personal one and depends on the ability of the patient to care for herself. The person should be able to benefit from therapy outside the hospital, the goal of which is to improve her mental condition to make her as independent as possible. Consumers with a high level of functioning do it routinely. The sooner the patient can get on with life independently, the better.

Table 14-2: Benefits of Living in Independently or Semi-Independently

The Relatives	The Patient
Less daily stress and family conflict	Less stress, greater privacy
More freedom	Improved sense of self-esteem, independence, self-reliance
Chance to recover from caregiver burnout	Good training for complete independence

Adapted from Mueser and Gingerich, *The Complete Family Guide to Schizophrenia.*

The decision concerning where a patient should live and receive care depends on many factors. These factors can, and most likely will, change over time and will require adjustment in therapy. The most important factor should be the patient's mental condition. In reality, insurance coverage and your ability to pay for different types of care will have an impact on the type of therapy a person may receive. Treatment in a private psychiatric hospital, for example, may be too expensive for many people.

When Living at Home Is Not a Good Idea

The well-being of both family members and patients should be considered when deciding where someone with schizophrenia should live. The living arrangements have to work for both parties. If the patient is not yet functioning at a level high enough to benefit from living at home with family members, consider another arrangement.

More Harm than Good

Resentment, anger, and lack of support in a domestic setting can seriously hinder progress against schizophrenia and other mental illnesses. It is bad for the person struggling with the disease and for those living with him.

Essential

Constant care is an obvious advantage of hospitalization. This is especially important if the person poses a threat to herself or others. In this case protective methods such as isolation and, in extreme cases, restraint, can only be used for a short time and performed in a hospital setting under close observation by highly specialized personnel until the patient is calmed and the threat passes.

A psychiatrist will examine the patient, evaluate the symptoms, and formulate a treatment plan. If a patient can receive better care initially in a hospital than in an outpatient setting, hospitalization is indicated.

No patient, however, should be hospitalized if he can receive adequate treatment in a less confining setting and adequate living arrangements outside the hospital can be arranged. Possible options range from full-time commitment to a psychiatric hospital to residential care or supervised independent living.

No Other Choice

Hospitalization is the obvious choice when a patient's symptoms become so severe he cannot be cared for effectively as an outpatient or he poses a danger to himself or others. The decision to hospitalize a patient depends on several considerations. One is the seriousness or severity of the illness.

Another is the availability of a social support network provided by family, friends, and/or other caregivers. The presence of an effective support group may make it possible for one patient to receive care at home while another patient with a similar illness may receive better treatment in a hospital.

Woolis advises that a person may not thrive at home if there is only one parent. The arrangement weakens the parent's relationship with the children, or siblings react negatively. Parents who are incapable of giving support and encouragement should not be primary caregivers. And, of course, anyone with schizophrenia who abuses street drugs or alcohol and is not in a drug treatment program should not live at home.

Full- and Part-Time Hospitalization

The severity of schizophrenia as an illness is indicated by the fact that it sends more people to the hospital than almost any other illness, according to the National Alliance for Research on Schizophrenia and Depression. Fortunately, hospital stays in psychiatric facilities average less than two weeks. If hospitalization is recommended, research different facilities and programs.

Questions to Ask when Visiting a Prospective Psychiatric Hospital

- How will you be kept informed of the patient's progress?
- How often will the patient see a psychiatrist?
- Who else will be working closely with the patient?
- What programs are offered?
- What kinds of recreation are offered?
- How many staff members are on-site during the day?
- How many staff members are on-site in the evening and overnight?

The answers you receive should satisfy you that the person you care for will receive thorough and appropriate treatment. If you are not satisfied with what you learn, keep looking for a more suitable facility.

Benefits of Hospitalization

If living at home is not an option, a patient may receive better care in a hospital before other living arrangements, such as a group home, can be found. If a patient is in the midst of a psychotic crisis, the treatment in a good hospital can provide immediate relief. After the medical staff has helped the patient overcome the crisis, he can begin to recover in an environment free of responsibilities and major outside stresses.

 Alert

Hospitals vary in quality. Some offer more services than others. Compare facilities you can afford. If you are familiar with the hospital you will use before you need it, both you and the patient may experience less stress if hospitalization becomes necessary.

The patient's psychiatrist will direct the care he receives in the hospital just as a cardiologist will direct a heart patient's care. If a patient enters a hospital with severe symptoms that require immediate treatment, he likely will receive medication.

If the patient does not require emergency treatment, or once a crisis is brought under control, he should have a complete physical examination. This exam, including a drug screen, urinalysis, general chemistry, and a complete blood count, will provide a good indication of the patient's state of health. It also could identify medical factors influencing psychotic or other symptoms, such as mental dullness or lethargy.

Treatments Available in a Psychiatric Hospital

After a patient is stabilized, a psychiatrist may prescribe a variety of therapies, which could include sessions with a primary therapist, group therapy sessions with other patients, and family therapy sessions that may include parents, spouses, children, siblings, caretakers, and even close friends.

Types of Mental Health Care Workers Involved in Therapy

- Psychiatrists
- Clinical psychologists
- Psychiatric nurses
- Rehabilitation therapists
- Social workers
- Physical therapists
- Drug and alcohol counselors
- Nutritionists

Source: the American Psychiatric Association

A specialist in addiction counseling can be consulted if the patient's crisis was precipitated by drug or alcohol use, or if the hospital staff discovers that the patient is dependent on drugs.

Essential

The skills a patient learns in residential care can make her feel better about herself. If a patient feels she is making progress in therapy, getting along with other residents, and learning how to care for her household and herself, then her self-confidence and self-esteem may increase.

It is common, but not necessarily universal, for patients to take antipsychotic drugs while attending therapy sessions. In most cases, the drug therapy will continue after the patient leaves the hospital. In therapy, patients learn skills to help them live independently. These can include hints for getting along better in the workplace and in social settings. Patients develop and practice routines to help them maintain personal hygiene and a clean, smoothly run home. As the patient's mental health improves, the mental health professionals and staff at the hospital will prepare a discharge plan. The plan should include details concerning the patient's medication, therapy, and outpatient care.

Part-Time Hospitalization

Partial hospitalization offers a less intensive treatment option than full-time hospital care. It involves attending activities, therapy, and programs at a hospital during the day. After receiving therapy and rehabilitation, the health care consumer returns home. Weekends may also be spent outside the hospital. This schedule allows patients to avoid the extra cost of overnight stays and interact with family and other members of the community when they are away from the hospital. Partial hospitalization may include the following services:

- Individual psychotherapy
- Group psychotherapy
- Social rehabilitation
- Vocational rehabilitation
- Education counseling and assistance

Source: the American Psychiatric Association

A patient is ready for partial hospitalization when he has benefited from therapy and rehabilitation designed to help him lead a more independent life. The support of family and/or others in the community can greatly increase his chances of success. The consumer may rely heavily on his outside support network when he is not attending sessions in the hospital.

Assisted Living

Assisted living is analogous to a retirement home that offers a range of on-site aide services. People who function very well and who need little outside assistance can live independent lives in their own rooms or apartments, but there will always be qualified staff nearby if they need help.

People who need more help can also live alone and receive more visits from assistants who live in the same building. The amount of aid a person gets is determined by his needs. The patient's state of recovery determines his degree of independence.

Hospitalizing Children

Children and teenagers represent a significant group of mental health care consumers. Like young adults with schizophrenia, some recover or go into remission. Others worsen with time. As with young adults, hospitalization is an option if symptoms become severe. The treatment plan developed for a child by the physician and hospital staff will address needs similar to those of adult patients. In addition, the plan should take the child's academic needs into account.

Factors to Consider for a Hospitalized Child

A minor should have access to all types of therapy—individual, group, family, and educational—that he needs during hospitalization. Social skills can be learned and practiced in activity therapy. If necessary, the child can be treated for alcohol and drug abuse. Some of the questions you and your doctor probably will want to answer when deciding whether hospitalization is required include the following:

- Does the child pose a real and immediate threat to himself or others?
- Is the child's behavior bizarre and destructive to those around him?
- Does the child require careful observation and monitoring while taking medication?
- Does the child need around-the-clock care to improve?
- Has the child failed to improve or recover in other, more open treatment facilities or environments?

Source: the American Psychiatric Association

Family therapy is very important for the child's future. You and other family members or guardians should take advantage of family therapy to learn the most effective techniques for communicating and working with the child. It also is important that you learn as much as you can about the nature of the child's illness, his current course of treatment, and what progress to expect in the future.

Getting Good Care for Your Child

Most likely, hospitalization will be a short-term experience for a child. One reason is the lack of long-term hospitals. Short hospital stays are possible with the assistance of antipsychotic drugs, but many children and others with schizophrenia would benefit from longer stays in facilities that could provide a secure environment, treatment, education, and therapy under one roof. For the most part, such facilities are too expensive for all but a small percentage of the population.

Consequently, finding good care can be a hit-or-miss experience. It takes effort and persistence to find the right doctor and other mental health care workers to work with you to help your child. Don't stop until you have found treatment that controls psychotic symptoms, a process that will not happen overnight. Seek out therapy programs that make a difference to your child. Always try to minimize stress in your child's life, but expect setbacks.

Legal Rights and Hospitalization

Eighty-eight percent of patients who enter a psychiatric hospital do so voluntarily, according to the National Alliance on Mental Illness. The 12 percent who are committed involuntarily must first be certified by a physician as needing hospitalization. The details of this process vary from state to state.

It is not easy to have someone involuntarily committed to a mental health facility or to force someone to undergo treatment. Strict laws protect the rights of people who resist hospitalization.

Evaluating the Need for Hospitalization

Check with local mental health services to find out if a mental health care provider will come to your home to conduct an evaluation. Be sure to talk to the visiting mental health worker privately to explain symptoms and changes in behavior you have observed. This is important if the patient might hide symptoms from the visiting professional.

The course of action becomes clearer—but not necessarily easier—when someone is having a psychotic episode. Because this situation obviously poses a threat to the patient and perhaps others, the police or other emergency responders can help you get the patient to a doctor who can perform an emergency psychiatric evaluation.

Involuntary Admissions

A doctor usually has the option of placing a patient into a hospital without her permission for an evaluation. This confinement is usually limited to a few days or a few weeks.

A judge should be informed of the involuntary admission. This requirement is mandated in many states. In some states, the testimony of one or two psychiatrists may be enough to involuntarily commit a patient who is too ill to appear in court. In all cases, it is crucial that a court of law be informed of an involuntary commitment and that the legal rights of the patient are protected before, during, and after hospitalization.

 Question

What is the procedure for committing someone to a psychiatric hospital?

It varies according to state. If you think it might be necessary to involuntarily commit someone, check with the patient's psychiatrist or other mental health adviser about the procedure for your state.

If a more thorough evaluation of the patient's mental health in the hospital indicates that the patient needs continued observation and/or intensive medical care, the hospitalization may be extended after a court hearing. The patient, a legal guardian, or a court-approved representative must be present at this court hearing.

The judge will decide whether or not hospitalization can be extended for a longer but finite period of time. After this time has elapsed, another court hearing will be required to extend the involuntary stay. Usually by this time, antipsychotic medications and/or therapy will have produced some positive results that allow a treatment plan to be developed so extended hospital stays can be discontinued. If the doctors recommend long-term commitment, they must justify their decision to the court. Psychiatrists might also determine that the patient can be treated adequately with partial hospitalization, providing the patient's mental condition will allow this less restrictive treatment option.

Outpatient Care

Following hospitalization, patients have a right to effective care provided by their community. You, as a caregiver, patient, or patient advocate, should receive certain basic benefits. Effective outpatient care should provide sufficient psychiatric monitoring, medical compliance, therapy, decent housing, and training in preparation for a job or volunteer position.

Essential

Among mental health care providers, a case manager is the person who oversees a consumer's treatment plan outside the hospital. A good case manager will ensure good treatment by going to bat for consumers when they run into obstacles as they work toward recovery.

The absence of an effective community care program can make it more difficult for someone to continue her medication and get effective therapy and training. This increases chances of symptoms, psychotic emergencies, hospitalizations, unemployment, homelessness, and even suicide.

No Secrets

A 1975 study showed the benefit of informing patients about recommended treatment options. Before their first visit to a psychiatric outpatient clinic, fifty people were asked what they thought about the upcoming consultation. The survey revealed a fear of social stigma and a fair amount of misunderstanding about the nature of the visit. Some of those questioned did not even know they were going to see a psychiatrist. Thirty percent of the people who were informed about the nature of the clinic never visited it. With patient education and explanations, however, the number of refusals fell to just 13 percent.

CHAPTER 15

What You Can Do to Aid Recovery

THE MOST IMPORTANT steps you can take are to recognize that your loved one has a mental health problem and to help him get treatment. That advice may sound obvious, but ignorance, suspicion, fear, embarrassment, and denial are serious handicaps for many people who are faced with this challenge. Even some health care providers who are unfamiliar with mental health topics may not recognize the seriousness of a patient's symptoms. These issues can lead to significant delays in treatment, which can make the illness more difficult to treat.

Attitude: Accept the Pain and Take Charge of Your Situation

The diagnosis of a serious illness can have different effects on people. In time, however, they can be reduced to two. You can passively accept the situation and take what comes along, or you can engage the threat and actively learn everything useful you can in order to fight it. An active fighter looks upon doctors and other mental health care providers as partners in the fight.

The Lessons of Hamilton Jordan

Hamilton Jordan was White House Chief of Staff in the Carter administration. Over the course of many years, he survived battles against three different forms of cancer: non-Hodgkin's lymphoma, prostate cancer, and skin cancer. At least two of his illnesses were probably caused by the plant poison Agent Orange, which he was exposed to while serving as a humanitarian volunteer in Vietnam. Jordan finally succumbed to a fourth type of cancer, mesothelioma, in 2008 at age sixty-three.

Essential

As a caregiver, you are working to save the quality of life of someone with schizophrenia. Bring all of your determination and resources to the job, as Jordan did to fight his multiple illnesses.

Jordan recounted how he survived for so many years against such long odds in his memoir, *No Such Thing as a Bad Day*. His book includes his top ten tips for cancer patients. Many of the tips Jordan offers apply to people facing a new life as a caregiver for someone with a serious disease such as schizophrenia.

Ten Tips for Dealing with a Severe Disease

1. Be an active partner in the medical decisions made about your life or the life of a someone you care for.
2. Seek and know the truth about the illness and the prognosis.
3. Get a second opinion.
4. Determine upfront how broad or narrow your physicians' experience is.
5. If the prognosis is poor, try to get to a top rated medical center or teaching hospital. Find experts engaged in cutting edge, experimental treatments.
6. Do not allow experts to project their values, goals, and expectations onto you. Don't let anyone tell you there is no chance of recovery as long as there is the chance that

new medications will be approved and new treatments developed.

7. Understand the economics of medical care. Know if care is being denied for financial reasons. Seek help from any person or agency who might be able to direct you to the best care possible.

8. Ultimately, find a doctor that you trust and believe in.

9. Treat your mind as well as your body. Taking care of yourself will help you care for your loved one. Protecting your loved one from stress may ease the burden of the disease.

10. Your attitude and beliefs are your most powerful weapons for fighting the disease.

Source: Adapted from Hamilton Jordan, *No Such Thing as a Bad Day*

Setting Realistic Goals of Recovery

No one can deny that hearing a diagnosis of schizophrenia will be an unsettling, life-changing event. Fifteen years ago, it would have been even worse. Although there is still no cure, our understanding of the disease and new combinations of therapies have placed patients and caregivers in a better position than many could have hoped for in the not-so-distant past.

Be Realistic

In her book *When Someone You Love Has a Mental Illness*, Rebecca Woolis suggests guidelines for setting goals for someone with a mental illness. She recommends first evaluating the person's ability to function in three areas:

- Living independently. How many of the daily chores required for living alone can the patient perform adequately?
- Interacting with others. How well does the person make and keep friends? How comfortable is he around others?
- Learning and working skills. What level of education and employment has the person attained?

Woolis suggests that a higher-functioning patient will score well in at least two of the areas, have symptoms under control enough to concentrate on improving skills, and will demonstrate a desire to progress.

She advises caregivers to get the patient to agree to concentrate on one or two skills contained in one of the life-skill areas—independent living, social interactions, and work/education. Break the short-term goal into small steps that the person has a good chance of completing. Knowing he can accomplish something and take steps toward living a fuller life will help motivate the patient to be proactive.

Small Steps

If someone is working hard to achieve small, short-term goals such as getting up on time to keep appointments or looking after his hygiene, don't worry about large, long-term goals. Be content to progress a step at a time. If he asks about his future, don't lie to him. Tell him you are not sure about the future but that you know you will be there to encourage him in his progress. Concentrate on improving the present.

Don't make the steps too difficult. Start with easily attained goals and increase the challenge if the person can handle it. Back off if he gets discouraged or frustrated. Redefine the goals after a time off.

Alert

A person can experience changes during the course of the illness. Symptoms may disappear and be replaced by others. Progress may accelerate and slow. As a caregiver, try to be sensitive to these changes. Adjust your behavior and set goals based on the current mental state and abilities of the person you are working with.

As an example, consider a person who lives by himself and has worked at a part-time job for eighteen months. He takes medications as prescribed and attends therapy but has no social life. If he agrees to work on increasing his social interactions, you might suggest he attend more get-togethers with other mental health care consumers and volunteers.

One short-term goal for the patient might be to talk to two people over the course of the next weekend. Another might be for him to find out if any of his coworkers has a hobby and then ask about them. You can coach him in ways to talk to someone without seeming nosey or pushy. Discuss the results, his feelings about them, and how he might adjust his attempts to connect to people the next time he tries.

Encouraging Someone to Seek Medical Treatment

As soon as you can, enlist the aid of the person who needs help. This may be possible if the person does not have psychotic symptoms. Let her know there is hope for a majority of patients diagnosed with schizophrenia. With treatment, she can work to be one of them.

Addressing the Issue of Stigma

If someone is worried about the stigma that is still attached to the labels "mentally ill" and "schizophrenia," it may cause her to resist treatment. Reassure her that mental illness can be treated effectively and that getting better is the best way to counter the opinions of misinformed or uninformed strangers or acquaintances.

Don't accept a stranger's conscious or unconscious decision to deny you respect. You have a choice of ignoring or correcting people who are uninformed enough to believe and perpetuate stereotypes. It is always a good idea to educate the general public, when possible, about the facts concerning psychiatric illnesses.

The patient is the one who matters, not the people who know nothing about what a person with schizophrenia experiences.

Reassure the patient that there is no weakness in overcoming a disease and that she will have help getting better.

Explaining Your Concern

The patient should know that your advice is based on the best information you can obtain. Let her know why you are encouraging her to seek help at this time. Be specific about the symptoms that make you think she could benefit from talking to a professional. Relate your concerns to specific aspects of her life. You might say, for example, "It looks like you don't do many of the things that used to make you happy. I'm concerned you may not be doing what you like. Perhaps we can find a way to make you feel better so you can do more of the things you liked doing."

It may help to talk to the people who work in the clinic, hospital, or doctor's office before you take the patient to her appointment. Ask them what will happen when the patient arrives. Then share that information in detail with the patient. If she knows what to expect, she will be more likely to participate. Speak steadily, supportively, and calmly. Let her know that you care and will support her all the way from her first treatment until she is well again.

Communication

How you talk to someone with schizophrenia depends, not surprisingly, on who you are talking to. Tailor your speech so that the patient will understand and will not be threatened by what you are saying. People whose intellectual functions are high may require little, if any, adjustment on your part. Communicating with someone who has intellectual impairments in some areas of his life will probably require some adjustments, with more understanding and patience from you. Don't speak down or use baby talk. Speak gently and slowly with a normal tone of voice. Keep sentences simple if the person seems confused or has trouble understanding. Problems with memory and concentration may be countered somewhat by repetition and using simple, short sentences.

You will have to learn what works best for the person you interact with. A neutral tone that conveys your emotional steadiness and reassurance is always recommended.

 Question

How can you communicate with someone who is in his own world?
You can try to get him to focus on you, but you may be competing with voices he is hearing or with excess and distorted sensory input that is overloading his brain. It is possible you will not be able to communicate with him when this happens. You may have to wait until he is more receptive.

Is Now the Right Time to Talk?

Your attitude will have a big effect on the tone of the interaction. Don't take insults and verbal explosions personally. This will help neutralize them. It won't be helpful if you force someone to engage in conversation if he is agitated or excited. If you know you can calm someone, try it, but otherwise let the person settle down emotionally before initiating a conversation.

It is not a good idea to challenge someone's delusion. You cannot change it. Your logic, reason, and argument may even be taken as more evidence that the delusion is real. It requires professional treatment to free someone with schizophrenia from delusions.

Don't expect a person with schizophrenia to think much about your problems. He has more to deal with than any person should have to handle. Any lack of concern for others is almost certainly a result of the disease. This is something else you should not take personally. It is normal to be saddened by this and other changes in personality, but it is often the unfortunate reality of the situation. Eventually you must accept it if you are to help the person you care for. You will need to rely on your own support group or network for friendship and companionship.

Offering Hope

It is unlikely that someone can face schizophrenia and not experience significant periods of depression, insecurity, and a diminished sense of worth. You won't cure anyone or bring him out of the gloom with cheery chatter, but you can reassure him that you are there for him. Remind him of any progress he has made in the past and tell him he will make progress again in the future. If the person is close to you, let him know that you love him and he will not be alone.

Essential

Without sounding condescending, congratulate a person trying to recover from schizophrenia whenever he achieves a goal or accomplishes something positive. Don't speak to an adult as if he were a child, but do speak simply and directly if he has cognitive difficulties. Avoid big words or convoluted sentences.

Social withdrawal is a common symptom of schizophrenia. It is a good idea to talk to someone to get him more engaged. A low-key approach may be preferable to a gung-ho call to action. Try framing the invitation as a way to regain some of the activities the consumer enjoyed before the illness, rather than as a way to combat isolation.

Sticking to a Helpful Course of Treatment

Without treatment, few people with schizophrenia would recover by themselves. Before the development of drugs that reduce severe symptoms of the disorder, schizophrenia was considered a chronic, degenerative disease. It is, in most cases, still a chronic disease, but with treatment the path is no longer relentlessly downward. Caregivers and consumers tell one story again and again: Giving up treatment is usually followed by a flare-up of symptoms and a resumption of the downward slide.

Don't Tolerate Substance Abuse

Substance abuse is, unfortunately, a common problem for people struggling with schizophrenia. If drug use by someone you care about is making her symptoms worse or her treatment less effective, seek help immediately. Ask the psychiatrist, social worker, or other mental health care provider how you can get her into a substance abuse program if necessary. Substance abuse is a serious challenge even for people who do not have schizophrenia. It often requires the intervention of family, friends, or law enforcement officials to initiate change. Its implications can be even worse for people with schizophrenia. It is crucial that someone with schizophrenia be directed to a program that will help free her of substance abuse problems.

Although it does not cause schizophrenia, the abuse of alcohol and other drugs can make the symptoms worse and lead someone to stop taking medications. People who are prone to psychosis do not respond well to the additional burden imposed by these recreational drugs.

Structure and Rules

If you can introduce structure into the daily routine of your loved one, it will help both of you. Along with structure and routine comes less stress and greater reassurance for the person struggling with schizophrenia. You and your loved one need to be sure that expectations are clearly stated and understood. You must also set clear limits and restrictions so you can share a living space in harmony.

House rules are one way to introduce structure and cut down on arguments and nagging. Consider getting your loved one to agree to a set of rules. Try to write them out together. Keep it short and include the most important concerns. The items on the list will be determined by the circumstances in your home. Here is an example:

Example of House Rules
- No drugs or alcohol
- Take medicine daily
- Shower daily and brush teeth

- No hitting or slamming anything except a punching bag
- Vacuum once a week
- Clean up after using the kitchen

Someone who is working to overcome the challenges of schizophrenia can benefit from activities that distract her from her symptoms. Inactivity and withdrawal make it easy for a person to be caught up in delusions and auditory hallucinations. Recreation, social interaction, hobbies, sports, and anything else that can help the patient alleviate the distractions of the disease can be beneficial.

When someone is ready to take part in activities, encourage her to participate in programs offered by mental health outpatient clinics or groups. If none are available, consider organizing projects with other people who are caring for their relatives.

Mastering the Health Care System

As a caregiver or assistant to a person with schizophrenia, you have the opportunity to not only help your loved one obtain the best medical care available but also to help him protect his rights. The National Mental Health Information Center, the Schizophrenia Society of Canada, and other organizations have compiled comprehensive lists of the rights and considerations every patient is entitled to. Some of these are laws and others are recommended rights that all consumers of mental health care should expect.

Right to Information

A patient undergoing psychiatric care and his caregiver should receive a complete explanation of his illness in understandable, nontechnical language. He should be told what symptoms his medications or treatments are meant to treat. This should include information about the risks and benefits of the recommended treatments as well as information about alternative treatments. He should have access to an interpreter if needed.

Patients should also expect the right to:

- Have a trusted family member or friend present during examinations, treatment, consultations, and other procedures
- Know why a psychiatrist is making a referral and whether the referral is for a second opinion or to get a more experienced opinion
- Have the opportunity to choose a treatment with which the patient and family agree
- Give informed consent to treatment, including prescribed medications (informed consent means the patient and/or his guardian has received full information about the pros and cons of treatment in understandable language)
- Learn the nature of communications between the psychiatrist and the physician who referred the patient
- Discuss topics related to the condition, voice concerns, express opinions, and make comments in addition to what the psychiatrist asks about or expresses interest in
- Have access to health records
- Obtain additional information about the disease from mental health care providers, including appropriate written information such as brochures and contact details of support groups
- Voluntarily stop treatment or medication at any time, provided the treatment is not mandated through a court order

Sources: the Schizophrenia Society of Canada and the National Mental Health Information Center

Essential

Everyone has the right to know how a doctor reached a diagnosis. Ask if a diagnosis is confirmed or is provisional, meaning the doctor is awaiting test results or more information. Find out what the implications of a provisional diagnosis are. Be sure to discuss the diagnosis with your psychiatrist and tell her if you disagree and why. Get a second opinion if you think it will help.

You should expect all of these rights and privileges during treatment. Realistically, that won't always be the case. A major problem faced by all caregivers of modest financial means is the shift in the last thirty years toward quick care.

Quick Care

The introduction of medications that can control psychotic symptoms has caused many insurance companies, HMOs, and government health plans to cut back on the amount of money they approve for treating mental illnesses. Long-term hospitalization is often seen as too expensive even if it would benefit a patient. It is more cost effective for health insurers to approve prescriptions for drugs and then follow up with short office visits. Some medical care providers and insurers follow this pattern. Others provide comprehensive services.

The best hospitals and treatment centers provide thorough, caring treatment, including therapy and medications. Standards of care differ by location. Caregivers report that it takes time, effort, and patience to find the best care, given their often limited resources and geographic restrictions.

Getting Good Psychiatric Care

In addition to feeling comfortable with a psychiatrist, a patient and his family have the right to a high level of care. Expect to be included in the plan for treating the person who needs help. All of your questions should be answered in language you can understand.

Choose a doctor who is experienced in treating people with schizophrenia and who appreciates the need to combine pharmacotherapy with different types of psychotherapies. In addition to knowing about the latest antipsychotic treatments and medications, the doctor should be thorough and organized. He should obtain a complete medical history by interviewing the patient and family. You should expect that both physical and mental concerns will be checked and treated. Follow-up visits and treatment sessions should be organized and arranged to fit your schedule and the patient's schedule as much as possible.

Alert

Your mental health care team may include some combination of psychiatrists, clinical psychologists, psychiatric nurses, psychiatric social workers, and a case manager. Their duties and roles in providing treatment and services should be clearly defined. If it appears there is any problem coordinating treatment, be sure to mention your concerns to whoever is leading the treatment.

Be sure that prescriptions are reviewed on a regular basis and adjusted as needed based on side effects and patient preference.

It is essential that your doctor care about the patient beyond the act of writing prescriptions for medications. If the psychiatrist sees the patient as an individual in need of help, he is more likely to refer you to outside sources of assistance, such as outpatient clinics and social aid groups that can help with housing, social support, and even financial aid. A consumer is more likely to respond to treatment offered by a thoughtful, empathetic health care provider.

CHAPTER 16

Success Stories and Case Histories

NOT ALL PATIENTS do as well as those whose stories are summarized in this section. In many cases, schizophrenia is controlled to the extent that people can care for themselves or get along well with the help of others. A lucky few recover completely or nearly so. The accounts in this chapter accurately reflect the experiences of real people who have struggled with schizophrenia or closely related illnesses. To maintain medical confidentiality, names and details concerning the patients have been changed unless they were the subjects of published books or memoirs.

The Difficulty of Predicting the Future

The most optimistic picture of schizophrenia is provided by the Society for Neuroscience, which claims that three out of four people affected by schizophrenia will be able to live as independent adults. It might be more accurate to estimate that three out of four will live independent or semi-independent lives. Even if this estimate is accurate, it tragically leaves 25 percent—approximately 500,000 people in the United States—who will not recover enough to reach this stage of independence.

No Guarantees

Scientists have followed many individuals with schizophrenia from the time the disease first appeared to old age. The outcomes for these individuals varied considerably. Unfortunately, our present understanding of the disease does not yet allow physicians to accurately predict the long-term outcome for every individual diagnosed with schizophrenia. Some researchers, however, have noted that patients who were mentally healthier before being diagnosed did better than those who had trouble functioning in social, school, and work settings before diagnosis.

Treatment Is Essential

In the early 1990s, it was estimated that around 40 percent of people with serious mental diseases, including schizophrenia, were not receiving treatment. It is among this group that you expect to find the most suffering, homelessness, incarceration, and increased instances of violence.

A few people with schizophrenia recover completely after a relatively few psychotic episodes. A small number are able to function most of the time without medication but still suffer intermittently from the disease. The majority will not do as well without treatment. They run a high risk of withdrawing into a private, tormented world of delusions and hallucinations unless they receive medical help.

 Question

How many patients with schizophrenia remain untreated?
Of the approximately 2 million U.S. citizens who live with schizophrenia, an estimated two-thirds are not receiving treatment at any one time, according to the National Alliance on Mental Illness. A series of research studies conducted between 1980 and 2001 indicates the figure may be somewhat lower, between 35 percent and 54 percent.

What Does Successful Schizophrenia Treatment Mean?

Successful schizophrenia treatment means different things to different people. Close to one in four people recover enough from schizophrenia to live productive independent or semi-independent lives. To a psychiatrist who did not know their previous history, some of these people might not even appear to be suffering from schizophrenia. Such improvement in mental health is often achieved with the support of antipsychotic medications that can control symptoms well in many people. When someone who previously dealt with the disease is free of symptoms for six months, he is said to be in remission. The longer a remission lasts, the better someone's future prospects are.

Regular visits to a psychiatrist may help ensure that everything continues to go well. If the patient is taking medications, their effects must be monitored so problems can be discussed and treatment adjusted. Discontinuing medication and other treatment greatly increases the chance of relapse.

Remissions and Other Outcomes

Remissions occur in a significant percentage of people diagnosed with schizophrenia. An older guideline predicting the fate of people with schizophrenia divided the population into thirds. One-third would have an excellent chance of complete recovery. One-third would experience healthy periods interspersed with recurring episodes of the disease. The least fortunate third would suffer from a chronic form of the disease and undergo a steady deterioration.

A more recent compilation of studies that followed the fate of schizophrenia patients divides the population into quarters. A study cited in E. Fuller Torrey's book *Surviving Schizophrenia*, compares outcomes one decade and three decades after onset of the disease.

After ten years, 25 percent of patients have recovered completely. Another 25 percent have shown significant improvement and can live independently for the most part. Another 25 percent show definite improvement but still need an active, well-developed social and therapeutic support network to function adequately. Fifteen percent require hospitalization, and 10 percent are deceased, often the victims of suicide.

Essential

Even during remission, the underlying predisposition to schizophrenia remains. It is important that people in remission take care of themselves to avoid excessive stress and continue treatment. Furthermore, the person in remission and people close to her will benefit by learning to recognize behavioral clues that might signal a return of disease symptoms.

After thirty years, the percentage of patients who recover completely—25 percent—does not change from the earlier study to the later one. The percentage that enters the next optimistic category—significant improvement with nearly independent living status—increases to 35 percent from 25 percent. This increase appears to result from a decrease in patients who show definite improvement but need an active, well-developed social and therapeutic support network; that category drops from 25 percent to 15 percent. Further progress is evident in the drop in unimproved, hospitalized patients, from 15 percent to 10 percent. The percentage of deaths rises to 15 percent from 10 percent. Again, most of these are due to suicide, according to Torrey.

Tips for Staying in Remission

Structure your life to minimize stress. Develop an ordered lifestyle; if possible, it should be built around what you must do and what you enjoy doing. Work to eliminate stresses that you don't need and can avoid; for instance, irritating acquaintances, self-imposed deadlines, expectations around the holidays, and attempts to impress others.

Try to bring structure and balance in your life. Try to find a comfortable sleep-wake rhythm that suits you and stick to this routine as much as possible.

Strive for a stress-free environment. At the same time, look for methods to cope with stress. Try to recognize the triggers for psychosis and be alert for new psychotic episodes. If you think something is going wrong, don't hesitate to seek help.

"Mary"

Mary's case is recounted by Alice Medalia, PhD, and Nadine Revheim, PhD, in *Dealing with Cognitive Dysfunction Associated with Psychiatric Disabilities: A Handbook for Families and Friends of Individuals with Psychiatric Disorders.*

Background and Goal

Mary was first hospitalized at age twenty and diagnosed with schizophrenia. Since then she has been in the hospital four more times and has lived in three community residences.

Her therapy includes attending a three-day-per-week continuing day treatment program and taking 4 mg of the atypical antipsychotic risperidone per day. She chose the treatment program over permanent residence in an adult home. She wants to volunteer at her local library, something compatible with her education, which includes two years of college.

Essential

Mary and her parents used the useful technique of identifying small problems and breaking their solutions into small steps. These exercises were designed to prepare Mary for improving her abilities so she can accomplish a specific, realistic goal. Remember: don't try to deal with schizophrenia as a whole. Break it down and attack the parts.

Mary shows signs of mild negative and cognitive problems that worry Mary and her parents. With the aid of a National Alliance on Mental Illness family group, her parents are beginning to learn how they can help their daughter overcome these challenges so she can attain her goal of working in the library.

Identifying Problems

Mary has four easily identified problems:

1. Difficulty getting out of bed in the morning
2. Neglect in caring for herself
3. Forgetfulness that causes her to miss doctor appointments, forget to take her medication, and forget other tasks
4. Speaking very little

Mary knows that her illness has dulled her thinking ability. Cognitive tests of her memory confirm her impression.

Taking Advantage of Therapy

Mary is working to improve her ability to concentrate and remember things, illustrated by her interest in taking part in a program offered at her part-time treatment program. The "Laughing and Learning" session promotes socializing with others. It uses exercises in the form of games that are designed to let her practice her ability to process information. This type of cognitive therapy has been shown to help people whose intellectual abilities have been affected by schizophrenia. This program has the added benefit of encouraging social interaction, another subject of therapy from which many patients benefit.

Improving Living Skills

Working with counselors, Mary is trying other approaches to improve enough to attain her goal of volunteering at her local library. To do this, she will have to develop more skills required for independent living. She'll have to get up on time, make herself presentable, and learn and remember tasks at the library.

Her therapist helped Mary start a day planner. It includes lists of tasks Mary can check off throughout the day as they are completed. Her therapist suggests that one of her tasks should be to review the next day's schedule. Other recommended tasks in the planner include setting her alarm clock for getting up in the morning and looking at her day planner. Her to-do list includes writing sticky notes to remind herself to tend to her personal hygiene: showering, brushing her teeth, and combing her hair. Sticky notes could also help her remember to take her risperidone once a day.

 Fact

> To compensate for her cognitive problems, Mary has been taught to use reminder aids to help her in her daily activities. These are not unlike the organization techniques used by busy people everywhere. The tasks and goals included in Mary's planners are appropriate for her current abilities. Keeping the items on her to-do list at the right level of difficulty will help keep her from getting frustrated.

If these habits are practiced, reinforced, and eventually adopted, Mary will be closer to living more independently. This will relieve the pressure on her parents, who will be freed from the task of frequently reminding Mary what she has to do.

Memory Aids

Mary's therapists encourage her to repeat any instructions she is given. This helps her comprehend verbal instructions and remember details, two cognitive abilities she knows she will need to work in a library. It also helps broaden her social skills.

Mary may be improving her problem solving and other cognitive skills by practicing on the family's computer. This activity exercises her memory because she needs to follow sequential steps when typing in computer commands and navigating the Internet, and it may help Mary develop the skills she needs to gain a more independent life with a part-time volunteer position.

"John"

John was interviewed in a psychiatric hospital after his illness came to the attention of his employers and acquaintances. He was very nervous before he was referred for treatment. He said the typical antipsychotic medication he received back then, Thorazine, slowed him down a bit but he was pleased he was no longer anxious or uptight.

During the interview he was well spoken and calm. Indeed, without hearing him describe his symptoms, it might not be easy, after just a short conversation, to recognize that he was ill unless he mentioned his delusions or hallucinations.

Background

When John was still in high school, he was referred to a school psychologist and hospitalized for a week after he heard the voice of his recently deceased grandmother urging him to join her. He said he did not feel ill in any way and was puzzled that doctors thought he was ill.

John graduated from high school and dropped out of college after eighteen months to get married. In his mid-twenties and working as a shipping clerk, he was referred to psychiatric care after his employers noticed he was not making any sense.

About six weeks before the interview, he began hearing voices that told him he had to save other people and himself. Initially, this scared him. Although he did not know whose voices he heard, he suspected they belonged to a messenger sent by God to tell him what was happening in the world.

The voices warned him that a big war was about to begin and spread around the world. The voices told him he had to warn people. He did what the voices urged him to do.

Twice he walked out of work to go to church at the command of the voices, which told him he would receive more instructions there. He sat all afternoon in the church.

John said television and radio newscasts were like puzzles to him. They provided the pieces of the puzzle and he had to solve them. The broadcasts told him what was going to happen and what part he would play. He was absolutely certain he had a role in the events he foresaw. John said the clues—what psychiatrists call delusions of reference—are in all news programs. John could not understand why other people couldn't see what he saw in the broadcasts. He believed anyone is capable intellectually of figuring out the puzzle, but only he had been told how to do it.

During the interview, he knew where he was and what month it was but was uncertain of the year and day. Asked to keep subtracting seven starting with the number 100, he was not able to keep an accurate count after the first result, ninety-three. He remembered what he had for breakfast the morning of the interview.

Predicted Outcome

John had a common form of schizophrenia, the paranoid subtype. His chances of recovery were good and the doctor told him that in time, he would be released from the hospital, something John was looking forward to. John's post-hospitalization goals included returning to school and teaching.

Lori Schiller

Lori Schiller began hearing voices around the same time as "John." Lori's journey through schizoaffective disorder, however, was much more traumatic than John's experience of paranoid schizophrenia. Lori tells her story in her memoir, *The Quiet Room*.

Lori's story is interesting and inspiring for many reasons. She skillfully conveys the personal experience of psychosis and the effects it has on patients and their families. It is also noteworthy because it depicts the tremendous turnaround effect the introduction of the atypical antipsychotic medication clozapine had on people like Lori.

Onset

While working as a counselor at summer camp in 1976, seventeen-year-old Lori began to notice some pleasant changes. Colors were richer and deeper. She embraced the changes.

Lori did not know it at the time, but these enhanced sensations were probably early signs that her brain was changing from a healthy state to one of illness. At this point in Lori's condition, the effects were vitalizing and enlivening. In later stages of schizophrenia, many patients experience overwhelming sensations that can be paralyzing. An abnormally enhanced sense of vision and hearing, for example, can make it very difficult to concentrate.

Auditory Hallucinations

That summer, the voices began. They told her she must die. She ran from them, literally, but they stayed with her. They tormented her for extended periods but subsided enough to allow her to graduate from high school with a 3.9 grade point average. In college they retreated to the background for a while, but they eventually became more insistent.

 Fact

Lori hid the fact that she heard voices for years. She struggled to maintain an appearance of normalcy with her roommates. Like the majority of people with a schizophrenia-like illness, she began smoking. She never really considered herself ill until years later.

During her later college years, Lori began to show signs of depression and mania, symptoms that, combined with her auditory hallucinations, would later lead to a diagnosis of schizoaffective disorder.

The voices became constant, day and night. They began telling her to hurt people, and she feared she might act on their orders. Finally, she sought help but could not bring herself to tell the therapist about the voices.

She feared she or any person she told about the voices would be harmed if she revealed their presence. After graduation, she attempted suicide and was hospitalized. After this, she stopped caring about her appearance.

She was treated with tranquilizers and other medications, and felt some initial improvement. However, the medications failed to help over time and she attempted suicide again. She developed the delusion that she could fly. In addition to her delusions and hallucinations, her symptoms included periods of excitement and high energy alternating with times of profound despair.

Hospitalization and Home

Due to the persistence of her severe symptoms, Lori was transferred to a long-term psychiatric hospital, where she stayed for six months. The medications the doctors gave her did not help her symptoms. She went home a few days before her twenty-fourth birthday.

The voices continued. Still, she was convinced she was not ill. She took a job as a waitress and began using cocaine. With her parent's encouragement, she entered a drug treatment program and overcame her dependency.

Lori took Thorazine and was able to take a part-time job as a mental health care assistant. Then, on a vacation to Europe, she stopped her medication. Three days later, the voices were back and she was longing for street drugs to distract her from them.

Outcome

Although Lori never responded exceptionally well to the typical antipsychotic medications available to her, they did help control her psychotic symptoms enough that she finally resolved to get better. She acknowledged she was ill and began participating actively in programs offered at her treatment facility.

Unchecked, Lori's psychotic symptoms could have caused her to fall apart, both psychologically and physically. She could have lost the ability to interact rationally with her environment. This steady decline in mental function can lead to a physical decline because the victim of the disease is unable to care for herself. She may stop bathing, eat little and poorly, and be unable to seek more than rudimentary shelter and safety. Fortunately, Lori eventually resumed taking medication and experienced significant recovery.

Besides her determination to get better, she was helped by meeting a doctor and a therapist she liked and came to trust. Then she heard about clozapine and insisted on trying it. Finally, after eighteen years, the voices subsided.

 ## Question

Do antipsychotic medications make voices go away?
They often do, but not always. They often significantly reduce their influence and effects on patients. No longer intimidated by them, a patient comes to realize through therapy that the source of the voices is herself. She can teach herself to ignore them or realize they are providing clues about her hidden feelings.

Lori still hears the voices but has learned, with the help of medication and therapy, to master them. She knows they are symptoms of her illness.

She experienced many of the problems that others with schizophrenia or closely related illnesses face. Aside from the core problems of psychosis and mood disorders, she smoked, abused drugs, denied she was ill, went off her medications, and resisted treatment. She was unfortunate in that traditional typical antipsychotic medications did not relieve her symptoms enough to allow her to get her life in order sooner. But she was fortunate enough to eventually find a drug that did.

Ken Steele

Ken suffered from severe schizophrenia for more than three decades. At one time he lived in an alley in San Francisco. Against incredible odds, he survived. He eventually recovered with the help of an atypical antipsychotic medication, Risperdal, and became an admired and leading advocate for the mentally ill. He told his story in *The Day the Voices Stopped: A Memoir of Madness and Hope.*

Early Start

Ken started hearing voices suddenly when he was fourteen years old. They told him he was useless, unworthy, and ugly. They urged him to kill himself. He tried to flee from them, but they never stopped tormenting him. He also experienced fleeting visual hallucinations. He attempted suicide and went from being a top student to a poor one before dropping out of school. Living at home, he spent most of his time in his room, alone. Told by his father that he would have to earn his own living when he reached age eighteen, Ken left home for New York City in 1966.

After leaving home he became a prostitute and was hospitalized after another suicide attempt. Doctors recognized that Ken suffered from schizophrenia at this time and treated him initially with too heavy doses of Thorazine. His parents abandoned him. He spent time in and out of hospitals, suffering as a victim of crime on the street and as an inmate in poorly run state hospitals.

Eventually Ken began to benefit from programs such as Medicaid and the treatment they helped pay for. In the early 1990s, he found a therapist he had confidence in.

Ken's therapist persuaded him to see a doctor, who recommended Risperdal. In August 1994, Ken agreed to try it because he liked the doctor. On his own, he took less than the recommended dose at first, but in November 1994 he began to take the prescribed dose of the new medicine. On May 3, 1995, after thirty-two years of incessant torment, the voices stopped.

Advocacy

Ken became a leading figure among advocates for the mentally ill. He published *New York City Voices: A Consumer Journal for Mental Health Advocacy*, and edited the newsletter of the New York City/Metropolitan area chapter of the National Alliance for the Mentally Ill. Before his death from heart failure at the age of fifty-two in 2000, he was recognized by patients and mental health professionals across the country for his efforts in promoting the cause of consumer rights and better understanding of the disease that he struggled with and eventually conquered.

Ken's case is exceptional. Not everyone has his motivation, intelligence, and empathy. Not everyone finds a medication that can do what Risperidal did for Ken. But many do. Not everyone has to be a leader. It is enough to never give up trying to overcome the burdens of the disease and gain some independence and self-esteem.

CHAPTER 17

How to Handle a Schizophrenia Emergency

THE FIRST PRIORITY during an emergency is to determine whether anyone—patient, relative, or bystander—is in danger. If you feel you are in danger, leave and summon help. If you feel the patient is in danger of harming herself, try to reassure and calm her if you can defuse the situation without putting yourself or anyone else in danger. Once the immediate threat has passed, arrange professional help.

Preparing for an Emergency

Mental health care professionals must learn to recognize warning signs that vary considerably from patient to patient (see Chapter 6). You, like others who care for people with mental disorders, will also have to keep track of warning signs and symptoms that might change as time passes. Such changes might not be easy to spot, depending on the nature of the symptom or warning signs. You have one advantage: you can become an expert concerning the one person you care for.

Learn to Spot Coming Crises if You Can

Changes may come on slowly and may not be easy to recognize at first. They are worth noting, however, because they might predict trouble. This is true if the changes are part of a pattern or part of a disruption of a pattern. It is important to learn to recognize and trust your intuition when observing someone you know well. If something does not seem right with her, be prepared to assist her. Early intervention can ward off the more serious consequences of a mental health crisis.

From Their Perspective

An emerging psychosis is an intensely personal and frightening event. This is a large part of the problem: often people don't talk about it or ask for help as it is progressing. They do not want to be seen as mentally ill or different from other people. Then, when the torment of the hallucinations and/or delusions reaches an unbearable level, the patient reacts in a frightened and frightening way. Any approach you make should be done in a low-key manner, away from others if possible.

Who to Call for Help

If you assist someone with schizophrenia, find the hotline crisis number for your area by visiting *http://mentalhealth.samhsa.gov/hotlines/state.asp*, which keeps an updated list of twenty-four-hour crisis lines organized by state. Find the name of your state and write down the number or numbers. Keep a copy in your wallet and around your home so it will be at hand if and when you need it. Program it into your cell phone and landline.

In addition, make sure you do the same for the National Suicide Prevention Lifeline, which offers immediate advice to anyone seeking mental health assistance twenty-four hours a day. The toll-free phone number is (800) 273-TALK (273-8255). Your call does not have to concern suicide. You can get advice concerning any mental health-related crisis including psychotic episodes. Your confidential call will be routed to one of more than 130 crisis centers around the United States. The National Suicide Prevention Lifeline also offers referrals to local mental health services and access to a crisis worker with whom you can talk about someone you want to help.

If you contact a psychiatrist, describe the symptoms completely. Don't assume that she can know anything other than what you report. Be her eyes and ears. Then you should express your concerns to her. Answer any questions the psychiatrist has and follow her advice.

What to Tell Emergency Responders

If you have to call the police or rescue squad, be sure you fill them in on the situation before they confront the patient. They need to know they are dealing with a mentally ill individual who is having a psychotic episode. They need to know if the person is threatening to harm himself or others. They need to know if the person is armed with any weapon, improvised or not, that he could use to injure himself or others. Tell them they are being asked for help in getting the patient to medical care, not to arrest him. Tell the police the name of the patient's doctor and where she practices.

Dealing with Aggressive Behavior

One study estimates that an adult with schizophrenia is fourteen times more likely to be attacked by a violent criminal than he is to be arrested as a violent offender. A much greater threat is the risk that people with schizophrenia pose to themselves; more people with schizophrenia harm themselves than harm others.

The threat of violence increases during psychotic episodes and in people with paranoid symptoms, which is another reason to encourage a person with the brain disease to adhere to his treatment plan. Alcohol and illegal drug use can increase the incidence of violence.

Rare Cases of Violence

For a small minority of patients, the troubling voices they experience and the perceived threats posed by some delusions have the potential to make patients a threat to others. These relatively rare cases often attract a great deal of publicity. As a result, they seem to the general public to occur much more frequently than they really do. Such occurrences might be compared to the rare event of a person who has a heart attack while driving and accidentally drives across a schoolyard, killing several people. When assaults do occur, the majority of them are directed against people close to the person with the disease, and they take place in the home.

 ## Question

How do you interact with a jittery patient?
If something seems to make the person uneasy, avoid doing it and try to insulate the patient from others who might upset her. Don't look at the person's eyes if it makes her nervous. Respect her personal space so she feels secure. Don't touch the person unless she indicates it is okay. Avoid subjects that are obviously upsetting.

Leave the patient and call for help from others better prepared to handle actual or imminent physical threats if the patient becomes aggressive. Paramedics are taught not to put themselves at risk to help others; if the emergency responder is injured, he cannot assist others. The same rule should apply to you if someone becomes hostile and poses a physical threat.

A person with schizophrenia may respond to a hallucination or delusion as if it were real. Try to anticipate this possibility. Understand that she may be responding to a very scary threat. You can help by not increasing her agitation. Instead, calm her, if possible, by being a calming influence. It is a good idea to:

- Have a ready means of exiting the situation. Always have an easy escape route planned to quickly get away from the situation if needed.
- Have the phone number of emergency services handy.
- Have the phone number of a reliable mental health care professional handy.

- Keep trying to get help if someone you call refuses to get involved.

- Brief the police, rescue squad, emergency medical technicians, mental health workers, or other emergency responders about the patient's medical history, diagnosis and needs.

- Explain to the patient who the emergency responders are, why they have come, and what they are going to do.

Adapted from the *Schizophrenia Bulletin.*

If a patient having a psychotic episode tells you something bad is going to happen or makes threats, assume the warnings are serious, particularly if the patient has delusions of persecution. Get assistance, but try to do it in a way that does not aggravate the patient's feeling of persecution. Calling the police or other assistance in the presence of a suspicious, aggressive patient may make her react more aggressively.

Involve the police as a last resort, but do not hesitate to do so if you are not able to defuse the crisis. Remember: keep your safety and the safety of others, including the patient, in mind at all times.

Don't Argue

It is more important to listen when dealing with someone in crisis than it is to impose your idea of "sense" or your opinions on him. It might be difficult not to correct a person who is convinced of an obviously false belief, or who is seeing or hearing something that is not real, but you will not help by challenging him. For him, it does not *seem* real, it *is* real.

At the same time, try not to be patronizing. It will not help, for example, if you agree with or encourage a paranoid person's conviction that others are threatening his in some way. The task requires empathy and a calming presence. Just like you, the patient may need to talk about her feelings and experiences. Listening to a patient discuss bizarre and troubling delusions can be difficult. It will not help if you pretend nothing is wrong. Explain that you understand why he feels the way he does and that it must be very stressful for him. Offer to help the patient find a way to relieve the source of the stress.

Alert

If someone's psychotic symptoms become severe, remain as calm as you can. Follow the steps in the patient's customized emergency plan if there is one. Determine whether the person is a threat to herself or others. Don't leave the patient alone if she might hurt herself. Contact someone the patient trusts and ask him to talk to the patient. And, of course, leave and call for help if you feel threatened in any way.

What You Should Do

Work with a doctor or other mental health professional to develop an emergency contingency plan or an advance directive/relapse prevention plan. These written guidelines should tell you what to do, whom to contact, and how to contact them in the event a patient's psychotic symptoms become overwhelming and may result in a crisis.

Speaking to Someone Having a Crisis

Speak slowly, calmly, and clearly to the person without talking down to her. If you are talking to an adult, address her as an adult. Avoid using a condescending or threatening tone. Try to project a moderating image. Keep your sentences simple and brief. Remember that a person in crisis is going through a highly disturbing experience that may involve threatening thoughts, voices, and/or visions. You do not want to add to his stress.

Follow the patient's lead if she will talk to you. Let her talk about herself and her feelings, beliefs, experiences, concerns, and fears. Be sympathetic and encouraging by letting her know, at the proper time, that there are ways to ease some of her concerns.

Sometimes, if someone is coherent, she can provide hints that may help you as her caregiver. For example, if she has had similar crises in the past, she may be able to tell you who or what helped her deal with them. Was there anyone who was particularly helpful? Was a particular place soothing? Did removing a particular source of stress help? Ask what she thinks will help her, and assist her in finding it.

Let Her Know She Has Options

If the person indicates she wants to seek psychiatric help, support her emotionally as you assist her in finding appropriate and competent care. People's ethnic, religious, and cultural background may influence their behavior when they are ill. Be sensitive to these influences when speaking to someone dealing with the disease.

Give the person every opportunity to know that he still has some control of his situation. Ask if you can sit in a certain place or if you can approach the person in crisis. If she asks for something, or asks you to do something, agree if you can be sure it will not compromise her own safety or that of others.

Dealing with Patients Who Won't Talk

Some patients will not want to talk about what bothers them. They may be confused, embarrassed, or too disturbed by their symptoms. Others may not trust certain individuals enough to open up to them. Don't insist or try to force someone to talk to you. Instead, tell her you will be available if she wants to talk later. Ask her if there is anyone she would feel comfortable talking to, and offer to put her in contact with that person if possible.

If the patient in crisis is not a threat to herself, there is no reason to stop her from moving, walking about, or fidgeting. It is a normal response to the situation she is living through. It will do no good if you grab, restrain, or hold on to her to restrict her movement unless you think she is in imminent danger of harming herself.

What to Avoid

Threatening the patient will only make her troubles, and perhaps yours, worse. It may even prompt him to protect himself from the perceived increased threat that you have added to his crisis. Instead of administering any form of discipline or threats, tell him you want to help him deal with what is happening.

Alert

A person experiencing a psychotic crisis may vigorously resist your attempts to comfort her or help her get professional help. Unless a doctor examines her and recommends treatment, a person cannot be compelled to enter a hospital. Never threaten or try to force a person into a hospital by yourself.

Support and Understanding

The following dialogue is an example of one approach for communicating with someone upset by a delusion that is interfering with her ability to attend treatment. In this case the patient suffers from delusions of reference, the belief that messages just for her are encoded in television news broadcasts.

Patient: Leave me alone! I have to hear this! No one understands I have to listen to the news or people will die. I will die. You will die.

You: I understand that is very upsetting for you. It is very stressful.

Patient: It is. I can't miss the broadcast. I can't go with you.

You: Maybe we could work out a way to go to therapy later and discuss this. Maybe it will help you deal with what you have to do. I'll be there to support you. I'll make sure the therapist listens to you. I know how difficult it is for you.

If the compromise works one time, be sure to mention it to the therapist. Remember, the feelings a person with psychosis has are completely justified in her mind. They are logical responses to the false stimuli her brain is generating. If a person with schizophrenia is hearing voices, they are real voices for that person. The same is true for visual hallucinations. It will not do any good if you deny the existence of a lurking, threatening, or frightful image that, for the psychotic patient, is right there in the room.

Fact

It won't help the person if you tell her what psychiatric disorder you think she is experiencing. A non-expert cannot distinguish between the scores of mental disorders that share common symptoms at different times but require different treatments and approaches. Instead of telling the person she is acting depressed, schizophrenic, psychotic, insane, mentally ill, disturbed, nuts, or crazy, explain that you are concerned about her well-being.

No matter how bizarre or troubling the delusions are, try not to respond emotionally if the patient discusses them. Never laugh at or make fun of a person because her ideas are odd, unrealistic, or fantastic. Try to offer reassurance without being condescending or judgmental.

Screaming, yelling, crying, and even throwing and breaking things do not constitute signs of imminent threat. They could be signs of coming violence, but they can also be acts of frustration. Trust your instincts. Leave if you feel at all uneasy.

What to Do if You Cannot Succeed

If you feel you will not be able to calm someone who is having a psychotic emergency, you have several options for finding help. If the patient agrees to travel, you can take him to a nearby hospital emergency room. You also may get help from a psychiatrist or other mental health care provider who has agreed to handle emergency calls. Another option is to call a qualified rescue or ambulance service whose members are trained to deal with psychiatric emergencies.

Learning from the Experience

The fact that a person has a disorder that incapacitates her mentally for short or long periods of time does not mean she deserves any less respect than another person does. Your actions and statements may still register with a person whose speech makes no sense to you. What you say can affect his willingness and ability to trust you. Do not let others mock, patronize, or insult a person who seems not to be in touch with reality or is acting bizarrely. It will only weaken your ability to help her now and in the future. If you promise a person something just to get a measure of control over him but fail to meet your obligation, you will have destroyed trust that might have been a great benefit later.

It's Not Personal

Do not take personally what a person in the midst of a psychotic crisis says to you. Her words or actions directed toward you in response to psychotic symptoms are not personal affronts. This can be very difficult to deal with, but it's very important you understand it. Such behavior is a symptom of the disease.

 Question

> **What should I do if someone's speech does not make sense?**
> Severe symptoms of psychosis can result in disorganized thinking and speech. Use simple, straightforward sentences to speak to a person who is not coherent. Be patient and repeat yourself as many times as you need to. Don't rush the person to respond to you. Try to be a steady, calming influence.

Don't be fooled by a lack of response from the person you are trying to help. A patient may show little reaction or emotion, but this does not mean she feels nothing. The same applies to her ability to understand. A failure to respond by nodding, making eye contact, or verbally agreeing or disagreeing does not necessarily indicate a lack of understanding.

What to Do After the Crisis

Taking care of yourself is as important as taking care of someone else. After the crisis is over and the person in crisis is receiving treatment, recognize that you have been through an emotional, and perhaps traumatic, experience. Don't ignore what happened by trying not to think about it. Talk to someone—a friend, relative, social worker, or therapist—who will understand.

 Fact

It is normal to be stressed and fearful. Abnormal situations evoke unusual reactions from people. You may not be used to how your body is responding to a crisis, but the response, although distressing, is normal.

The American Counseling Association offers other suggestions for coping after going through a crisis. It advises you to listen to others who have experienced a similar crisis and recommends that you talk to a counselor. This is particularly true if you experience nightmares, insomnia, or social withdrawal, and have trouble focusing. These are normal reactions for people who have survived a crisis. Try to be patient and not take out your stress on others. Try to remember that taking care of yourself is as important as taking care of someone else.

CHAPTER 18

Support for the Caregiver

CAREGIVERS HAVE IT hard. Research by the National Alliance on Mental Illness suggests that approximately 41 percent of caregivers have been caring for a loved one for more than a decade. Eighty percent have a hard time obtaining services for the people they look after and 63 percent cannot find enough time for themselves.

Problems of the Caregiver

Unless they take extraordinary care of themselves, many caregivers face high levels of stress, burnout, and financial problems. They get frustrated by insurance companies, health care centers, and paperwork. They live on edge around someone who is subject to psychotic relapses. They often feel a pervading sense that they are responsible for it all. That is not true, of course. But parents, for instance, feel responsible for their children; if a child has schizophrenia, it is not unusual for feelings of regret and guilt to linger in the background.

Do You Have to Be a Caregiver?

Your answer is probably yes, but it doesn't have to be. At a minimum you must care for a minor if you are her legal guardian. If the person in need of help is older, you have a legal and moral obligation to prevent her from harming herself or others. But these responsibilities can be less taxing than those faced by people caring for minor children.

The mental capacity of the person you care for will influence the degree of your involvement. For example, if her level of functioning is high but she is overly dependent on you, it might be better for both parties if you arrange to cut back on your help and shift the burden of care more onto her, her case manager, her psychiatrist, or her therapist.

If, by contrast, the patient's level of functioning is low, you may need to step in to protect the person from himself and ensure that his basic needs are being met. You may be able to do this with the person's consent or you may need to obtain the legal power from a court of law (see Chapter 11). In this situation, you should seek the assistance of mental health care professionals and therapists. Let them know when you can no longer handle the burden and ask them to suggest possible solutions. Also, be sure to alert them to any suspicions of illegal drug use so the patient can be treated for substance abuse.

Not Everyone Can Handle It

Remember that different people have different capacities for handling stress and responsibilities. You are within your rights to cut back on your contact with a person whose symptoms flare up and become especially difficult to deal with. Again, make sure she is not a threat to herself and others before you step away and allow others to help. You are not obligated by law or moral ethics to allow someone else—even someone you love—to create chaos in your life.

Alert

Your friend or relative may have schizophrenia, but you still are entitled to a life of your own. It is okay to seek help if you feel you can no longer provide the level of care you feel your loved one needs. Do not let schizophrenia destroy both of you.

There won't always be a professional ready or able to step in when you are overwhelmed, but you should use your community's programs to your best advantage. Your best option is to learn everything you can about the system and what resources it can offer you and the patient. See Chapter 11 for legal options that might help you.

Caregiver Stress

Stress increases for the caregiver as the severity of the patient's symptoms increases. Negative symptoms and disorganized behavior common in schizophrenia have been shown to significantly increase the caregiver's burden. Make sure you take care of yourself. Watch for the following signs of stress and work to remedy them.

Signs of Stress in Caregivers
- Anger and frustration
- Denial
- Fatigue and exhaustion
- Sleep disturbance
- Social withdrawal
- Feeling irritable
- Difficulty with concentration and attention
- Anxiety and stress
- Depression
- Health deterioration

Adapted from Sharon L. Johnson's *Therapist's Guide to Clinical Intervention.*

Caregivers feel tension, distress, and a sense of being overwhelmed. It is important, therefore, that you find the best psychoeducational programs, social support, and therapy for yourself to help you deal with the challenge you face.

Try to Escape Somehow

There are multiple ways to counter stress and burnout. Unfortunately, many of them require money or resources. It may be convenient to turn to someone else while you take a break, but it can also be costly. If you, like many others, don't have enough money to buy free time, you can still strive to find some activities you can do alone. Plan something for yourself when the person you care for is attending therapy sessions or doctor's appointments.

If all you can do is go for a walk by yourself, it still is something you can use to escape, both physically and mentally. This can benefit you tremendously. Make dates with acquaintances or friends for thirty or sixty minutes at a time if you can manage it. Seek out positive, supportive people at self-help group meetings or in other gatherings. Don't allow yourself to be consumed by your role as a caregiver.

Coping with Daily Stresses

One way to improve your ability to decrease stress in the life of someone you care for is to decrease stress in your own life. This presents an obvious paradox. Stress reduction can be a significant challenge for anyone. It often requires time, effort, and even counseling or training to achieve. How can you decrease everyday stress while you are caring for someone with a serious mental illness?

When Things Get Too Hot

It is to be expected that the trying experiences of dealing with schizophrenia will result in times of frustration and anger for both the patient and family members. Train yourself to recognize when you are shifting from conversation and supportive interaction to emotional conflict. Learn to walk away when things get too intense. Tell your loved one that you are taking a break and will talk to him later. If the situation requires an immediate decision, stall for time until you can regain a healthy emotional distance from the topic.

Dealing with the effects of a disease like schizophrenia requires you to distance yourself from your emotional brain, the part of the brain that takes things personally. This is difficult to achieve. As a good parent or close relative, you can't cut someone off emotionally, but try to be clear in your own mind when you are dealing with the consequences of the disease as opposed to dealing with your loved one. The first requires distance, the second empathy.

Essential

Try to maintain an emotional distance from the disease while continuing to love the person affected by it. The symptoms of schizophrenia will try your patience, challenge you, frighten you, and even insult you. Realize that this is not the intention of the person struggling with schizophrenia. Keeping a loving distance will make you a better caregiver.

You have a harder job than do nurses or doctors, who have learned to separate potentially crippling empathy from professional concern. A doctor normally would not operate on a friend or family member, simply because she has personal feelings that could interfere with her surgical performance. But you may have to care for someone you are emotionally attached to. Once mastered, this distancing strategy will also make it easier for you to keep from becoming pessimistic in the face of setbacks and failures.

Get a Private Life

As a caregiver, much of your time necessarily will be devoted to your friend or loved one. It is easy to neglect yourself while caring for someone else. As difficult as it is, you will benefit by keeping a to-do list and a daily or weekly schedule that is for you alone.

Don't try to squeeze your life into the schedule you maintain for the person you care for. Keep your own schedule. Use it to make time for yourself. If necessary, ask someone else to sit in for you while you take a day, afternoon, or even a half hour off to do something for yourself.

Another way to reduce the risk of caregiver burnout is to keep or develop a social support network just for you. These can be friends, people who share a common interest in a hobby, coworkers, or other people in a caregiver support group.

Get Away If You Can

Taking a break takes insight, planning, and resources. You need insight to know when to escape from a situation that often imposes a steady level of stress. Insight helps you overcome feelings of guilt that some people feel when they confuse a well-deserved break with abandonment of their charge. The caregiver must be able to consciously give himself permission to withdraw for a short time.

Planning for your temporary absence requires time and effort. The replacement caregiver must be taught about medications, daily schedules, symptoms, and other information that will make the substitution work. Finally, the tired caregiver needs either money to hire help or the volunteer services of someone to take over his tasks for the length of the break.

Get a Healthy Life

Your health is as important as the health of the person you care for. It may take more conscious effort for you to achieve it because of your additional responsibilities, but it will be worth it. If you are healthy and strong, you will feel better, handle stress better, and be capable of giving better care. Get a yearly physical exam, exercise regularly, eat nutritious foods, and get enough rest and sleep.

Therapy is another option to consider. A good therapist can provide helpful insights and techniques for improving your ability to handle the challenges you face in your personal life, at your job, and in your role as a caregiver.

Essential

Take advantage of a family or psychoeducation program if you have access to one. This type of training improves the ability of people to cope with the stresses of caring for a person with schizophrenia. A good program will help you deal with both positive and negative symptoms.

Find Relaxation

Stress and relaxation are mutually exclusive. The body cannot be stressed and relaxed at the same time. Any time you can find to relax—through exercise, yoga, meditation, or entertainment—will provide at least a temporary escape from stress. Discipline and a regular schedule of stress-reducing pastimes can help you stay relaxed for longer periods throughout the day, even while you deal with stressful tasks.

Ways to Reduce Stress

- Get enough sleep
- Get good nutrition
- Find ways to laugh
- Find ways to be entertained
- Exercise
- Practice deep breathing or meditation

Adapted from Sharon L. Johnson's *Therapist's Guide to Clinical Intervention.*

Coping with the Stigma of Mental Illness

Stigma is a mark of shame or discredit imposed by some people onto others. In most cases, it is caused by lack of knowledge. Many people are unfamiliar with the symptoms and signs of schizophrenia. Many are ignorant of the biological basis of the brain disease. Some uninformed people have trouble distinguishing some symptoms of schizophrenia from alcohol or drug intoxication.

In the late 1990s, interviews with people caring for relatives with schizophrenia revealed that they suffered from the stigma of being associated with someone with schizophrenia. Stigma can add to caregiver stress. The greater the burden a caregiver feels, the greater her risk of developing depression and lasting health problems.

If it becomes a problem, find someone to discuss the stigma. If you can't find an understanding friend, seek the help of a therapist or mental health care professional.

Consequences of Stigma

Because of the stigma surrounding mental illness, you may be ignored or gossiped about. In extreme cases, you may be illegally fired or not hired for a job or denied housing. Some physicians have been shown to take the medical complaints of people with mental illness less seriously than those of other patients. Some police officers and other governmental officials may do the same.

Taking It Personally

The worst effect of stigma occurs when it sticks to a person with schizophrenia and she believes she is socially inferior. Adoption of this self-defeating attitude can have devastating effects on self-image, sense of worth, self-confidence, and ability to recover. Stigma can have the same effect on caregivers. This is an issue you can discuss with a good therapist or a trusted adviser.

Dealing with Prejudice and Ignorance

You cannot change everyone's attitude. You can try to educate and inform those you come in contact with informally, and you can join organizations to work to increase understanding on a wider scale. These are important efforts if you have the energy and time to devote to them. They will not change the fact, however, that during your day-to-day struggles you will encounter people who perpetuate the stigma against people overcoming psychiatric illnesses.

 Fact

Uninformed members of the general public easily misinterpret many of the symptoms of schizophrenia. Negative symptoms involving lack of emotional expression and motivation, for example, may look like signs of laziness or of a weak personality. Of course, they are really symptoms of the brain disease.

The challenges presented by uninformed individuals who promote harmful, stereotyped ideas about psychiatric illnesses will be your problem more than theirs. Therefore it is as important for you to learn how to deal with your reactions to stigma as it is for you to try to change this unfortunate fact of life. You can educate others, but you can't completely eliminate the ignorance behind the stigma.

Possible Sources of Stigma
- Belief that patients are violent
- Fear of what is not understood; ignorance of the disease
- Negative media images of the mentally ill
- Fear of being associated with mental illness
- Unease with anything different

Seek the advice of a friend, therapist, or social worker. Share your feelings and frustrations with her. Talk to her about strategies for dealing with the problems you face. Listen to what she has to say.

Stigma's Effect on You as a Caregiver
Ultimately, dealing with stigma is a personal problem for which you must find a personal solution. You must recognize how you respond to the insult and how you let it affect you. This is a difficult concept to realize. It requires considerable personal strength. You may need help reaching a mental state that enables you to care for your loved one and deal with negative attitudes with minimal effect on your morale. If you can't win over someone who is prejudiced against the mentally ill, let his ignorance pass around you.

Get on with the task of convincing yourself or the person you care for that some progress and recovery are possible. Continue your efforts to improve the care you are giving. Continue to seek benefits from self-help groups, therapy, and/or stress reduction programs.

Fighting Back
If stigma affects employment, housing, or other services, you can first confront the person or agency that is denying you or your

loved one what is legally yours. If you receive no satisfaction, you have two choices. You can try someplace else—another employer or landlord, for example—or you can appeal to a regulatory agency or a court of law.

Paying for Mental Health Care

Unless you are independently wealthy, you will probably rely on health insurance or government programs to pay for mental health care. There are multiple sources of benefits available to you. A psychiatric social worker or your case manager may be able to guide you to programs and benefits for which you may qualify.

Potential Sources of Health Benefits

- Private health insurance or health maintenance organization
- Veterans administration benefits
- Social security disability insurance
- Supplemental security income
- Public assistance (welfare)
- Medicare
- Medicaid

Community Mental Health Centers (CMHCs), located in every state, may also provide treatment opportunities. They accept payment based on your insurance coverage, income or financial resources, and eligibility for other types of assistance.

Private Insurance and Veterans Administration Benefits

Private health insurance and health maintenance organization (HMO) plans are provided by a private insurance company or agency. Insurance is usually obtained through an employer because group rates are less expensive than those for individual policies. Individuals can also sign up on their own. Employers who do not offer a full health insurance plan may pay some of the cost of subscribing to a health plan.

 Question

What is a clinical social worker?
A clinical social worker is trained to help clients obtain mental health resources. He can determine eligibility and need. In some cases, he may work as a case manager to coordinate care and services provided by multiple agencies, provide information, refer you to other sources of help, and intercede for you when dealing with government and insurance agency red tape.

You should receive a contract that explains the details of your benefits when you sign up for health care coverage. Many people either don't read their contracts or gloss over them. Don't make that mistake. Read the contract carefully, especially the parts that define coverage for mental health benefits. Find out exactly what your mental health care benefits are.

Health insurance coverage varies greatly according to the insurance provider and how much your employer is willing to pay to help defray your costs. It may cover nearly all of your medical needs or it may provide only partial coverage for the most serious. The amount you have to pay when you use the services can also vary widely. It is important that you know exactly what you signed up for and, if possible, begin supplementing your coverage to cover holes in your policy. If that is not feasible, start investigating other options.

Veterans Affairs Benefits

If a veteran is affected by schizophrenia, she may be eligible for Department of Veterans Affairs (VA) benefits. Contact the VA at (800) 827-1000 to determine if you or someone you care for qualifies. You can search for nearby VA treatment facilities online at *www.va.gov/directory/guide/home.asp*. VA medical care is paid for by general tax revenues. The VA has its own doctors, who work at VA hospitals.

Social Security

Social security disability insurance (SSDI) and supplemental security income (SSI) are government programs that may provide financial assistance if you qualify. In 2002, more than one in four people receiving SSDI benefits had a mental disorder, totaling 1.7 million people at a cost of $18 billion. If a patient worked in the past and accumulated credits with the social security system, he may be eligible to receive financial assistance regardless of his present income. You might also investigate the possibility that a parent's contribution to social security can qualify an ill child for benefits.

If SSDI is not an option and you don't have much money or income, you might qualify for SSI. In 2002, nearly one in three people receiving SSI had a mental disorder, totaling 1.6 million people at a cost of approximately $8.2 billion.

Contact the Social Security Administration Office in your area to find out which, if either, of these programs might help you. To find the nearest office, you can call the automated telephone service at (800) 772-1213 or enter your zip code into the Social Security Office Locator website at *https://secure.ssa.gov/apps6z/FOLO/fo001.jsp.*

Public Assistance (Welfare)

Welfare, like schizophrenia, has a stigma attached to it. And like the stigma associated with schizophrenia, it is unfounded and unfair. The stigma is associated with healthy people, capable of working, who were accused of abusing the program.

Low-income patients have a right to this basic government assistance program. Take advantage of it if you qualify. You will need to check your phone book for the Office of Public Assistance nearest you or ask your case manager or other health care provider for information.

Alert

If you have no insurance or if your financial means are limited, ask your case manager if there are any patient assistance programs in your state that can help you obtain medications free or at a reduced rate.

Medicare and Medicaid

Medicare (medical insurance for the elderly) is another program offered through the Social Security Administration. If you have been collecting SSDI benefits for a couple of years, ask if you qualify for this program.

Medicaid programs (medical insurance for low-income patients) are administered by individual states, which determine what services are offered and who can receive them. Contact your local state health department for information about your eligibility and potential benefits. You can find that information on the Health and Human Service's Centers for Medicare and Medicaid Services website: *www .cms.hhs.gov.*

CHAPTER 19

Advocating for Better Understanding and Treatment

YOU DON'T NEED an office or a title to be an advocate for better mental health care services and education. Whenever you tell your story to someone and mention your efforts to get better treatment, find housing, or deal with stress, you are serving as an advocate by educating your neighbors and community. When you organize with others who are doing the same thing at public events, you increase the possibility of reaching more people.

Established Advocacy Groups

There are scores of groups devoted to sharing information about schizophrenia and advocating for better treatment. It might be a good idea to start with the largest and work your way down to the smaller groups. You will pick up information first from established, reliable sources. As you learn more, you will be better able to judge the quality of advice and information offered by newer and smaller groups and organizations.

When you visit websites of self-help groups or other organizations, look for a list of references or sources that you can use to verify the information or stories. Check the sponsor of the site or book. Is it a reputable institution, organization, or publisher? Do the people offering the information have experience with the disease? Do they have professional credentials?

NAMI

The National Alliance on Mental Illness (*www.nami.org*) describes itself as "the nation's largest grassroots organization for people with mental illness and their families." It has local affiliate chapters all over the United States that can provide you with an established stage for getting involved and finding people to share experiences, support, and information.

The Treatment Advocacy Center

The Treatment Advocacy Center (*www.treatmentadvocacycen ter.org*) was founded by noted schizophrenia expert E. Fuller Torrey, MD. This nonprofit organization's goal is to ensure proper treatment of mental illness as efficiently and quickly as possible. It provides useful general, medical, and legal resources. You can find information on research topics, news stories, legal actions, relevant political stories, and personal accounts on the group's website.

Schizophrenia.com

Schizophrenia.com (*www.schizophrenia.com*), founded in 1995, is a volunteer-run group composed mostly of people who have cared for loved ones who have been diagnosed with schizophrenia. Although most of these people do not have medical or mental health backgrounds, their strength lies in their personal experiences with schizophrenia and the significant amount of research they have done. The site relies on the advice of qualified experts and offers a place for caregivers, families, and patients with firsthand knowledge of the disease to share information and experience.

Local Support Groups

You may be able to find or start a self-help group in your area. You just need other people with interests and experiences similar to yours. Self-help groups can be therapeutic beyond the relief provided by a visit to a professional therapist's or doctor's office. Groups can provide emotional support and a forum for the exchange of helpful ideas.

Benefits

It is very helpful to be reminded that you are not alone as you deal with schizophrenia. Share experiences. Talk about successes and setbacks. Trade the names of good and bad sources of treatment in your area. Arrange to help each other out with driving and other tasks. Find people you can call when you need to talk to someone. You may also meet allies in your effort to educate the community about schizophrenia or in your advocacy for better treatment and research.

Start a Group

If there isn't already a self-help group in your area, consider getting some people together. You can find potential members by leaving invitations at local treatment centers or hospitals. Visit the website of the National Mental Health Consumers' Self-Help Clearinghouse (*www.mhselfhelp.org*). This organization helps consumers who are interested in organizing self-help and advocacy groups.

Educating Your Neighbors

Not much will change unless the general public learns more about schizophrenia and mental illnesses. Neither the news media nor the entertainment industry can be relied upon to educate the public about psychiatric disorders. That leaves the task to schools, government, and private organizations. Unfortunately, it is not a priority for schools. Government agencies such as the National Institute of Mental Health provide good information for those who seek it out, but its clients are usually people who are directly affected by mental illness, not members of the general public. That leaves advocates and potential advocates to do the job.

Knowledge Gap

A NAMI survey indicated that the number of U.S. citizens living with schizophrenia is double the number of Americans living with HIV/AIDS. Despite this, the survey indicates that most people don't know much about the mental illness that afflicts millions of their peers. The same poll indicated that nearly half of the respondents were uneasy about the idea of dating someone with a history of schizophrenia.

 Fact

Mental disease is still a hidden fact of everyday life for millions of people. The surgeon general's 1999 report on mental health indicated that more than one in five people in the United States have a "diagnosable" mental disorder. Only one-third of these people seek or receive treatment.

After the survey's release, NAMI expressed concern regarding the potential negative impact of Americans' lack of knowledge about and suspicion toward schizophrenia.

Advantages of a Knowledgeable Public

The earlier psychotic symptoms are detected and treated, the better the outcome can be for the patient. While family members are often in the best position to spot developing trouble, there are many others, including teachers, coaches, school officials, friends, and acquaintances, who may also be close enough to detect emerging signs of illness. It is important that these people know the basic signs of mental illness.

The less people know about something, the more likely they are to fear it. Increased public awareness can reduce the stigma surrounding schizophrenia. It educates more people in the community, who may then be able to notice signs of trouble and help those who have undiagnosed schizophrenia seek treatment sooner. It can remove the shame that many people wrongly associate with mental illness. This sense of shame often keeps individuals from seeking help, but greater public understanding and acceptance of schizophrenia can encourage people to seek treatment. You can help further the spread of information by educating anyone who comes into frequent contact with young people. Sponsor meetings and informal gatherings to spread information about schizophrenia and other mental illnesses.

Services that Need Improvement

Finding effective treatments and resources for patients with schizophrenia can be frustrating and challenging. This is why the most important goal for mental health advocates is securing better treatment through coordination and increased funding of psychiatric care programs.

Plenty to Choose From

Researchers have repeatedly shown the value of therapy or psychosocial interventions, rehabilitation services, and proper medication. These measures undeniably improve the lives of patients, and by extension, their caregivers. Access to these effective treatments, unfortunately, is not nearly as available as it needs to be to help everyone who needs them. The same can be said of social programs and policies that mandate treatment in the community. Without it, hospitalization is often the only option for undertreated people suffering from schizophrenia. Not all communities have crisis management teams ready to serve those who need immediate help.

 Fact

Researchers claim that around 60 percent of people with schizophrenia live in poverty and 5 percent end up homeless. There are organizations and professionals who are dedicated to helping disadvantaged communities seek help for mental illnesses. However, with no widespread, effective social support system in place, these people become easy targets for criminals.

The recent advances in both pharmacology and psychotherapy are not readily available to many who suffer from schizophrenia.

In addition, much work remains to be done to establish programs that make psychiatric care available to those who are most severely affected by the disease.

Help for Families

Much more effort is needed to capitalize on the benefits that come from educating the families of people with schizophrenia. The sooner patients and relatives start educating themselves, the more significant the benefits. Unfortunately, such opportunities often are missed for lack of funding.

Correcting these weaknesses in the mental health care system will require the work of advocates who recognize the problems and know the solutions. The advocates must be knowledgeable and politically astute enough to get the attention of lawmakers.

Essential

There are many threats to patient-doctor confidentiality today. Expanded use of computers and data storage banks is one area of concern. Another is the trend to deny medical services or access to insurance coverage based on past history. Genetic testing may soon provide another reason medical confidentiality must be strengthened by legislation.

You can help by getting involved in your community and teaming up with people who have access to politicians. Acquaint yourself with the facts concerning the number of people who could benefit from improved counseling services and find out exactly how much it will cost to implement such services.

Back this up with projections showing the cost to the community if such programs are not available. This may be difficult to quantify because medical economists have not yet provided definitive estimates for how much money it costs society for family members to bear the burden of schizophrenia.

The Neglected

The Department of Justice estimates that up to 61 percent of prisoners in U.S. jails and prisons—63,000 people—are mentally ill. Nearly half had received no mental health treatment prior to arrest, and only 20 percent had been treated during the preceding year. About one-third of state prisoners and one-quarter of federal prisoners with mental illness received treatment after incarceration. Critics complain that mental health care behind bars is lacking in quality and quantity.

This type of neglect might be traced to several sources: lack of money for treatment, lack of concern by the public, and lack of understanding that mental illness often leads to jail for people who cannot get treatment or won't accept it. With very few psychiatric hospitals available for such people, jail becomes society's psychiatric hospital. This area is in desperate need of correction and advocacy attention.

MentalHelp.net provides some useful background information on this topic in Allan Schwartz's article "Imprisoning the Mentally Ill" (*www.mentalhelp.net/poc/view_doc.php?type=doc&id=14284*). For ideas on what you can do and for more information on this topic, visit the Ohio Legal Rights Service website (*http://olrs.ohio.gov/asp/pub_jailrts.asp*) and the American Friends Service Committee Criminal Justice Program site at *www.prisoneradvocacy.org*.

Organizing

Government must play a central role in ensuring better treatment for the mentally ill. Apart from pharmaceutical companies, private industry has little to gain from finding better ways to care for and treat people in need of mental health care. Patient advocates must pressure elected officials to provide programs to help those disadvantaged by brain diseases such as schizophrenia.

PACTs

In assertive case management programs or assertive community treatment (PACT or ACT) programs, health care professionals are paid to go into the field to deliver treatment. Even patients who have stopped coming in for therapy can benefit from such programs.

The professionals visit homes, hangouts, and other places where they might find patients who need treatment but aren't getting it. Such programs have been shown to decrease hospitalizations, thereby saving communities money. However, such programs need political backing to attain and maintain funding.

Far too few people who need PACT benefits have access to them. Lobbying to establish a PACT program in your community could bring benefits that will help both patients and their families.

No Shortage of Projects

In *Surviving Schizophrenia*, E. Fuller Torrey lists more than forty ways you as an advocate can improve mental health care services, which he describes as being, for the most part, "mediocre to abysmal" in the United States. The suggestions he offers are so varied, there is a good chance you will find at least one that will fit your interest and skills.

If you enjoy writing, for example, you might:

- Gather information about mental health resources in your town or county and make it available to others online or in pamphlet form.
- Rank all the facilities that provide mental health care in your state. Share your report. Keep it up to date as the information changes.
- Collect key information about laws governing court-ordered commitment in your state and get it into the hands of anyone who might need it.
- Research and publish a summary of the confidentiality laws in your state.
- Counter misinformation about, insensitivity toward, and ignorance of mental illness by writing to newspapers,

television and radio stations, and other media outlets when you hear something that is not accurate, true, or respectful concerning mental illness and mental health care.

- Write to your local and state representatives concerning mental health issues and policies. Find out who and where to write on the government's official website at *www.usa .gov/Contact/Elected.shtml.*

If you enjoy organizing events or programs, consider:

- Signing up local business and institutions to offer part-time or volunteer jobs to people with mental illness. Get the word out to the mental illness community after you have secured some promises to help.
- Establish a self-help or social group to bring caregivers together.
- Arrange programs to bring together people with mental illness and the general community. Ideas include sporting events, hobby clubs, or fundraisers. Fundraisers don't have to benefit a mental health care program. You can generate goodwill and better understanding of mental illness if you raise funds for other community needs using the efforts of people living with schizophrenia. This is a way for people dealing with schizophrenia to be accepted by the community as equals.
- Identify outstanding mental health care providers and administrators, journalists who have written responsibly and honestly about mental health issues, and local volunteers who have contributed to the welfare of others. Establish awards to honor them or work with local groups to see that they receive credit and appreciation.

Politicking

Do you enjoy politics? Do you have "people skills?" Are you good at persuasion? There is so much to be done that you will always have an opportunity to practice these skills as a political advocate for the mentally ill. The most obvious way to get involved is to run for office, but you can be just as effective if you organize others. Learn the rules of lobbying lawmakers, and get voters organized.

Local Projects

Torrey's suggestions include many projects you can do without leaving your local community. For example, find out if there are obstacles to establishing group homes for people with mental illness in your neighborhood. If so, work to get the zoning laws changed. You will also need to change the minds of many of your neighbors. Approach them and listen to what they have to say about the proposal. Expect opposition. Expect the formation of lobbying groups opposed to the idea. If you can keep the debate civil, this is a great opportunity for educating the public. With success, you might someday establish a much-needed place for people who need a safe place to recover.

You can multiply your influence by working to place good people in influential positions. Locate all mental health boards in your community, right up to the state level. Identify good candidates, including consumers, organizers, and advocates, and work to get them appointed to the boards and other committees that influence mental health care policies on the local and state levels. Back local representatives who have supported mental health reform in the past.

State and Federal Projects

Torrey suggests offering voter support to state and federal representatives who have a good record of supporting mental health programs. Work for their re-election and recruit others to do the same.

Find out how much your state spends on treatment programs for people with schizophrenia and other mental health problems. Meet with state representatives to ask for money to fill in any gaps.

Does your state have an adequate bill of rights guaranteeing good care and treatment for consumers of mental health care? If so, does it need revision? Consult lawyers about drafting a good one and then take it to state representatives to ask for their help getting it implemented. On the federal level, you can lobby lawmakers to improve Medicaid and other health care coverage for consumers.

 Alert

> Businesses that offer health insurance to fifty or more employees will have to provide equal benefits for mental health care and other illnesses starting on January 1, 2010. This breakthrough follows a dozen years of lobbying by mental health care advocates. It should mean the end of higher co-payments, higher deductibles, and restrictions on treatment options for mental illnesses and addiction.

This is just a sample of the activities in which your contributions could make a difference in the lives of many people. Once you become involved in mental health care issues, the number of projects you could potentially participate in will increase quickly.

CHAPTER 20

The Promise of Future Research

ADVANCES IN OUR understanding of schizophrenia itself and improvements in the drugs and therapies used to treat it mean that schizophrenia patients and their caregivers have much to look forward to. Caregivers, however, cannot wait years for greater understanding of the disease and for new treatments to reach the psychiatrist's office and the mental health clinic. They have to act now with what is known about the disease and its treatments today.

Schizophrenia Research

It is not clear how long it may take before a cure for schizophrenia is discovered, if there ever is one. The "easy" diseases were cured a long time ago. Now medicine is dealing with the most difficult, challenging conditions, which often represent complexes of diseases such as cancer and mental illness.

Are More Genetic Insights the Answer?

The genetic origins of schizophrenia will continue to be an important area of research. Scientists are narrowing down regions of DNA that are clearly different in many patients with schizophrenia. The identification of specific genes that are closely associated with schizophrenia will give medical researchers valuable new biological targets for developing new treatments. The more scientists know about the disease, the better able they will be to counter its effects.

Early Detection

At this time, there is no way to diagnose schizophrenia using a laboratory test. A diagnosis is made on the basis of a patient's symptoms. A reliable, generally applicable clinical test would be a great advantage for spotting the disease early, beginning treatment without delay, and lessening the toll this mental illness can take on consumers and their families.

Because schizophrenia is so complex, the development of a single lab test may be unlikely. It is possible, however, that a pattern of test results—perhaps including genetic, brain imaging, and other indicators that are still undefined—could someday be helpful in diagnosing and predicting the outcome of the disease. Identifying people at risk using these and psychological testing methods might provide a way to intercept the disease before symptoms appear and become fixed in the brain.

The Need for More Basic Research

The development of superior medications that can better treat negative symptoms will probably require a better understanding of the disease process itself. That means better understanding of the basic biology of the brain.

If scientists can identify more of the pathways and functions that are affected by schizophrenia, they will be more likely to create medications that specifically target the critical abnormalities underlying the disease.

In the short term, hope lies in the advances we can expect to see in more effective and safer treatments for schizophrenia and other difficult health care challenges. These improvements will follow continued basic scientific research in the fields of genetics, behavior, and neurobiology. Two obvious fields of fruitful research will be genetic research and noninvasive imaging studies of brain structure and function.

Alert

Progress in medicine is like figuring out what is wrong with a sagging wall. First, you need to know how the wall is constructed, where the supports are, and what materials are present. Then you can diagnose the problem. If you know nothing about walls, you won't be able to figure out why the wall is failing or how to fix it.

Luck Doesn't Count for Much

There is always a very slim chance that serendipity—a lucky accident or unexpected observation recognized by a prepared mind—will yield a new insight that will lead to another big leap in our understanding and treatment of schizophrenia.

Serendipity has played a major role in scientific discovery in the past. Today, however, overwhelming control of scientific inquiry is in the hands of federal funding agencies and for-profit companies. This makes serendipitous or unexpected discoveries significantly less likely.

Granting Favors

Many researchers report that in order to receive funding for their grant applications, they have to have a significant percentage of the work already done, complete with results they can share in the grant application. True exploratory research means a scientist does not know what she will discover when she sets out on a course of inquiry. That is the rare exception today, not the rule. Granting agencies want to know exactly what they will be getting for their money. This emphasis on predictable research might not serve consumers as well as grant administrators assume it does.

No one seriously believes planned serendipity is the best way to speed up our knowledge of diseases like schizophrenia. Giving scientists greater flexibility and choice in how and what they will research, however, might stimulate some fresh insights that could speed up the incremental progress we've seen in recent years.

Trends in Government Research Funding

In the last ten years, the budget of the National Institute of Mental Health (NIMH) has increased around sixfold, from $230 million to $1.4 billion. Unfortunately, factors such as the economy and other government spending priorities are resulting in cuts in federal funding of health care and mental illness prevention programs, according to NIMH.

In addition, only a small fraction of the NIMH budget is dedicated to schizophrenia research. Critics charge it is disproportionately low given the prevalence, severity, and cost of schizophrenia. Even if the percentage of funding devoted to schizophrenia research increases in the future, it means much research time and opportunity has already been lost. Future progress is being slowed by poor funding and poor allocation of funds. It is an area where advocates could make a difference by getting the attention of members of Congress.

Need for Better Medications

Progress in treating people with schizophrenia took a giant leap forward sixty years ago with the greatest advance in biological psychiatry in the history of medicine: the introduction of the typical antipsychotic drugs to treat psychosis. Advances in the treatment of schizophrenia have been less revolutionary and more incremental in the last quarter century. These small steps have made huge differences in the lives of hundreds of thousands of patients, but too many patients are still left out. The future outlook will be good if progress continues as it has, but incremental advances, by definition, take a long time to amount to a revolution.

Positive Progress and Negative Holdovers

One of the most notable steps forward in the last twenty years was the introduction of atypical antipsychotic medications. This has led to greater choice of medications with different, and arguably improved, side effect profiles. It has delivered effective treatment to people who were not helped by earlier drugs. Innovative and effective therapy programs also account for much of the recent progress.

Fact

Research for the development of better drugs with fewer side effects is an ongoing effort. Current antipsychotic medications are good, but they could be better. The newer drugs are said to be more effective and better tolerated than the older drugs, but their side effects can still be dangerous for some patients. Several studies have indicated that newer, more expensive drugs are not as superior to older drugs as once thought.

Current and future research should improve our understanding of the lingering side effects of antipsychotic medication. This knowledge could enable physicians to predict who is most at risk for adverse drug reactions. Patients then could be started sooner on medications they would have a better chance of tolerating, eliminating the need to employ a hit-or-miss strategy.

One lasting problem is the medical community's inability to effectively treat negative symptoms as well as positive ones. The typical antipsychotic drugs have little or no effect on negative symptoms. The atypical antipsychotics have some effect on these difficult, residual effects of the disease, but it is not enough.

Developing New Medications

Drug companies won't invest millions of dollars in potential new medications unless someone can make a good argument that they will work. In other words, the industry waits until there is a good scientific basis for developing new profit-making products.

Unfortunately, the cause or causes of schizophrenia are still not well understood. As a result, many companies have limited themselves to bringing out drugs that are often only slightly different versions of what is already available.

Pharmaceutical companies finance some research studies that are not directly related to a particular drug's action, but economics prevent them from being big players in the pursuit of basic scientific knowledge. Without more basic research, the identification of promising new targets for advancing schizophrenia treatments will be delayed.

Hope for Cognition

Cognitive dysfunction and negative symptoms are key areas of treatment in need of fresh approaches. In response to this need, NIMH started the Measurement and Treatment Research to Improve Cognition in Schizophrenia (MATRICS) program as a way to stimulate academic scientists and pharmaceutical companies to identify biological targets for new drugs that will improve intellectual function in people struggling with schizophrenia. It is possible that developments in the future will result in multiple medications, each effective against some symptoms of the disease.

The Drug Pipeline

The drug pipeline contains dozens of new drug candidates for treating the symptoms of schizophrenia. Many are likely to prove ineffective, unsafe, or otherwise inappropriate for use in humans, but some will make it onto the market. Because schizophrenia is such an individualistic disease, the availability of new medications is always a source of hope for patients who might respond to something novel if older, existing medications don't work.

Newer antipsychotic drugs such as clozapine have made a big difference in the lives of many people with schizophrenia and their families. Despite clozapine's lack of disturbing neurological side effects and its ability to help people who don't respond to other antipsychotic drugs, the newer atypical drugs have never fully lived up to the early hopes that pharmaceutical companies and many psychiatrists had for them. They have their own side effects, and it's not clear how effective they are at reducing cognitive symptoms and sometimes negative symptoms.

 Question

How long does it take for a new treatment to become available?
While the time can vary, it is often unacceptably long, according to experts in the medical and mental health community. The Institute of Medicine's report "Crossing the Quality Chasm: A New Health System for the 21st Century" estimates that the time elapsed between the discovery of a useful new treatment and its introduction into routine, daily medical practice can be as long as fifteen to twenty years.

Dozens of Candidates

In 2008 there were approximately forty-five new drugs for treating schizophrenia in development. Many of the studies testing these potential treatments are open to consumers who wish to participate in them.

At the time of this writing, all except one are similar to existing antipsychotic drugs in their biochemical effects. Prospective new drugs directed at truly novel biochemical targets have not yet produced any promising results.

Dozens more drug candidates are actively being investigated in laboratories but have not yet advanced to the stage at which they can be tested in humans. Some are related to familiar drugs. Some may eventually be selected for further treatment based on new approaches, such as their ability to interact with genes suspected of being involved in schizophrenia.

Animal Models of the Disease

Drug screening programs are hindered by the lack of good animal models of the disease. Some drugs, such as PCP (angel dust), produce schizophrenia-like symptoms in humans. Some researchers treat animals with these drugs and test the effects of candidate medications on them. This is about as close as scientists can come to reproducing schizophrenia in the laboratory, something that would greatly enhance progress.

No one expects to see a lab rat with schizophrenia. But if scientists could learn more specific details about the biochemistry of the disease, they might be able to mimic or approximate those changes in laboratory animals. Drugs could then be tested in these animals to see if they could affect the particular biochemical feature linked to schizophrenia in humans.

Hope

Ken Steele, patient and advocate, ended his memoir with his hope for the future. "In this new century," he wrote, "mentally ill people will have the science, the organized voting strength, and the means to leave our ghettos of isolation behind us. We will finally join with the mainstream community, where we'll be able to live as independent individuals and not as a group of people who are known and feared by the names of our illnesses."

That will happen if patients, friends, and families push for more funding for research, education programs for the public, and treatment options for everyone who has a mental illness. It will take a long time and much effort. But it will never be as difficult as living with schizophrenia.

Glossary

Acute psychotic episode
A psychotic episode that seems to occur suddenly with no prior indication or hints that it is about to happen.

Acute schizophrenia
The sudden appearance of schizophrenia symptoms that have not been present or the worsening of symptoms over a short period of time, usually days.

Adherence
Faithfully sticking to a treatment plan, including taking medications and attending therapy.

Adverse reaction
See Side effect

Affect
Emotional expressions of inner feelings made visible to others by movement and position of facial features or other indications of body language. Examples are smiles, frowns, shaking of the head, etc.

Affective disorder
See mood disorder

Agranulocytosis
A life-threatening loss of white blood cells, which fight infection. It is a complication affecting about 1 percent of patients taking the atypical antipsychotic drug clozapine.

Akathisia
A side effect of some antipsychotic medications, causing restlessness, which is demonstrated by an inability to sit for any significant length of time and a feeling of quivering muscles.

Alogia
A decreased ability to speak, a negative symptom of schizophrenia reflecting a lack of ease in thinking and speaking.

Anergia
Lack of energy.

Anhedonia
The inability to derive pleasure from, or take an interest in, nearly anything.

Anosognosia
A person's inability to recognize that he is ill; lack of insight into one's own psychiatric or other physical illness or deficit. This is a common symptom of schizophrenia. Other conditions similar to schizophrenia make a person unable to recognize that he is blind when he really is, or that his arm is paralyzed when it really is.

Auditory hallucination
A common symptom of schizophrenia in which a person hears sounds, noises, or voices that no one else can hear and that have no external source.

Bipolar disorder
A mood disorder that cycles between depression and mania. It used to be called manic-depression or manic-depressive illness.

Blunted affect
Showing limited emotional responses or a significantly reduced intensity and range of emotional expression.

Catatonia
A symptom of a rare form of schizophrenia characterized by immobility or repetitive movements. Sometimes a patient with catatonia may show signs of excitation.

Catatonic schizophrenia
A rare subtype of schizophrenia characterized by an extreme psychological separation from one's surroundings. The disturbance can range from trance-like stupor, complete unresponsiveness, excitement, or the assumption of odd postures. There can be quick changes between excited behavior and stupor. Patients may be mute or they may echo repeatedly a word or words spoken by others. Sometimes mannerisms are repeated in a stereotyped way.

Chronic schizophrenia
A form of the disease in which symptoms linger at a relatively milder level without significant periods of remission.

Clang
Abnormal speech observed in schizophrenia during which the sound of a word influences the future choice of words more than does the context

of the conversation. For example, a patient may say "You have nothing to gain. The pain comes from rain."

Clinical trial
A medical research study conducted on a group of subjects to determine the safety and effectiveness of experimental new drugs or treatments.

Clozapine
The first atypical antipsychotic medication. It has the ability to help many patients who are not helped by other antipsychotic medications. It can cause a potentially fatal blood disease in one out of a hundred people.

Cognitive
Intellectual, as opposed to emotional, mental processes including understanding, evaluating, remembering, and reasoning.

Cognitive-behavioral therapy
A type of therapy shown to increase the coping and functional abilities of many people dealing with schizophrenia.

Combination therapy
A commonly used strategy that simultaneously employs psychosocial and medical therapy to treat schizophrenia.

Delusion
An unshakable belief in something that is not true or real. Evidence that a healthy person would recognize as contradictory will not persuade someone with a delusion to change her belief. Bizarre delusions are delusions that are not possible or plausible. Examples include the belief that extraterrestrial creatures have implanted a device in someone's brain in order to listen to

her thoughts or to use her brain power in order to fly their spaceship. Another example may be the belief by a male patient that he is pregnant with twins.

Depression
See Major depressive disorder

Derailment
A symptom of schizophrenia involving conversation that rapidly changes from one topic to another with little meaningful connection for the listener; also referred to as loose associations.

Disorganized schizophrenia
A severe subtype of schizophrenia in which patients lack systematized delusions but are incoherent and show symptoms of inappropriate, blunted, or silly emotions.

Dopamine
A chemical messenger in the brain that has long been implicated in schizophrenia. Many antipsychotic drugs decrease the activity of this neurotransmitter.

DSM-IV
The American Psychiatric Association's Diagnostic and Statistical Manual of Mental Disorders, fourth edition. It lists the standard criteria used to classify and diagnose mental disorders. It is used by mental health professionals and insurance companies to define the diagnoses of patients.

Early treatment
A treatment strategy that stresses recognizing symptoms when they are still mild and treating them as soon as possible. It has been shown to improve the outcome for patients.

Echolalia
A symptom of schizophrenia involving the repetition or echoing of something said by another person, repeatedly, without any apparent meaning or purpose.

Echopraxia
A symptom of schizophrenia involving the repetitive imitation of another person's movement.

Euphoria
In mood or psychotic disorders, a pathological state of elation unrelated or barely related to outside events that would justify the feeling of extreme joy.

Extrapyramidal symptoms
Parkinson's disease-like symptoms associated with older antipsychotic medications including slowed movement, loss of facial expression, shakiness in the limbs, arms held at the sides when walking, muscular rigidity, uncontrolled contractions of muscles affecting posture, and involuntary movements often involving the tongue and lips.

Family psychoeducation
A training program that teaches family members or friends about schizophrenia and how to help someone with schizophrenia at home or outside the hospital. Such training has been shown to have significant benefits for both patients and caregivers.

Flat affect
The lack of emotional expression in the face or voice.

Glutamate
A chemical messenger in the brain that has been implicated in schizophrenia.

Gray matter
Brain substance consisting of nerve cells. Often referred to by nonspecialists as the part of the brain used to think.

Guardian
A person over the age of eighteen years or an organization appointed by a court to act in the best interest of a person who is incapacitated physically or mentally. The guardian has the responsibility to make decisions for the person and to provide for his personal needs. In the case of a mentally ill person, responsibilities would also include arrangement of appropriate, professional treatment.

Hallucination
A positive symptom of schizophrenia that may involve any of the five senses (hearing, seeing, touch, smelling, or tasting) in which a person perceives something to be there when nothing is and no one else can sense it. It is experienced by the person in the same way events are perceived during a dream, except in this case, the person is awake. Patients with schizophrenia most commonly hear things or see things that are not there. Hallucinations of touch, smell, or taste are very rarely present in schizophrenia.

Heredity
All the characteristics and potential characteristics of physical qualities handed down from parent to child through genetic material contained in genes.

ICD 10
The International Statistical Classification of Diseases and Related Health Problems, 10th revision; the international standard diagnostic classification for general epidemiological and health management purposes compiled by the World Health Organization. Schizophrenia and related disorders are described in Chapter V of the most recent edition.

Illusion
The misperception of the nature or identity of something that does exist (unlike hallucinations, in which it is imagined). An example would be the misperception of a wallpaper pattern as being somebody's face, or of symbols as representing the solution of a certain problem.

Inappropriate affect
Emotional demonstrations that do not match the situation that elicits them; for example, laughing at something sad or crying at something funny.

Loose associations
See Derailment

Major depressive disorder (also known as depression)
A mood disorder producing emotional symptoms of overwhelming feelings of despair, hopelessness, and sadness along with several other physical symptoms, which persist daily for an extended period of at least two weeks. It is a disease that interferes with the ability to work, sleep, eat, and enjoy once pleasurable activities.

Mania

A period of extreme euphoria and often unrealistic enthusiasm resulting from a mood disorder. Manic "highs" are often characterized by unrestrained energy and grandiose ambition, sometimes accompanied by agitation and extreme excitability. Speech reflects the rapid coming and going of ideas. It is one of the phases of the so-called manic-depressive illness, which is currently known as bipolar disorder.

Manic episode

A period of mania.

Medication schedule

A plan describing how and when prescribed medications should be taken. It includes the names of the medications and their dosages. Sometimes called a medication regimen.

Mixed episode

A period of manic-depressive illness or bipolar disorder during which a person has symptoms of both mania and depression at the same time. This can result in someone experiencing despair while feeling highly keyed up and severely irritable.

Mood disorders

A group of mental disorders that usually involve abnormalities of mood, causing depression, mania, or a mixed state of both. They include bipolar disorder, major depressive disorder, mood disorder due to a general medical condition, and substance-induced (intoxication/withdrawal) mood disorder, among others.

National Alliance on Mental Illness (NAMI)

A leading educational and advocacy group, founded by parents of children with mental illness in 1979.

Negative symptoms

A major subcategory of schizophrenia symptoms that includes decreased intellectual, emotional, or behavioral expression. People with negative symptoms may seem withdrawn, unresponsive, uninterested in, and uninvolved with, their surroundings. They may keep to themselves and express little emotion.

Neologism

An invented word, found in the speech of some people with schizophrenia.

Neuroleptic agent

An older term applied to the original or typical antipsychotic drugs such as Haldol and chlorpromazine. The term refers to the neurological side effects associated with this class of drug.

Neuroleptic malignant syndrome

A serious, rare side effect of antipsychotic drug treatment producing sweating, fever, blood pressure changes, rigid muscles, stupor, and other neurological problems. It requires immediate medical treatment.

Neuron

A nerve cell. The contact points between nerve cells are gaps called synapses, which are believed to be the site of action of antipsychotic drugs.

Neurotransmitters

Chemical messengers in the nervous system that carry information between nerve cells. Abnormalities in neurotransmitter function appear to play an important role in schizophrenia and other mood and mental disorders. Antipsychotic drugs appear to work by adjusting the function of one or more selected neurotransmitters.

NIH
National Institutes of Health, the leading federal government agency funding and directing medical research in the United States.

NIMH
A part of the NIH, the National Institute of Mental Health is the leading federal government agency funding and directing mental health research in the United States.

Noncompliance
Failure to take medicine and/or to participate in treatment as prescribed by a physician. In many cases, noncompliance results in recurrence of psychotic symptoms. Failure to accept any treatment can result in severe symptoms and mental decline.

Paranoia
An unfounded feeling of being threatened, resulting in fear, suspicion, hostility, or distrust of others.

Paranoid-type symptoms
False beliefs that make a person feel she is being persecuted, cheated, spied on, plotted against, secretly ridiculed, or harassed. One in three schizophrenia patients show signs of paranoid symptoms.

Positive symptoms
Symptoms of schizophrenia that appear to be excessive versions of normal behavior, thinking, or feeling. They are called positive because they are evident as the presence of something that is not normally present (compared with negative symptoms, which are subtractions, or the absence, of certain functions that are normally present). Hallucinations, delusions, and disorganized thinking are examples of positive symptoms.

Prognosis
The predicted outcome of a disease based on the experiences of similar cases in the past and special circumstances of the patient's case.

Psychosis
A loss of contact with reality due to delusions, hallucinations, disorganized speech, disorganized behavior, or catatonic behavior.

Psychotherapist
A trained professional who treats people with mental disorders by addressing psychological problems. Psychotherapists educate patients and teach them techniques to help them understand and control their thoughts, emotions, or behaviors.

Psychotherapy
A technique applied by a psychotherapist to help patients as described in the previous entry. There are several different types of psychotherapy.

Psychotic episode
A time when a person experiences severe and disturbing forms of hallucinations, delusions, or other psychotic

symptoms. Sometimes unexpected with rapid onset, these are very stressful for both patient and family. Usually controlled by antipsychotic medication.

Psychotic symptom

A feature of psychotic disorders including schizophrenia. Examples include hearing voices or other hallucinations, delusions, and severely disordered thinking.

Remission

A period during which a patient has no symptoms of the disease.

Residual schizophrenia

One of the five different types of schizophrenia, characterized by the absence of prominent delusion, hallucinations, disorganized speech, and grossly disorganized or catatonic behavior. Evidence of persistent schizophrenia instead of a full remission is based on negative symptoms or only mild and faded psychotic symptoms.

Schizoaffective disorder

A mental disorder with lasting major depressive, manic, or mixed episodes along with psychotic symptoms characteristic of schizophrenia: delusions, hallucinations, and disorganized speech and behavior. It must include a period of at least two weeks during which the patient experienced the psychotic symptoms without any prominent depressive or manic symptoms.

Schizophrenia

A complex brain disease, or perhaps a group of psychotic disorders, that can lead to the deterioration of social and personal functioning as a result of disorganized thinking, delusions, hallucinations, and social withdrawal, as well as other symptoms.

Schizophreniform disorder

A diagnosis for patients whose symptoms are identical to those of schizophrenia except that they have been present for more than one month but less than six months.

Side effect

Any unintended and unwanted reaction to a medication. They can range from harmless and annoying to serious and life-threatening.

SSDI

Social security disability insurance.

SSI

Supplemental security income.

Symptom

A behavior or other indication of the presence of a disease or disorder.

Tardive dyskinesia

A potential side effect, most often associated with long-term use of older antipsychotic medications, producing involuntary movements. They frequently involve the tongue, mouth, lips, and muscles in the face, but may also occur anywhere else in the body.

Thought disorder

A symptom of schizophrenia that may involve the form or the content of a person's thoughts. Thought disorder prevents patients from thinking rationally and logically. Thoughts are disconnected and out of order, sped up or slowed down. Speech and communication also are affected. Delusions are considered a thought disorder that involves thought content.

Ventricles

Also called cerebral ventricles, these are spaces or cavities normally found in the brain. Ventricles may be enlarged in some people with schizophrenia, a finding believed to reflect the role of abnormal brain developmental in the cause of the disease.

White matter

Brain tissue that consists mostly of nerve fibers and the light-colored insulating material, myelin, that covers them.

Resources

Books and Other Publications

Adamec, Christine. *How to Live with a Mentally Ill Person: A Handbook of Day-to-Day Strategies.* New York: John Wiley, 1996.

Alexander, Franz G., and Sheldon T. Selesnick. *The History of Psychiatry: An Evaluation of Psychiatric Thought and Practice from Prehistoric Times to the Present.* New York: Harper and Row, 1966.

Amador, Xavier. *I Am Not Sick, I Don't Need Help! How to Help Someone with Mental Illness Accept Treatment.* Peconic, NY: Vida Press, 2007.

American Psychiatric Association. *Diagnostic and Statistical Manual of Mental Disorders.* 4th ed. Text Revision. Washington, DC: American Psychiatric Association, 2000.

Beam, Alex. *Gracefully Insane: The Rise and Fall of America's Premier Mental Hospital.* New York: Public Affairs, 2001.

Bloom, Floyd E., M. Flint Beal, and David J. Kupfer, eds. *The Dana Guide to Brain Health.* (New York: Dana Press, 2003.)

Caldwell, Anne E. *Origins of Psychopharmacology from CPZ to LSD.* Springfield, IL: Charles C. Thomas, 1970.

Comer, Ronald J. *Fundamentals of Abnormal Psychology.* New York: Worth Publishers, 2004.

Division of Community Psychiatry, University of British Columbia. *Early Psychosis: A Guide for Physicians.* Vancouver, Canada: The University of British Columbia, 2000.

Gorman, Jack M. *The Essential Guide to Psychiatric Drugs.* New York: St. Martin's Griffin, 2007.

Gur, Raquel E., and Ann Braden Johnson. *If Your Adolescent Has Schizophrenia: An Essential Resource for Parents.* New York: Oxford University Press, 2006.

Howard, Pierce J. *The Owner's Manual for the Brain: Everyday Applications from Mind-Brain Research.* Austin, TX: Bard Press, 2006.

Jordan, Hamilton. *No Such Thing as a Bad Day: A Memoir.* Atlanta, GA: Longstreet Press, 2000.

Medalia, Alice, and Nadine Revheim. *Dealing with Cognitive Dysfunction Associated with Psychiatric Disabilities: A Handbook for Families and Friends of Individuals with Psychiatric Disorders.* New York: The New York State Office of Mental Health Family Liaison Bureau, 2002.

Mueser, Kim T., and Susan Gingerich. *The Complete Family Guide to Schizophrenia: Helping Your Loved One Get the Most Out of Life.* New York: Guilford Press, 2006. A manual with many helpful hints and worksheets for caregivers.

National Institute of Mental Health. *Medications for Mental Illness.* Bethesda, MD: NIMH Public Information and Communications Branch, 2005, addendum update 2007.

Schiller, Lori, and Amanda Bennett. *The Quiet Room: A Journey out of the Torment of Madness.* New York: Warner Books, 1994. A good account of a brave woman's experience with schizoaffective disorder. Well-written account told through the eyes of parents and child.

Steele, Ken. *The Day the Voices Stopped: A Memoir of Madness and Hope.* With Claire Berman. New York: Basic Books, 2001. A well-written and inspiring story of an exceptional person.

Stone, Alan A., and Sue Smart Stone, eds. *The Abnormal Personality Through Literature.* Englewood Cliffs, NJ: Prentice Hall, 1966. This anthology is full of interesting insights and commentary covering many forms of mental illness.

Torrey, E. Fuller. *Surviving Schizophrenia: A Manual for Families, Patients, and Providers*. New York: Harper Collins, 2006. Now in its fifth edition, this is one of the most thorough books on schizophrenia, written for consumers by someone who knows the disease better than most. It is one of the best books available on the subject.

Woolis, Rebecca. *When Someone You Love Has a Mental Illness: A Handbook for Family, Friends, and Caregivers*. New York: Jeremy P. Tarcher/Putnam, 2003. This excellent book is full of useful suggestions, tips, and information.

Useful Websites

American Academy of Child & Adolescent Psychiatry (AACAP)
3615 Wisconsin Ave., N.W., Washington, DC 20016-3007;
phone (202) 966-7300
www.aacap.org

American Psychiatric Association (APA)
1000 Wilson Blvd., Suite 1825, Arlington, VA 22209;
phone (703) 907-7300
www.HealthyMinds.org

British Columbia Schizophrenia Society
www.bcss.org

CenterWatch Clinical Trials Listing Service, Clinical Trials: Schizophrenia and Schizoaffective Disorders
A good source of information concerning clinical trials.
www.centerwatch.com/patient/studies/cat135.html

ClinicalTrials.gov
A service of The U.S. National Institutes of Health. ClinicalTrials.gov is "a registry of federally and privately supported clinical trials conducted in the United States and around the world."
www.clinicaltrials.gov/ct2/home

Living with Schizophrenia Community
A service provided by NAMI, this site offers information, support, and
ways to find other people going through what you are going through.

www.nami.org/Template.cfm?Section=Schizophrenia&Template=/
TaggedPage/TaggedPageDisplay.cfm&TPLID=19&ContentID=38851

Mental Health America (formerly NMHA)
2000 N. Beauregard Street, 6th Floor, Alexandria, VA 22311; phone
(800) 969-NMHA (969-6642)

www.nmha.org

National Alliance for Research on Schizophrenia and Depression
NARSAD supports scientific research into mental illnesses. Call
NARSAD's infoline at (800) 829-8289 to ask about mental disorders,
types of specialists, local support groups, or related questions, or
contact them at 60 Cutter Mill Road, Suite 404, Great Neck, New York
11021; fax (516) 487-6930; e-mail *info@narsad.org*.

www.narsad.org

The National Alliance on Mental Illness (NAMI)
NAMI claims to be "the nation's largest grassroots organization for
people with mental illness and their families." Colonial Place Three,
2107 Wilson Blvd., Suite 300, Arlington, VA 22201; phone (703) 524-
7600. Information Helpline: (800) 950-NAMI (950-6264)

www.nami.org

National Institute of Mental Health (NIMH)
Public Information Branch, 6001 Executive Boulevard, Room 8184,
MSC 9663 Bethesda, MD 20892; phone (866) 615-6464.

www.nimh.nih.gov

National Mental Health Consumers' Self-Help Clearinghouse
A good resource for new and veteran advocates of better mental
health care. 1211 Chestnut Street, Suite 1207, Philadelphia, PA 19107;
phone (800) 553-4539; fax (215) 636-6312; e-mail *info@mhselfhelp.org*.

www.mhselfhelp.org

Substance Abuse and Mental Health Services Administration (SAMHSA)

http://mentalhealth.samhsa.gov

Substance Abuse and Mental Health Services Administration Mental Health Services Locator

http://mentalhealth.samhsa.gov/databases

Schizophrenia.com Home Page

www.schizophrenia.com

National Federation of Families for Children's Mental Health

www.ffcmh.org

Schizophrenia Society of Canada
4 Fort Street, Winnipeg, MB CSC 104; phone (204) 786-1616; fax (204) 783-4898.

www.schizophrenia.ca

The Treatment Advocacy Center (TAC)
Helpful information about assisted treatment. 200 N. Glebe Road, Suite 730, Arlington, VA 22203; phone (703) 294-6001/6002; fax (703) 294-6010; e-mail *info@treatmentadvocacycenter.org.*

www.treatmentadvocacycenter.org

U.S. Pharmacopeia Drug Error Finder

www.usp.org/hqi/similarProducts/drugErrorFinderTool.html

WebMD Schizophrenia Health Center

www.webmd.com/schizophrenia/default.htm

World Health Organization's International Statistical Classification of Diseases and Related Health Problems, 10th Revision

www.who.int/classifications/apps/icd/icd10online

Early Treatment Clinics in the United States and Canada

The following list includes some of the most prominent early treatment clinics in North America. It does not include all of them, so check your local listings if you do not see one in your immediate area.

California

The Staglin Music Festival Center for the Assessment and Prevention of Prodromal States

Departments of Psychology and Psychiatry & Biobehavioral Sciences
University of California, Los Angeles
Semel Institute for Neuroscience and Human Behavior
300 Building Medical Plaza, Los Angeles, CA 90095
(310) 206-3466 phone
(310) 794-9517 fax
www.capps.ucla.edu

Prodrome Assessment Research and Treatment (PART) Program

The Langley Porter Psychiatric Institute
University of California, San Francisco (UCSF)
401 Parnassus Avenue
Box 0984-PAR
San Francisco, CA 94143
(415) 476-7278 phone
(415) 476-7320 fax
http://psych.ucsf.edu/research.aspx?id=1328

Cognitive Assessment and Risk Evaluation (CARE) Program

Medical Center Outpatient Psychiatry Clinic
University of California, San Diego
140 Arbor Drive, Fourth Floor
San Diego, California 92103
(619) 725-3516 phone
(619) 260-8437 fax
care@ucsd.edu
www.ucsdcareprogram.com

The EDAPT Clinic for Early Diagnosis and Preventive Treatment of Psychotic Illness
University of California, Davis Medical Center
(916) 734-2964 phone
www.earlypsychosis.ucdavis.edu

Connecticut

Prevention through Risk Identification, Management, & Education
Postal Address: PRIME Research Clinic
Yale Psychiatric Research
P.O. Box 208098
New Haven, CT 06520
Street Address: 301 Cedar Street, 2nd Floor
New Haven, CT 06519-1611
(866) AT-PRIME (287-7463)
primecl@mail.med.yale.edu
http://info.med.yale.edu/psych/clinics/prime/pintro.html

Illinois

First Episode Psychosis Clinic at the University of Illinois Medical Center at Chicago
(312) 355-5234 phone
http://ccm.psych.uic.edu/Need Doctor/FEPClinic/FEPClinic.aspx

Maine

Portland Identification and Early Referral (PIER), a program of the Maine Medical Center
295 Park Avenue, Portland, ME 04102
(877) 880-3377 phone
(207) 662-2004 phone
(207) 662-3300 fax
www.preventmentalillness.org/pier_home.html

Maryland

Maryland Psychiatric Research Center
Schizophrenia Related Disorders Program
P.O. Box 21247
Baltimore, MD 21228
(410) 402-6820 phone
(410) 402-6023 fax
http://medschool.umaryland.edu/MPRC/schizophrenia.asp

Massachusetts

The First-Episode and Early Psychosis Program (FEPP) at Massachusetts General Hospital
(617) 912-7800 phone
schizophrenia@partners.org

The Massachusetts Mental Health Center's Prevention and Recovery in Early Psychosis (PREP)
(617) 626-9559 phone
www.massmentalhealth center.org/clinicalservices/ programsandservices-prep.htm

Michigan

Services for Treatment in Early Psychoses (STEP), affiliated with the Wayne State University Department of Psychiatry and Behavioral Neurosciences
(888) 362-7792 phone
www.med.wayne .edu/psychiatry/step

New York

The Center of Prevention & Evaluation (COPE) of the Columbia University Department of Psychiatry / New York State Psychiatric Institute
(212) 543-5874 phone
www.cumc.columbia.edu/dept/ pi/research/clinics/pc.html

The Lieber Schizophrenia Research Clinic (LSRC) at the New York State Psychiatric Institute on the Columbia-Presbyterian Medical Campus
(212) 543-5418 phone
(212) 543-5537 fax
http://nyspi.org/Kolb/ResStudy/ Lieber.htm

The Recognition and Prevention Program (RAP) of the Zucker Hillside Hospital
(718) 470-8115 phone
www.nslijhs.com/body.cfm?id= 4977&oTopID=4958&PLinkID=66

North Carolina

Prevention through Risk Identification, Management and Education (PRIME), affiliated with the University of North Carolina at Chapel Hill School of Medicine
(877) PRIME19 phone
(919) 843-7746 phone
www.prime.unc.edu

Outreach and Support Intervention Services (OASIS), provided by the Department of Psychiatry at the University of North Carolina at Chapel Hill School of Medicine
(919) 929-2311 phone
www.psychiatry.unc.edu/oasis

Oregon

The Early Assessment and Support Team (EAST) of the Mid-Valley Behavioral Care Network
(888) 327-8817 phone
(503) 584-4837 fax
www.eastcommunity.org

Early Treatment Clinics in Canada

Centre for Addiction and Mental Health
1001 Queen Street West and 60 White Squirrel Way (Queen and Ossington)
Toronto, Ontario M6J 1H4 Canada
(416) 535-8501 phone
www.camh.net

The Champlain District Regional First Episode Psychosis Program of the Ottawa Hospital
(613) 722-7000 phone
www.ottawahospital.on.ca/patient/visit/clinics/psychosis-e.asp

The Prevention and Early Intervention Program for Psychoses (PEPP) of the London Health Sciences Centre and the University of Western Ontario
(519) 667-6777
www.pepp.ca/index.html
pepp@lhsc.on.ca

The Early Psychosis Intervention (EPI) Program

Fraser South area: (604) 538-4278
Fraser East area: (866) 870-7847
Fraser North area: (604) 777-8386
www.psychosissucks.ca/epi

Vancouver/Richmond EPI
207-2250 Commercial Drive
Vancouver, British Columbia V5N 5P9 Canada
(604) 225-2211 phone
www.hopevancouver.com

The Prevention and Early Intervention Program for Psychoses (PEPP–Montréal) of the Douglas Hospital Mental Health University Institute
FBC Pavilion, Second Floor, Rm.: F-2120
6875 LaSalle Blvd.
Borough of Verdun
Montreal, Quebec H4H 1R3, Canada
(514) 761-6131, ext. 4121 phone
(888) 4453 phone
(514) 888-4064 fax
www.douglas.qc.ca/clinical-services/adults/specialized/pepp.asp?l=e

The Early Psychosis Treatment Service (EPTS), run by Calgary Health Region and the Alberta Mental Health Board

Foothills Medical Centre
1403 - 29 Street NW
Calgary, Alberta, Canada T2N
2T9
(403) 944-4836 phone
(403) 944-4008 fax
www.calgaryhealthregion.ca/
mh/EPTP/epp/about.htm

Early Psychosis Program, provided by the Department of
Psychiatry, Faculty of Medicine,
Dalhousie University, Halifax,
Nova Scotia Canada
Nova Scotia Early Psychosis
Program
Abbie J. Lane Memorial Building
5909 Veteran's Memorial Lane
Halifax, NS B3H 2E2 Canada
(902) 473-2976 phone
(902) 473-3456 fax
nseppweb@dal.ca
http://earlypsychosis.medicine
.dal.ca

Top Psychiatric Hospitals in the United States

U.S. News & World Report ranks psychiatric hospitals (excluding military or veterans' hospitals) based on their reputation among physicians who responded to the magazine's survey.

California
Stanford Hospital and Clinics
    300 Pasteur Drive
    Palo Alto, CA 94304
    (650) 723-4000
    www.stanfordhospital.com

UCLA's Neuropsychiatric Hospital
    10833 Le Conte Avenue
    Los Angeles, CA 90095
    (310) 825-9111
    www.uclahealth.org

University of California, San Francisco Medical Center
    500 Parnassus Avenue
    San Francisco, CA 94143
    (415) 476-1000
    www.ucsfhealth.org

Connecticut
Yale-New Haven Hospital
    20 York Street
    New Haven, CT 06510
    (203) 688-4242
    www.ynhh.org

Georgia
Emory University Hospital
    1364 Clifton Road NE
    Atlanta, GA 30322
    (404) 712-2000
    www.emoryhealthcare.org

Maryland
Johns Hopkins Hospital
    600 North Wolfe Street
    Baltimore, MD 21287
    (410) 955-5000
    www.hopkinsmedicine.org

Sheppard and Enoch Pratt
Hospital
    6501 North Charles Street
    Baltimore, MD 21285
    (410) 938-3000
    www.sheppardpratt.org

Massachusetts

Austen Riggs Center
    25 Main Street
    Stockbridge, MA 01262
    (413) 298-5511
    www.austenriggs.org

Massachusetts General Hospital
    55 Fruit Street
    Boston, MA 02114
    (617) 726-2000
    www.massgeneral.org

McLean Hospital
    115 Mill Street
    Belmont, MA 02478
    (617) 855-2000
    www.mclean.harvard.edu

Minnesota

Mayo Clinic
    1216 Second Street SW
    Rochester, MN 55902
    (507) 255-5123
    www.mayoclinic.org

Missouri

Barnes-Jewish Hospital/Wash-
ington University, St. Louis
    1 Barnes-Jewish Hospital Plaza
    Saint Louis, MO 63110
    (314) 747-3000
    www.barnesjewish.org

New York

Long Island Jewish Medical
Center
    270-05 76th Avenue
    New Hyde Park, NY 11040
    (718) 470-7000
    www.lij.edu

Mount Sinai Medical Center
    One Gustave L. Levy Place
    New York, NY 10029
    (212) 241-6500
    www.mountsinai.org

New York-Presbyterian University Hospital of Columbia and
Cornell
    525 East 68th Street
    New York, NY 10021
    (212) 746-5454
    www.nyp.org

NYU Medical Center
    550 First Avenue
    New York, NY 10016
    (212) 263-7300
    www.nyumedicalcenter.org

North Carolina
Duke University Medical Center
Erwin Road
Durham, NC 27710
(919) 684-8111
www.mc.duke.edu

Pennsylvania
UPMC-University of Pittsburgh Medical Center
200 Lothrop Street
Pittsburgh, PA 15213
(800) 533-8762
www.upmc.com

Texas
Menninger Clinic
2801 Gessner Drive
Houston, TX 77080
(713) 275-5000
www.menningerclinic.com

Methodist Hospital
6565 Fannin Street
Houston, TX 77030
(713) 790-3311
www.methodisthealth.com

Index